QuickBooks® 2003 For Dummies®

Keeping Your Debits and Credits Straight

Assets = Liabilities + Owner's Equity. The natural balance for asset accou... natural balance for liability and owner's equity accounts is on the right (c... accounts and expense accounts that add or deduct from other accounts to ... a net amount.

Account Type	Debits	Credits
Assets	Increase asset accounts	Decrease asset accounts
Liabilities	Decrease liability accounts	Increase liability accounts
Owner's equity	Decrease owner's equity accounts	Increase owner's equity accounts
Income	Decrease income accounts	Increase income accounts
Expenses	Increase expense accounts	Decrease expense accounts

Speedy Keyboard Shortcuts

Press This PC Shortcut	And QuickBooks Does This
Ctrl+A	Displays the Chart of Accounts window
Ctrl+C	Copies your selection to the clipboard
Ctrl+F	Displays the Find window
Ctrl+G	Goes to the other side of a transfer transaction
Ctrl+I	Displays the Create Invoice window
Ctrl+J	Displays the Customer:Job List window
Ctrl+M	Memorizes a transaction
Ctrl+N	Creates a new <fill in the blank> where fill in the blank is whatever is active at the time
Ctrl+P	Almost always prints the currently active register, list, or form
Ctrl+Q	Creates and displays a QuickReport on the selected transaction
Ctrl+R	Displays the Register window
Crtl+T	Displays the memorized transaction list
Ctrl+V	Pastes the contents of the clipboard
Ctrl+W	Displays the Write Checks window
Ctrl+X	Moves your selection to the clipboard
Ctrl+Z	Undoes your last action — usually
Ctrl+Ins	Inserts a line into a list of items or expenses
Ctrl+Del	Deletes the selected line from a list of items or expenses

For Dummies: Bestselling Book Series for Beginners

QuickBooks® 2003 For Dummies®

Cheat Sheet

Some User Interface Tricks

- To get help, click the How Do I? button in the upper-right corner of the dialog box and choose a topic from the drop-down menu.
- To move quickly to a specific list box entry, press the letter.
- To select a list box entry and choose a dialog box's suggested command button, double-click the entry.
- To move the insertion point to the beginning of a field, press Home.
- To move the insertion point to the end of a field, press End.
- QuickBooks locks the active window into place and then displays a list of windows in its Navigator pane, which is like another little window. To move to a listed window, just click it.
- To remove the Navigator, choose View➪Open Window List. (You can move the other locked pane which lists windows, called the Shortcuts List, by choosing Lists➪Shortcut List.)
- To tell QuickBooks to use windows like every other program does, choose View➪Multiple Windows.

Some Calculation and Editing Tricks

If the selection cursor is on amount field, you can use these symbol keys to make calculations:

Press	What Happens
+	To add the number you just typed to the next number you type
-	To subtract the next number you type from the number you just typed
*	To multiply the number you just typed by the next number you type
/	To divide the number you just typed by the next number you type

If the selection cursor is on a date field, you can use these tricks to edit the date:

Press	What Happens
+	Adds one day to the date shown
t	Replaces the date shown with today's date
–	Subtracts one day from the date shown
y	Changes the date to the first day in the year
r	Changes the date to the last day in the year
m	Changes the date to the first day in the month
h	Changes the date to the last day in the month

Right-Click to Perform Common Tasks

To perform a common task related to a window, you can use the right-mouse button to display a shortcut menu. In a register, select and right-click a specific transaction; in a list, right-click an item; in a form, display a transaction and right-click a blank area of the form. QuickBooks displays a shortcut menu of common commands for the particular transaction, item, or window. For example, it often displays commands for memorizing or voiding the transaction, or creating a QuickReport on the transaction. The commands differ based on the type of transaction you select.

For Dummies: Bestselling Book Series for Beginners

QuickBooks® 2003

FOR

DUMMIES®

by Stephen L. Nelson, MBA, CPA

Wiley Publishing, Inc.

QuickBooks® 2003 For Dummies®

Published by
Wiley Publishing, Inc.
909 Third Avenue
New York, NY 10022

www.wiley.com

Copyright © 2003 by Wiley Publishing, Inc., Indianapolis, Indiana

Published by Wiley Publishing, Inc., Indianapolis, Indiana

Published simultaneously in Canada

For general information on our other products and services or to obtain technical support, please contact our Customer Care Department within the U.S. at 800-762-2974, outside the U.S. at 317-572-3993, or fax 317-572-4002.

Wiley also publishes its books in a variety of electronic formats. Some content that appears in print may not be available in electronic books.

Library of Congress Control Number: 2002117704

ISBN: 0-7645-1986-7

Manufactured in the United States of America

10 9 8 7 6 5 4 3 2 1

1B/RU/QR/QT/IN

Wiley Publishing, Inc. is a trademark of Wiley Publishing, Inc.

About the Author

Stephen L. Nelson, MBA, CPA, has a simple purpose in life: He wants to help you (and people like you) manage your business finances by using computers. Oh, sure, this personal mandate won't win him a Nobel Prize or anything, but it's his own little contribution to the world.

Steve's education and experiences mesh nicely with his special purpose. He has a B.S. in accounting and an MBA in finance. He's a CPA in Redmond, Washington. He used to work as a senior consultant and CPA with Arthur Andersen & Co. (er, yeah, that Arthur Andersen — but hey it was 20 years ago). Steve, whose books have sold more than 4 million copies in English and have been translated into 11 other languages, is also the bestselling author of *Quicken 2002 For Dummies* (from Wiley Publishing, Inc.).

Dedication

To the entrepreneurs and small-business people of the world. You folks create most of the new jobs.

Author's Acknowledgments

Hey, reader, lots of folks spent lots of time working on this book to make QuickBooks easier for you. You should know who these people are. You may just possibly meet one of them someday at a produce shop, squeezing cantaloupe, eating grapes, and looking for the perfect peach.

Those folks include my acquisitions editor, Bob Woerner, and my editors, Christine Berman, Nicole Sholly, and Diana Conover. And without Michael Patrick Chaffey, the technical editor, this book wouldn't have been possible.

Thanks to all for a job well-done!

Publisher's Acknowledgments

We're proud of this book; please send us your comments through our online registration form located at www.dummies.com/register/.

Some of the people who helped bring this book to market include the following:

Acquisitions, Editorial, and Media Development

Project Editor: Christine Berman

Acquisitions Editor: Bob Woerner

Copy Editors: Nicole Sholly, Diana Conover

Technical Editor: Michael Patrick Chaffey, OCP, CPA

Editorial Manager: Leah Cameron

Media Development Supervisor: Richard Graves

Editorial Assistant: Amanda Foxworth

Cartoons: Rich Tennant, www.the5thwave.com

Production

Project Coordinator: Kristie Rees

Layout and Graphics: Carrie Foster, Stephanie D. Jumper, Gabriele McCann, Kristin McMullan, Tiffany Muth, Jackie Nicholas, Janet Seib, Jeremey Unger, Erin Zeltner

Proofreaders: John Tyler Connoley, John Greenough, Angel Perez, Carl Pierce

Indexer: TECHBOOKS Production Services

Special Help Rebecca Senninger

Publishing and Editorial for Technology Dummies

Richard Swadley, Vice President and Executive Group Publisher

Andy Cummings, Vice President and Publisher

Mary C. Corder, Editorial Director

Publishing for Consumer Dummies

Diane Graves Steele, Vice President and Publisher

Joyce Pepple, Acquisitions Director

Composition Services

Gerry Fahey, Vice President of Production Services

Debbie Stailey, Director of Composition Services

Contents at a Glance

Table of Contents

Introduction

I think that running, or working in, a small business is one of the coolest things a person can do. Really. I mean it. Sure, sometimes the environment is dangerous. Kind of like the Old West. But it's also an environment in which you have the opportunity to make tons of money. And it's an environment in which you can build a company or a job that fits you. In comparison, many brothers and sisters working in big-company corporate America are furiously trying to fit their round pegs into painfully square holes. Yuck.

You're wondering, of course, what any of this has to do with this book or with QuickBooks. Quite a lot, actually. The whole purpose of this book is to make it easier for you to run or work in a small business by using QuickBooks.

About QuickBooks

Let me start off with a minor but useful point. QuickBooks comes in several different flavors: QuickBooks Basic, QuickBooks Pro, QuickBooks Premier, and QuickBooks Premier: Accountants Edition.

This book, however, talks about QuickBooks Premier.

Does this mean that I've somehow left you adrift if you've got one of these other flavors? No way. I wouldn't do that to you. QuickBooks Premier is a superset of QuickBooks Basic and QuickBooks Pro, so by describing how you use QuickBooks Premier, I also tell you how to use the other flavors of QuickBooks.

What's more, for the readers of this book, there's no discernible difference between QuickBooks Pro and either flavor of QuickBooks Premier. You're not reading this book to prepare for the C.P.A. exam, right? Right. The extra whistles and bells that make QuickBooks Premier, well, "premier" are all things that only accountants care about: remote access to QuickBooks and your QuickBooks data, reversing general entries, extra security for general ledger closings, and so on.

The bottom line? Yes, there are several flavors of QuickBooks, but if you're just trying to get started and want to use QuickBooks, this book works for QuickBooks Basic, QuickBooks Pro, and QuickBooks Premier.

About This Book

This book isn't meant to be read from cover to cover like some Harry Potter page turner. Instead, it's organized into tiny, no-sweat descriptions of how you do the things you need to do. If you're the sort of person who just doesn't feel right not reading a book from cover to cover, you can, of course, go ahead and read this thing from front to back. You can start reading Chapter 1 and continue all the way to the end (which means through Chapter 21 and the appendixes).

I actually don't think this from-start-to-finish approach is bad, because I tell you a bunch of stuff. I tried to write the book in such a way that the experience isn't as bad as you might think, and I really do think you get good value from your reading.

But you also can use this book like an encyclopedia. If you want to know about a subject, you can look it up in the table of contents or the index. Then you can flip to the correct chapter or page and read as much as you need or enjoy. No muss, no fuss.

I should, however, mention one thing: Accounting software programs require you to do a certain amount of preparation before you can use them to get real work done. If you haven't started to use QuickBooks yet, I recommend that you read through the first few chapters of this book to find out what you need to do first.

Hey. There's something else I should tell you. I have fiddled a bit with the Windows display settings. For example, I've noodled around with the font settings and most of the colors. The benefit is that the pictures in this book are easy to read. And that's good. But the cost of all this is that my pictures look a little bit different than what you see on your screen. And that's not good. In the end, however, what the publisher has found is that people are really happier with increased readability. Anyway, I just thought I should mention this here, up front, in case you had any question about it.

What You Can Safely Ignore

Sometimes I provide step-by-step descriptions of tasks. I feel very bad about having to do this. So to make things easier for you, I describe the tasks by using bold text. That way, you know exactly what you're supposed to do. I also provide a more detailed explanation in the text that follows the step. You can skip the text that accompanies the step-by-step boldfaced directions if you already understand the process.

Here's an example that shows what I mean:

1. **Press Enter.**

    Find the key that's labeled Enter or Return. Extend your index finger so that it rests ever so gently on the Enter key. In one sure, fluid motion, press the Enter key by using your index finger. Then release your finger.

Okay, that example is kind of extreme. I never actually go into that much detail. But you get the idea. If you know how to press Enter, you can just do that and not read further. If you need help — maybe with the finger part or something — just read the nitty-gritty details.

Can you skip anything else? Let me see now. . . . You can skip the Technical Stuff icons, too. The information next to these icons is really there only for those of you who like that kind of stuff.

For that matter, I guess that you can safely ignore the stuff next to the Tip icons, too — even if the accumulated wisdom, gleaned from long hours slaving over a hot keyboard, could save you much weeping and gnashing of teeth. If you're someone who enjoys trying to do something another way, go ahead and read the tips.

What You Should Not Ignore (Unless You're a Masochist)

Don't skip the Warning icons. They're the ones flagged with the picture of the nineteenth-century bomb. They describe some things that you really shouldn't do.

Out of respect for you, I'm not going to put stuff such as "don't smoke" next to these icons. I figure that you're an adult. You can make your own lifestyle decisions. So I'm reserving the Warning icons for more urgent and immediate dangers — things akin to "Don't smoke while you're filling your car with gasoline."

Three Foolish Assumptions

I'm making three assumptions:

- ✔ You have a PC with Microsoft Windows 95 or later or Windows NT 4.0 or higher. (I took pictures of the QuickBooks windows and dialog boxes while using Windows XP, in case you're interested.)

- ✔ You know a little bit about how to work with your computer.

- ✔ You have or will buy a copy of QuickBooks, QuickBooks Pro, or QuickBooks Premier for each computer on which you want to run the program.

Personally, I use QuickBooks Premier, so this book includes some features unique to the Pro and Premier versions. If you're trying to decide which version to buy, I should tell you that QuickBooks Pro and Premier include networking capabilities (which I describe in Chapter 3) and the ability to create estimates and bids (which I describe in Appendix C). The standard version of QuickBooks doesn't include these features.

This book works for QuickBooks 2003, although in a pinch you could probably also use it for QuickBooks 2002. (I've got to say, however, that if you have QuickBooks 2002, you might instead want to return this book and trade it in for *QuickBooks 2002 For Dummies* by yours truly, which is also published by Wiley Publishing, Inc.)

By the way, if you haven't already installed QuickBooks and need help, refer to Appendix A, which tells you how to install QuickBooks in ten easy steps. And if you're just starting out with Microsoft Windows, peruse Chapter 1 of the Windows User's Guide or one of these books on your flavor of Windows, such as *Small Business Windows 98 For Dummies*, which I wrote; or *Windows 98 For Dummies*, *Windows 2000 Professional For Dummies*, *Microsoft Windows Me For Dummies*, or *Windows XP For Dummies* by Andy Rathbone (all published by Wiley Publishing, Inc.).

How This Book 1s Organized

This book is divided into five mostly coherent parts.

Part 1: You Gotta Start Someplace

Part I covers some up-front stuff that you need to take care of before you can start using QuickBooks. This part also introduces the networking capabilities of QuickBooks Pro. I promise I won't waste your time here. I just want to make sure that you get off on the right foot.

Part II: Daily Chores

The second part of this book explains how you use QuickBooks for your daily financial record keeping: preparing customer invoices, recording sales, and paying bills. That kind of stuff.

I guess you could say that these chores are just data entry stuff. And you'd be correct. But you'll be amazed at how much easier QuickBooks will make your life. QuickBooks is a really cool program.

Part III: Stuff You Do Every So Often

Part III talks about the kinds of things you should do at the end of the week, the end of the month, or the end of the year. This part explains, for example, how you print checks, explore QuickBooks online resources, do payroll, balance your bank account, create reports, take care of some housekeeping tasks, and create a business budget.

While I'm on the subject, I also want to categorically deny that Part III contains any secret messages that you can decipher by reading backward. Yllaer.

Part IV: The Part of Tens

Gravity isn't just a good idea; it's a law.

By tradition, the same is true for this part of a *For Dummies* book. The Part of Tens provides a collection of lists: ten tips for Webifying your business, ten things you should do if you own a business, ten things to do when you next visit Acapulco — oops, sorry about that last one. Wrong book.

By the way, also by tradition, these ten-item lists don't need to have exactly ten items. You know the concept of a baker's dozen, right? You order a dozen doughnuts but get thirteen for the same price. Well, *For Dummies* ten-item lists have roughly ten items. (If Dummies Man — the bug-eyed, paleface guy suffering from triangle-shaped-head syndrome who appears on the cover of this book and on icons throughout these pages — were running the bakery, a ten-doughnut order might mean that you get anywhere from eight to thirteen doughnuts.) Do you believe that I'm an accountant? So exacting that it's scary.

Part V: Appendixes

An unwritten rule says that computer books have appendixes, so I've included four. Appendix A tells you how to install QuickBooks in ten easy steps. Appendix B explains small business accounting, provides a short biography of an Italian monk, and explains double-entry bookkeeping. Appendix C describes how you use the Timer program, which is included with the Pro version of QuickBooks, to keep track of the time you spend on projects.

Conventions Used in This Book

To make the best use of your time and energy, you should know about the conventions I use in this book.

When I want you to type something such as **with a stupid grin, Martin watched the tall blonde strut into the bar and order grappa**, it's in bold letters. When I want you to type something that's short and uncomplicated, such as **Jennifer**, it still appears in boldface type.

By the way, except for passwords, you don't have to worry about the case of the stuff you type in QuickBooks. If I tell you to type **Jennifer**, you can type **JENNIFER**. Or you can follow poet e. e. cummings' lead and type **jennifer**.

Whenever I tell you to choose a command from a menu, I say something like, "Choose Lists⇨Items," which simply means to first choose the Lists menu and then choose Items. The ⇨ separates one part of the command from the next part.

You can choose menus and commands and select dialog box elements with the mouse. Just click the thing you want to select.

While we're on the subject of conventions, let me also mention something about QuickBooks conventions because it turns out that there's not really any good place to point this out. QuickBooks doesn't use document windows the same way that other Windows programs do. Instead, it locks the active window into place and then displays a list of windows in its Navigator pane, which is like another little window. To move to a listed window, you click it.

You can tell QuickBooks to use windows like every other program does, however, by choosing View⇨Multiple Windows. You can even remove the Navigators pane by choosing View⇨Open Window List. (You can also move the other locked pane, which lists windows and is called the Shortcuts List, by choosing View⇨Shortcut List.)

Special Icons

Like many computer books, this book uses icons, or little pictures, to flag things that don't quite fit into the flow of things:

Sometimes, I use made-up examples (along with examples from my own experience) to help you understand how some topic or area of QuickBooks helps you and your business. Just my way of continuing the giving.

An alert that I'm covering some topic or procedure that requires a certain amount of caution on your point.

This icon is just a friendly reminder to do something.

This icon points out nerdy technical material that you may want to skip (or read, if you're feeling particularly bright).

Whee! Here's a shortcut to make your life easier!

And this icon is a friendly reminder not to do something . . . or else.

Part I
You Gotta Start Someplace

The 5th Wave — By Rich Tennant

"COOKED BOOKS? LET ME JUST SAY YOU COULD SERVE THIS PROFIT AND LOSS STATEMENT WITH A FRUITY ZINFANDEL AND NOT BE OUT OF PLACE."

In this part . . .

All accounting programs — including QuickBooks — make you do a bunch of preliminary stuff. Sure, this is sort of a bummer. But getting depressed about it won't make things go any faster. So if you want to get up and go with QuickBooks — and if you want to find out about the cool network features QuickBooks offers — peruse the chapters in this first part. I promise that I'll get you through this stuff as quickly as possible.

Chapter 1

The Big Interview

In This Chapter

▶ Getting ready to do the big interview

▶ Not getting discouraged about the big interview

▶ Surviving the big interview

▶ Telling your friends all sorts of war stories about the big interview

▶ Making the accrual-accounting adjustment

▶ Supplying the missing numbers

1 know that you're eager to get started. You've got a business to run. But before you can start using QuickBooks, you need to do some up-front work. Specifically, you need to prepare for the *QuickBooks EasyStep Interview,* and then you need to walk through the EasyStep Interview. (The EasyStep Interview is just a thorough question-and-answer session that QuickBooks uses to set itself up for you.) After you finish with the EasyStep Interview, you also probably need to fiddle with QuickBooks to get everything working just right. In this chapter, I describe how you do all this stuff.

I assume that you know how Windows works. If you don't, take the time to read Chapter 1 of your Windows User's Guide. Or try the appropriate edition of *Windows For Dummies* (by Andy Rathbone and published by Wiley Publishing, Inc.).

Getting Ready for the Big Interview

You need to complete three tasks to get ready for the EasyStep Interview:

✔ You need to make an important decision about your conversion date (the date you convert from your old accounting system to QuickBooks).

✔ You need to prepare a trial balance as of the conversion date.

✔ You need to go on a scavenger hunt to collect a bunch of stuff that you'll need or find handy for the interview.

The big decision

Before you even start fiddling with your computer or the QuickBooks software, you need to choose the date — the so-called *conversion date* — on which you want to begin using QuickBooks for your financial record keeping.

This decision is hugely important because the conversion date that you choose dramatically affects both the work you have to do in order to get QuickBooks running smoothly and the initial usefulness of the financial information that you collect and record by using QuickBooks.

You've got three basic choices you can make:

- **The right way:** You can convert at the beginning of your accounting year (which is almost certainly the same as the beginning of the calendar year). This way is the right way for two reasons. First, converting at the beginning of the year requires the least amount of work from you. Second, it means that you have all the current year's financial information in one system.

- **The slightly awkward way:** You can convert at the beginning of some interim accounting period (probably the beginning of some month or quarter). This approach works, but it's slightly awkward because you have to plug your year-to-date income and expenses numbers from the old system into the new system. (If you don't know what an interim accounting period is, read Appendix B.)

- **The my-way-or-the-highway way:** You can convert at some time other than what I call the right way and the slightly awkward way. Specifically, you can choose to convert whenever you jolly well feel like it. You create a bunch of unnecessary work for yourself if you take this approach, and you pull out a bunch of your hair in the process. But you also have the satisfaction of knowing that through it all, you did it your way — without any help from me.

I recommend the right way. What this choice means is that if it's late in the year — say, October — I suggest that you just wait until January 1 of the next year to convert. If it's still early in the year, you can also retroactively convert as of the beginning of the year. (If you do this, you need to go back and do your financial record keeping for the first part of the current year by using QuickBooks: entering sales, recording purchases, and so on.)

If it's sometime in the middle of the year — say, Memorial Day or later — then you probably want to use the slightly awkward way. (I'm actually going to use the slightly awkward way in this chapter because if you see how to convert to QuickBooks by using the slightly awkward way, you know how to use both the right way and the slightly awkward way.)

The trial balance of the century

After you decide when you want to convert, you need a *trial balance*.

"Yikes," you say. "What's a trial balance?" Well, a trial balance simply lists all your assets, liabilities, and owner's equity account balances as well as the year-to-date income and expense numbers on a specified date (which, not coincidentally, happens to be the conversion date). You need this data for the EasyStep Interview and for some fiddling around that you need to do after you complete the EasyStep Interview.

Creating a trial balance doesn't have to be as hard as it sounds. If you've been using another small-business accounting system, such as Intuit's simpler Quicken product or Computer Associates' Simply Accounting program, you may be able to have your old system produce a trial balance on the conversion date. In that case, you can get the balances from your old system. (You can consider yourself lucky if this is the case.)

If your old system is rather informal (perhaps it's a shoe box full of receipts) or if it tracks only cash (perhaps you've been using Quicken), you need to do a bit more work:

- ✔ To get your cash balance, you need to reconcile your bank account or bank accounts (if you've got more than one bank account) as of the conversion date.

- ✔ To get your accounts receivable balance, you need to tally up the total of all your unpaid customer invoices.

- ✔ To get your other asset account balances, you need to know what each asset originally cost. For depreciable fixed assets, you also need to provide any accumulated depreciation that you've charged. (*Accumulated depreciation* is just the total depreciation that you've charged on an asset.)

  By the way, refer to Appendix B if you have questions about accounting or accounting terminology, such as *depreciation*.

- ✔ To get your liability account balances, you need to know how much you owe on each liability. If you trust your *creditors* — the people that you owe the money to — you may also be able to get this information from their statements.

You don't need to worry about the owner's equity accounts. QuickBooks can calculate your owner's equity account balances for you, based on the difference between your total assets and your total liabilities. This method is a bit sloppy, and accountants may not like it, but it's a pretty good compromise. (If you do have detailed account balances for your owner's equity accounts, use these figures — and know that you're one in a million.)

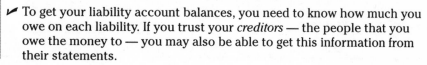

If you're using the slightly awkward way to convert to QuickBooks — in other words, if your conversion date is some date other than the beginning of the accounting year — then you also need to provide year-to-date income and expense balances. To get your income, cost of goods sold, expenses, other income, and other expense account balances, you need to calculate the year-to-date amount of each account. If you can get this information from your old system, that's super. If not, you need to get it manually. (If you suddenly have images of yourself sitting at your desk, late at night, tapping away on a ten-key, you're probably right. What's more, you probably also need to allocate half of another Saturday to getting up and running with QuickBooks.)

Just for fun, I've created the sample trial balance shown in Table 1-1. This table shows you what a trial balance looks like if you convert at some time other than at the beginning of the accounting year.

Table 1-1	A "Slightly Awkward Way" Sample Trial Balance		
Trial Balance Information		*Debit*	*Credit*
Assets			
Checking		$5,000	
Fixed assets		$60,000	
Accumulated depreciation (fixed assets)			$2,000
Liabilities information			
Loan payable			$10,000
Owner's equity and income statement information			
Opening bal equity			$20,000
Sales			$60,000
Cost of goods sold		$20,000	
Supplies expense		$2,100	
Rent expense		$4,900	
Totals		$92,000	$92,000

If you're converting at the very beginning of the accounting year, your trial balance looks instead like the one shown in Table 1-2. Notice that this trial balance doesn't have any year-to-date income or expense balances.

About those debits and credits

Don't get freaked out about those debits and credits. You just need to keep them straight for a few minutes. Here's the scoop: For assets and expenses, a *debit balance* is the same thing as a positive balance. So a cash debit balance of $5,000 means that you have $5,000 in your account. And $20,000 of cost of goods sold means that you incurred $20,000 of costs of goods expense. For assets and expenses, a *credit balance* is the same thing as a negative balance. So, if you have a cash balance of –$5,000, your account is overdrawn by $5,000. In the sample trial balance shown in Table 1-1, the accumulated depreciation shows a credit balance of $2,000, which is, in effect, a negative account balance.

For liabilities, owner's equity accounts, and income accounts, things are flip-flopped. A credit balance is the same thing as a positive balance. So, an accounts payable credit balance of $2,000 means that you owe your creditors $2,000. A bank loan credit balance of $10,000 means that you owe the bank $10,000. And a sales account credit balance of $60,000 means that you've enjoyed $60,000 of sales.

I know that I keep saying this, but do remember that those income and expense account balances are year-to-date figures. They exist *only* if the conversion date is after the start of the financial year.

Table 1-2	A "Right Way" Sample Trial Balance		
Trial Balance Information		*Debit*	*Credit*
Assets			
Checking		$5,000	
Fixed assets		$60,000	
Accumulated depreciation (fixed assets)			$2,000
Liabilities information			
Loan payable			$10,000
Owner's equity and income statement information			
Opening bal equity			$53,000
Totals		$65,000	$65,000

The mother of all scavenger hunts

Even after you've decided when you want to convert to QuickBooks and have come up with a trial balance, you still need to collect a bunch of additional information. I'm just going to list these items in laundry-list fashion. What you want to do is find all this stuff and then pile it up (neatly) in a big stack next to the computer.

- ✔ **Last year's federal tax return:** QuickBooks asks which federal income tax form you use to file your tax return and also about your taxpayer identification number. Last year's federal tax return is the easiest place to find this stuff.

- ✔ **Copies of your most recent state and federal payroll tax returns:** If you prepare payroll for employees, QuickBooks wants to know about the federal and state payroll tax rates you pay as well as some other stuff.

- ✔ **Copies of all the unpaid invoices that your customers (or clients or patients or whatever) owe you as of the conversion date:** I guess this is probably obvious, but the total accounts receivable balance shown on your trial balance needs to match the total of the unpaid customer invoices.

- ✔ **Copies of all unpaid invoices that you owe your vendors as of the conversion date:** Again, this is probably obvious, but the total accounts payable balance shown on your trial balance needs to match the total of the unpaid vendor invoices.

- ✔ **A detailed listing of any inventory items you're holding for resale:** This list should include not only inventory item descriptions and quantities, but also the initial purchase prices and the anticipated sales prices. In other words, if you sell porcelain wombats and you've got 1,200 of these beauties in inventory, you need to know exactly what you paid for them.

- ✔ **Copies of the prior year's W-2 statements, W-4 statements for anybody you've hired since the beginning of the prior year, detailed information about any payroll tax liabilities you owe as of the conversion date, and detailed information about the payroll tax deposits you've made since the beginning of the year:** You need the information shown on these forms to adequately and accurately set up the QuickBooks payroll feature. I don't want to scare you, but this is probably the most tedious part of setting up QuickBooks.

- ✔ **If you're retroactively converting as of the beginning of the year, you need a list of all the transactions that have occurred since the beginning of the year: sales, purchases, payroll transactions, and everything and anything else:** If you do the right way conversion retroactively, you need to re-enter each of these transactions into the new system. You actually enter the information after you complete the EasyStep Interview that I describe later in this chapter. But you may as well get all this information together now, while you're searching for the rest of the scavenger hunt items.

If you take the slightly awkward way, you don't need to find the last item that I've described in the previous list. You can just use the year-to-date income and expense numbers from the trial balance.

Doing the EasyStep Interview

After you decide when you want to convert, you prepare a trial balance as of the conversion date, and you collect the additional raw data that you need, you're ready to step through the EasyStep Interview.

Before you begin the interview, you have to start QuickBooks 2003. To do so, choose Start➪Programs and then click the menu choices that lead to QuickBooks. (For example, I choose Start➪Programs➪QuickBooks Premier➪ QuickBooks Premier.)

QuickBooks actually comes in several flavors. The most common flavors are: QuickBooks Basic, QuickBooks Pro, and QuickBooks Premier. These three programs differ in a couple of significant ways: QuickBooks Pro adds the advanced job-costing and time-estimating features, which I briefly describe in Appendix C. It also includes the ability to share a QuickBooks file over a network, as I describe in Chapter 3. QuickBooks Premier adds features to QuickBooks Pro for accountants and auditors who want to use QuickBooks for rather large small businesses. I used QuickBooks Premier for writing this book, by the way, so the figures you see here may look a wee bit different from what you see on-screen in one or two special cases. But other than minor cosmetic differences, the three programs work the same way.

If this is the first time you've started QuickBooks, QuickBooks displays a message box that asks you how you want to start. For example, you can click a button that indicates you want to open a sample data file. What I suggest you do, however, is jump right into the fray. If you've never used QuickBooks before — the likely case if you've started your reading here — click the Set Up A New Data File For A Company button, which starts the EasyStep Interview. (If you've already been using either an earlier version of QuickBooks or Quicken, click the buttons corresponding to these choices. QuickBooks then starts an abbreviated version of the EasyStep Interview.)

The real fun begins at this point. The EasyStep Interview starts automatically, displaying the dialog box shown in Figure 1-1.

If you're not starting QuickBooks for the first time but you want to step through the EasyStep Interview to set up a new company anyway, choose File➪New Company. Or, if you want to step through the interview for a company you've already set up (but perhaps set up incorrectly or incompletely), choose File➪EasyStep Interview.

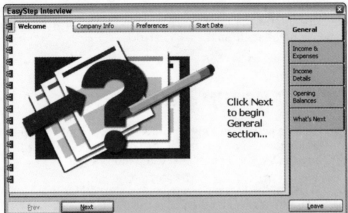

Figure 1-1:
The
EasyStep
Interview
dialog box.

To begin the interview, click the Next button. The next page of dialog box information asks whether you're upgrading from a previous version of Quicken or QuickBooks. You're probably not (or you wouldn't be reading this chapter), so click the No, I'm Not Upgrading option and then continue with the interview by clicking the Next button. Each time you finish a page of the interview, click the Next button to continue.

After QuickBooks starts, you may also see a message box that asks whether you want to register QuickBooks. You can use the product roughly a couple dozen times and then — whammo — either you register it or you can't use it. I don't like being forced to do something, but getting worked up about having to register QuickBooks is a waste of time. The simplest option is to just register. Here's how: When QuickBooks displays the message box that asks whether you want to register, click Online to register online or Phone to register over the phone. If you go with the phone option, QuickBooks displays another dialog box that gives you a telephone number to call and provides a space for you to enter your registration number. (You can get your registration number from your invoice if you bought QuickBooks from Intuit or over the phone when you call to register.)

I'm not going to provide you with a blow-by-blow account of what happens when you take the interview. A much better approach is for me to provide you with a handful of key tips that you can read now and then use later (during the interview) to make the process as easy and as fast as possible.

Tip 1: Learn the interview protocol

For the most part, to complete the EasyStep Interview, all you do is fill in text boxes with the information that QuickBooks requests (see Figure 1-2) or answer questions by clicking buttons clearly marked Yes or No.

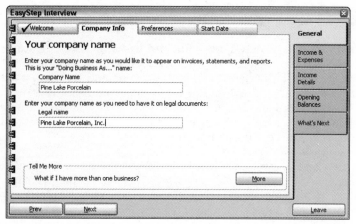

Figure 1-2:
Enter your
company's
trade name
and legal
name in this
dialog box.

If you ever decide that you want to change some piece of information that you've entered on a previous page of the EasyStep Interview dialog box, you can just click the Prev button to back up. If you get partway through the interview process and decide that it's not worth the time, just click the Leave button in the lower-right corner, and QuickBooks closes the EasyStep Interview dialog box. And, if after leaving the interview, you realize that you've made a mistake, all you have to do is choose File➪EasyStep Interview and then use the tabs shown in Figure 1-2 to go back and change something you entered.

Here are a few extra notes that may come in handy:

- ✔ The EasyStep Interview dialog box appears every time you start a new company (which you do by choosing File➪New Company).

- ✔ Note that when you click the tabs on the right side of the EasyStep Interview dialog box, the tabs at the top change accordingly. This change comes in handy when you're leafing through the 60 or 70 pages of information that appear in the EasyStep Interview dialog box.

- ✔ QuickBooks purposely makes deleting a company you create in QuickBooks hard, so don't make up an imaginary company to play with unless you're familiar enough with your operating system to delete files.

Tip 2: Take your time

As you step through the interview process, the EasyStep Interview dialog box displays a bunch of different pages with suggestions, instructions, and advice. Take the time to read this information. Click the Help button if you have questions. If the EasyStep Interview suggests that you view some related document with helpful information, do so.

Tip 3: Get industry-specific advice

Industry-specific advice is one of the handiest QuickBooks features. For example, are you a rancher or a farmer? QuickBooks includes a detailed online document that describes some of the unique accounting challenges your business faces, provides tips for making your record keeping easier, and points out QuickBooks features that may be of particular interest to someone like you. Are you a retailer? A manufacturer? A writer? A consultant? You can get this same sort of information, too.

QuickBooks displays industry-specific tips and tidbits of information throughout the interview. Keep your eyes peeled for the green arrows that mark these little hints. Let me mention one other quick pointer about this industry-specific information stuff: You may not understand everything you read. That's okay. You still want to read the tips and maybe jot them down on a piece of paper as you go along. As you work with QuickBooks and find out more about it, you'll find that more and more of the information provided in the industry-specific tips makes sense.

To view a document of industry-specific information at any time, click Info & Support on the Navigation bar and click the Industry-Specific Information hyperlink. Click the List Of Industries hyperlink, and then select your industry from the list in the Help window that QuickBooks displays. To print a copy of the information, click the Options button and choose Print Topic from the drop-down menu.

Some of the hyperlinks lead to resources at the QuickBooks Web site (www.quickbooks.com), so you may be prompted to make an Internet connection to access that information.

Tip 4: Accept the suggested filename and location

A few minutes into the EasyStep Interview, QuickBooks asks you to specify a name and location for the file that it uses to store your accounting information (see Figure 1-3). I can think of no good reason why you need to fiddle with or change the suggested filename or location. Don't do it. Let QuickBooks name the QuickBooks file whatever it wants and let QuickBooks store the file wherever it wants.

Figure 1-3:
The Save As
dialog box
lets you
change the
suggested
filename
and
location, but
I don't
recommend
doing so.

Tip 5: Go with the suggested chart of accounts

Immediately after you name the file that QuickBooks uses for storing your financial information, the EasyStep Interview displays a dialog box that shows a list of accounts that QuickBooks wants to use for tracking your business's financial condition. This dialog box also asks whether the list of accounts is the one that you want to use. Unless you know quite a bit about accounting and are willing to learn just as much about QuickBooks, I recommend that you accept the suggested chart of accounts. You make your future record keeping much easier by doing so.

Tip 6: Consider tracking all your expenses with your checkbook

You get two choices regarding how to record your expenses:

- ✔ By using just your checkbook
- ✔ By creating a bills-to-pay list

QuickBooks asks this question in the dialog box page shown in Figure 1-4. I want to be careful about what I say next because the decision you make in this dialog box can really screw up your business. But here's my suggestion: I think that you should consider taking the first option — the one that says you want to record bills by using your checkbook. You choose the first option, which I'm hesitantly recommending here, by clicking the Enter the Checks Directly button.

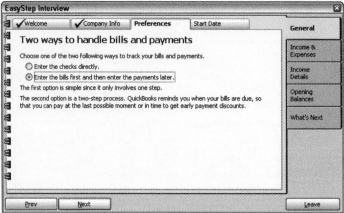

Figure 1-4:
Simplify
your bill
paying by
choosing to
record bills
when you
write
checks.

Now before you rush off to the next EasyStep Interview question, confident and happy in my suggestion, let me tell you about the implicit trade-off you're making. If you choose the Enter the Checks Directly option, you do simplify your record keeping — which is why I suggest that you take this route. But the catch is that you can't track your unpaid bills as closely. Until you sit down to actually write checks for your bills, you don't really know (precisely) how much money you owe vendors. What's more, you can't separate the actual incurring of some expense from the cash outflow that pays the expense. So, by taking the Enter the Checks Directly option, you're unable to do finely tuned accrual-basis accounting (unless you pay bills when you incur them). And you aren't able to closely monitor the money that you owe to vendors.

In my business, by the way, I do use the Enter the Checks Directly option. I do so to simplify my record keeping. But I'm probably a little unusual (at least for a small business) for a couple of reasons. First, almost all my expenses get negotiated up front and then get fixed by contract. (With the help of other writers and a team of editors and desktop publishers, I write and package books and technical reference materials.) For this reason, I don't use and don't need to use QuickBooks to keep track of and remind me about my unpaid bills. In effect, the negotiations and contracts do that.

Second, I've actually been in business for quite a while — more than 15 years, in fact. So I don't have the cash flow problems that many (most?) small businesses have, which means that if I want to produce an accurate profit and loss statement or an accurate balance sheet — one that includes all my expenses — I can just pay all my unpaid bills.

I guess the bottom line here is this: If you don't need to use QuickBooks to closely monitor your unpaid bills and if you don't mind the profit-calculation precision that you lose because of the lag between the time you incur some expense and the time you pay the bill by writing a check, go ahead and use the Enter the Checks Directly option. This choice greatly simplifies one area of your record keeping. Otherwise, go with the second option. (To choose the second option, mark Enter the Bills First and Then Enter the Payments Later, shown in Figure 1-4.)

Tip 7: Add accounts you need

As you step through the interview's questions, QuickBooks asks a few times whether you want to add an account (see Figure 1-5). Go ahead and do this — and feel comfortable doing so. Adding accounts isn't hard. (You need an account for each individual asset, liability, income, or expense amount you want to track.)

Figure 1-5:
During the EasyStep Interview, QuickBooks asks whether you want to add accounts.

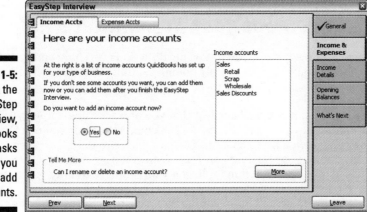

Tip 8: Provide inventory, customer, vendor, and other financial information

The last part of the EasyStep Interview asks you to describe in detail your inventory, your customer receivables, your vendor payables, and most (maybe all) of the other business assets and business liabilities that your firm owns or owes.

Provide this information in detail, and be very careful so that what you enter is correct and makes sense. If your current accounting system doesn't provide this data or seems rifled with errors and inconsistencies, you want to clean up your financial records before you enter this information into QuickBooks.

The Rest of the Story

Throughout the preceding sections in this chapter, I describe how you prepare for and then step through the EasyStep Interview. But even after the EasyStep Interview is over, you probably need to take care of two other little jobs:

✔ If you want to use accrual-basis accounting, you need to make an adjustment.

✔ You need to describe your current business finances.

These chores aren't time-consuming, but they are the two most complicated tasks that you need to do to set up QuickBooks. (If you're not sure what the big deal is about accrual-basis accounting, I respectfully suggest that you take a break here and read Appendix B.)

Should you get your accountant's help?

Oh, shoot. I don't know. If you follow my directions carefully and your business's financial affairs aren't wildly complex, I think that you can probably figure out all this stuff on your own.

Having said that, however, I suggest that you at least think about getting your accountant's help at this juncture. Your accountant can do a much better job of giving you advice that may be specific to your situation. The accountant probably knows your business and can keep you from making a terrible mess of things, just in case you don't follow my directions carefully.

By the way, if you do call upon your accountant to help you with the tasks in this chapter, bookmark the page with the sidebar "For accountants only" (elsewhere in this chapter) and ask your financial wizard to read it. The sidebar summarizes what you've accomplished thus far. (If you're going to do all this stuff yourself, reading the technical stuff sidebar isn't a bad idea.)

Just so you know, one of the things that, as a C.P.A, I do for my clients is help them set up QuickBooks. You almost certainly live in some other area of the country, so this seems somewhat irrelevant; but because I do this, I can give you a couple of pieces of useful information about getting a C.P.A.'s help in setting up. First, your C.P.A., assuming he or she already knows QuickBooks, should be able to help you through the setup process in a couple of hours. So, your C.P.A. will do it (or help you do it) much faster than you can on your own. Second, an hour or so of tutoring from your C.P.A. should mean that you get enough help to record all your usual transactions. With just this help, you can find out how to pay your bills, how to invoice customers exactly the way you want, and how to produce reports. I used to pooh-pooh this kind of hand-holding, but the older (and hopefully wiser) I get, the more I see that business owners and bookkeepers benefit from this up-front help. A bit of planning and expert advice in the beginning can save you a whole lot of trouble later on.

Adjusting for accrual-basis accounting

If you want to use accrual-basis accounting — and I recommend that you do — you need to camouflage a couple of goofy accounts, called *suspense accounts,* that QuickBooks creates when you set up the Item, Customer, and Vendor Lists. (Accrual-basis accounting more accurately measures your profits and financial condition by using a handful of accounting tricks, so you really do want to use accrual-basis account. Check out Appendix B for more information.)

Figure 1-6 shows the example trial balance after I've entered the inventory, accounts receivable, and accounts payable balances. (These account balances get set up indirectly, as noted in the nearby sidebar containing information for accountants. When you set up your Item, Customer, and Vendor Lists, you also create account balances for inventory, accounts receivable, and accounts payable.)

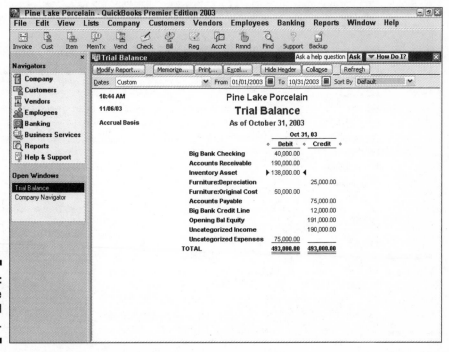

Figure 1-6:
A sample trial balance.

You can produce your own half-complete trial balance from inside QuickBooks by choosing Reports⇨Accountants & Taxes⇨Trial Balance. QuickBooks displays the trial balance report in a document window.

If you need to do so, enter the conversion date in the From and To date boxes by clicking these date boxes and typing the conversion date in MM/DD/YYYY fashion. Figure 1-6, for example, shows the conversion date 10/31/03 in the To box. You can set the From box to any value. The From to To range just needs to end with the conversion date. Make a note of the credit and debit balances shown for the Uncategorized Income and Uncategorized Expenses accounts.

If you want, you can print the report by clicking the Print button and then, when QuickBooks displays the Print Report dialog box, by clicking its Print button. Yes, you click *two* Print buttons.

After you have the conversion date balances for the Uncategorized Income and Uncategorized Expenses accounts, you're ready to make the accrual accounting adjustment. To do so, follow these steps:

1. **Choose Lists⇨Chart of Accounts to display that window.**

   QuickBooks displays the Chart of Accounts window, as shown in Figure 1-7.

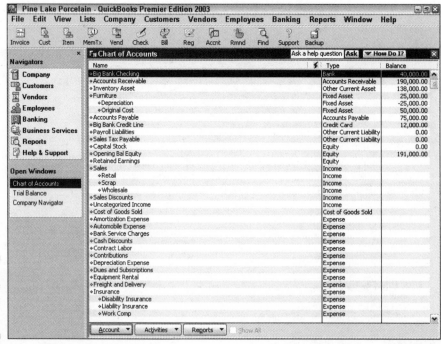

Figure 1-7:
The Chart of
Accounts
window.

2. **Double-click Opening Bal Equity in the Chart of Accounts list to display that account.**

   Opening Bal Equity is listed after the liability accounts. QuickBooks displays the register — just a list of transactions — for the account named Opening Bal Equity. Figure 1-8, coincidentally, shows this register.

3. **Select the next empty row of the register if it isn't already selected (although it probably is).**

   You can select a row by clicking it, or you can use the up- or down-arrow key to move to the next empty row.

4. **Type the conversion date in the Date field.**

   Move the cursor to the Date field (if it isn't already there) and type the date. Use the MM/DD/YY format. For example, you can type either **103103** or **10/31/03** to enter October 31, 2003.

5. **Type the Uncategorized Income account balance (from the trial balance report) in the Increase field.**

   In Figure 1-6, for example, the Uncategorized Income account balance is $190,000. In this case, click the Increase field and type **190000** in the field. (You don't need to include the dollar sign or the comma; QuickBooks adds the punctuation for you.)

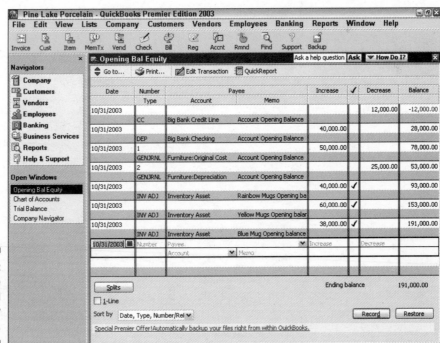

Figure 1-8:
The Opening Bal Equity register.

6. **Type** Uncategorized Income **(the account name) in the Account field.**

    Select the Account field, which is on the row under the word Payee, and begin typing **Uncategorized Income**, the account name. As soon as you type enough of the name for QuickBooks to figure out what you're typing, it fills in the rest of the name for you. When this happens, you can stop typing.

7. **Click the Record button to record the Uncategorized Income adjustment transaction.**

8. **Again, select the next empty row of the register.**

    Click it or use the up- or down-arrow key.

TECHNICAL STUFF

For accountants only

If you're reading this sidebar, I assume that you're an accountant who's been asked to help your client with the last piece of the QuickBooks conversion. Of course, you understand double-entry bookkeeping and presumably you're familiar with the general mechanics involved in converting to new accounting systems. With those two caveats, you're ready to start.

First, your client has probably already installed QuickBooks and then, by running something called the EasyStep Interview, partially set up a chart of accounts and loaded three master files: the Item List, the Customer List, and the Vendor List. The Item List master file describes the inventory account balances. (QuickBooks uses an average costing assumption.) The Customer List master file describes the accounts receivable balances. The Vendor List master file describes the accounts payable balances. Because your client has set up these master files, QuickBooks has made three journal entries, which I describe in the following paragraphs. (I'm using Xs to represent numbers, in case you're not familiar with this convention.)

To set up the conversion date inventory balance (if inventory exists), QuickBooks has created the following entry:

	Debit	Credit
Inventory Asset	$X,XXX	
Opening Bal Equity		$X,XXX

To set up the conversion date accounts receivable (A/R) balance (if A/R exists), QuickBooks has created the following entry:

	Debit	Credit
Accounts Receivable	$X,XXX	
Uncategorized Income		$X,XXX

To set up the conversion date accounts payable (A/P) balance (if A/P exists), QuickBooks has created the following entry:

	Debit	Credit
Accounts Payable		$X,XXX
Uncategorized Expenses	$X,XXX	

To complete the picture, you need to do two little housekeeping chores. If your client plans to use accrual-basis accounting, you need to get rid of the credit to the Uncategorized Income account and the debit to the Uncategorized Expenses account. (These two accounts are really just suspense accounts.) And you need to load the rest of the trial balance. I describe the steps for accomplishing these tasks in the section "Supplying the missing numbers," elsewhere in this chapter.

9. **Type the conversion date in the Date field.**

   Move the cursor to the Date field (if it isn't already there) and type the date. You use the MM/DD/YY format. You can type **10/31/03**, for example, to enter October 31, 2003.

10. **Type the Uncategorized Expenses account balance in the Decrease field.**

    In Figure 1-6, for example, the Uncategorized Expenses account balance is $75,000. In this case, you click the Decrease field and then type **75000** in the field. I've said this before, but I'll say it again because you're just starting out: You don't need to include any punctuation, such as a dollar sign or comma.

11. **Type** Uncategorized Expenses **(the account name) in the Account field.**

    Select the Account field, which is on the second line of the register transaction, and begin typing **Uncategorized Expenses**, the account name. As soon as you type enough of the name for QuickBooks to figure out what you're typing, it fills in the rest of the name for you.

12. **Click the Record button to record the Uncategorized Expenses adjustment transaction.**

    Figure 1-9 shows the Opening Bal Equity register with the correction transactions. The correction transactions are numbered with a 3 and a 4. See them? They're in the middle of the register.

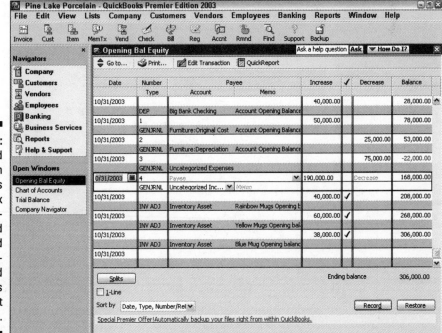

Figure 1-9: The third and fourth transactions shown fix the uncategorized income and uncategorized expenses account balances.

You can close the Opening Bal Equity register, too, at this point. You're finished with it. (One way to close it is to click the Close button — this is the little button with an X in the upper-right corner of the register window.)

You can check your work thus far — and checking it *is* a good idea — by producing another copy of the trial balance report. What you want to check are the Uncategorized Income and Uncategorized Expenses account balances. They should both be zero — as shown in Figure 1-10.

You can produce a trial balance by choosing Reports➪Accountant & Taxes➪ Trial Balance. QuickBooks displays the trial balance report in a document window. If you need to enter the conversion date in the From and To date boxes, click the boxes and type the conversion date in MM/DD/YY fashion in both boxes.

If the Uncategorized Income and the Uncategorized Expenses account balances don't show zero, you (with my help, of course) may have botched the accrual adjustment. To fix the mistake, redisplay the Opening Bal Equity register, select the adjustment transactions, and then check the account, amount, and field (increase or decrease). If one of the fields is wrong, select the field and replace its contents by typing over them.

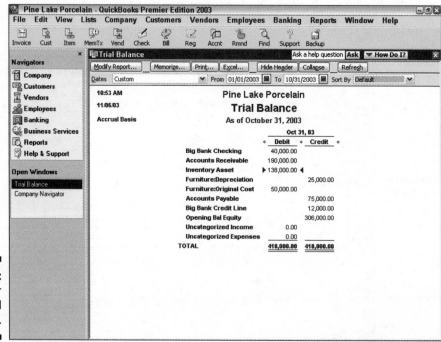

Figure 1-10: Another sample trial balance.

Supplying the missing numbers

You're almost done. Really. Your only other task is to enter the rest of the trial balance into QuickBooks. To perform this task, of course, you need to already have a trial balance as of the conversion date. But you should have one. (I talk about this earlier in the chapter; see the section, "The trial balance of the century.") Follow these steps:

1. **Display the General Journal Entry window.**

   Choose the Company➪Make Journal Entry command. QuickBooks displays the General Journal Entry window, as shown in Figure 1-11.

2. **Type the conversion date in the Date field.**

   Move the cursor to the Date field (if it isn't already there) and type the date. As you may know by now, you use the MM/DD/YY format. For example, type **10/31/03** for October 31, 2003. (Or **103103**, if you don't want to put the slashes in.)

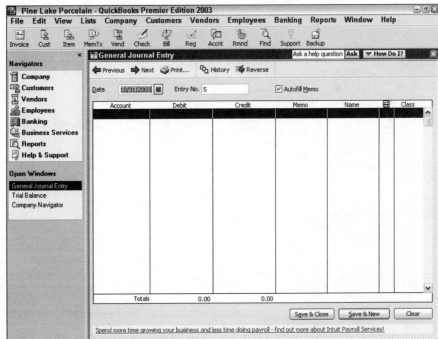

Figure 1-11: The empty General Journal Entry window.

3. **Type each trial balance account and balance that isn't already in the half-completed trial balance.**

   Okay. This step sounds confusing. But remember that you've already entered your cash, accounts receivable, inventory, and accounts payable account balances, as well as most other liability account balances and a portion of the Opening Bal Equity account balance as part of the EasyStep Interview.

   So what you need to do now is enter the rest of the trial balance: specifically, the year-to-date income and expense account balances and the remaining portion of the Opening Bal Equity. To enter each account and balance, use a row of the General Journal Entry window's list box. Figure 1-12 shows how this window looks after you enter the rest of the trial balance into the list box rows.

4. **Click Save & New to record the general journal entries that set up the rest of your trial balance.**

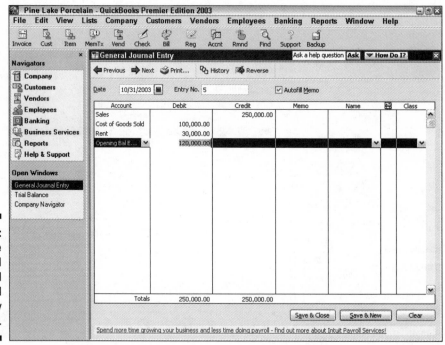

Figure 1-12: The completed General Journal Entry window.

Checking your work one more time

Checking your work again is a good idea. Produce another copy of the trial balance report, as shown in Figure 1-13. What you want to check is that the QuickBooks trial balance is the same one that you wanted to enter.

Remember that you can produce a trial balance by choosing Reports⇨ Accountant & Taxes⇨Trial Balance. Be sure to enter the conversion date in the From and To date boxes. If the QuickBooks trial balance report agrees with what your records show, you're finished.

If the QuickBooks trial balance doesn't agree with what your records show, you need to fix the problem. Fixing it is a bit awkward but not complicated. Choose Reports⇨Accountant & Taxes⇨Journal. QuickBooks displays a report or journal that lists all the transactions that you or QuickBooks has entered as part of setting up. (The Dates, From, and To text boxes need to specify the

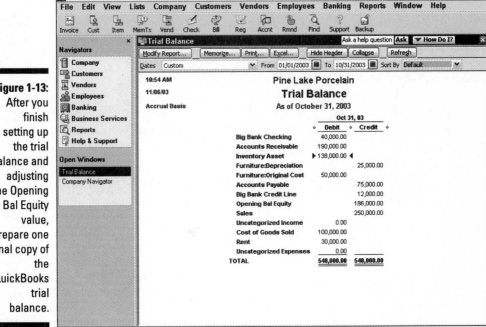

Figure 1-13: After you finish setting up the trial balance and adjusting the Opening Bal Equity value, prepare one final copy of the QuickBooks trial balance.

conversion date.) Scroll through the list of transactions until you get to the last one. The last transaction is the one that you entered to set up the rest of the trial balance, and it names recognizable accounts and uses familiar debit and credit amounts. Double-click this transaction. QuickBooks redisplays the General Journal Entry window with the botched transaction. Find the mistake and then fix the erroneous account or amount by clicking it and typing the correct account or amount.

Congratulations! You're done.

Chapter 2

Lots of Lists

In This Chapter

▶ Adding items to the Item list

▶ Adding employees to the Employee list

▶ Adding new customers and jobs

▶ Adding new vendors

▶ Understanding and using the other lists

*I*f you've just finished going through the EasyStep Interview (see Chapter 1), don't look at the title of this chapter and think to yourself that you're ready to throw in the towel because you're sick and tired of creating lists. As a matter of fact, if you've just finished the EasyStep Interview and carefully entered the names of all your products, employees, customers, and vendors into lists, you can kick up your heels and relax because you probably don't even need to read this chapter just yet. The lists that you need are already set up. But as time goes by, I bet you'll find that your lists need updating. You will get new customers and begin working with new vendors. You may even hire a new employee. In this chapter, I describe how you add to the lists that you've created in the EasyStep Interview.

I recommend that you periodically check your trial balance, especially after you (or someone else!) add to your lists, to make sure that you haven't created uncategorized transactions by entering balances for inventory items, customers, or vendors. You can produce a trial balance by choosing Reports⇨Accountant & Taxes⇨Trial Balance.

The Magic and Mystery of Items

Before you start adding to your Item list, I need to tell you that QuickBooks isn't very smart about its view of what you sell. It thinks that anything you stick on a sales invoice or a purchase order is something you're selling.

If you sell blue, yellow, and red coffee mugs, for example, you probably figure (and correctly so) that you need to add descriptions of each of these items to the Item list: blue mug, yellow mug, and red mug. But if you add freight charges to an invoice, QuickBooks thinks that you're adding another mug. And if you add sales tax to an invoice, well, guess what? QuickBooks again thinks that you're adding another mug.

This wacky definition of items is confusing at first. But just remember one thing and you'll be okay: You aren't the one who's stupid. QuickBooks is. No, I'm not saying that QuickBooks is a bad program. It's a wonderful accounting program and a great tool. What I'm saying is that QuickBooks is only a dumb computer program. It's not an artificial intelligence program. It doesn't pick up on the little subtleties of business — such as the fact that, even though you charge customers for freight, you're not really in the shipping business.

Each entry on the invoice or purchase order — the mugs you sell, the subtotal, the discount, the freight charges, and the sales tax — is an *item*. Yes, I know. This setup is weird. But getting used to the wackiness now makes the discussions that follow much easier to understand.

If you want to see a sample invoice, take a peek at Figure 2-1. See those first three items: Rainbow Mugs, Yellow Mugs, and Blue Mugs? You can see the sense of calling them *items,* right? All of these mugs are things you sell. But then suppose that you give frequent buyers of your merchandize a 10 percent discount. In order to include this discount in your accounting, you need to add a Subtotal item to tally the sale and then a Discount item to calculate the discount. Figure 2-1 also shows this. See it? Kind of weird, right? And then look at the Shipping item — which charges the customer $50 for freight. Yep, that's right: another item. In sum, everything that appears on an invoice or a purchase is an item that needs to be described in your item list.

I describe creating invoices in Chapter 4 and creating purchase orders in Chapter 7.

Adding items you may include on invoices

To add invoice or purchase order items to the Item Code list, follow these steps:

1. **Choose Lists➪Item List.**

   QuickBooks, with restrained but obvious enthusiasm, displays the Item List window, as shown in Figure 2-2.

2. **Click the Item button at the bottom of the Item List window and choose New from the drop-down menu.**

   QuickBooks displays the New Item window, as shown in Figure 2-3.

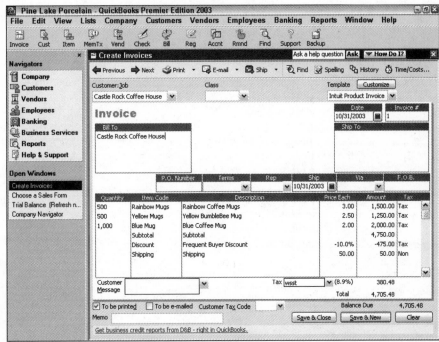

Figure 2-1:
A sample
QuickBooks
invoice.

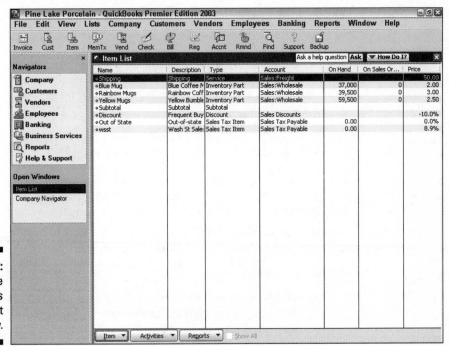

Figure 2-2:
The
QuickBooks
Item List
window.

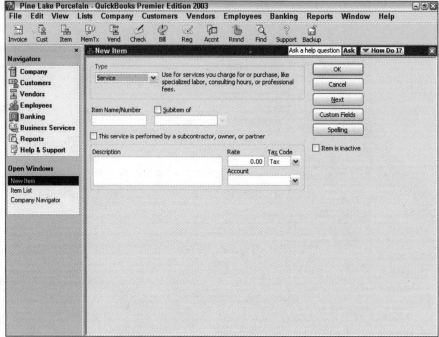

Figure 2-3:
The
QuickBooks
New Item
window.

3. Categorize the item.

Select an item type from the Type drop-down list box. The Item list that you see is dependent on the type of business you told QuickBooks you were in when you set up the program, so use the following as a sample — the amount and type of items you need depend on the business you're in. Select one of the following item types by clicking the name in the list:

- **Service:** Select this type if you charge for a service — such as an hour of labor or a repair job.

- **Inventory Part:** Select this type if what you sell is something that you buy from someone else. If you sell thingamajigs that you purchase from the manufacturer Thingamajigs Amalgamated, for example, you specify the item type as Inventory Part. (For more information on using QuickBooks to track inventory, see Chapter 7.)

- **Inventory Assembly:** Select this type if what you sell is something that you make. In other words, if you buy raw materials or other components and then assemble these things to create your finished product, the finished product is an inventory assembly item.

- **Non-Inventory Part:** Select this type if what you sell is something that you don't want to track as inventory. (You usually don't use this item type for products that you sell, by the way. Instead, you use it for items that you buy for the business and need to include on purchase orders.)

- **Other Charge:** Select this item type for things such as freight and handling charges that you include on invoices.

- **Subtotal:** This item type adds everything before you subtract any discount, add the sales tax, and so on.

- **Group:** Use this item type to enter a bunch of items (which are already on the list) at one time. This item is a nice timesaver. For example, if you commonly sell sets of items, you don't have to specify those items individually every time you write an invoice.

- **Discount:** This item type calculates an amount to be subtracted from a subtotal.

- **Payment:** This option is wacky, but if your invoice sometimes includes an entry that reduces the invoice total — customer deposits, for example — select this item type. If you're confused by this item type, just ignore it.

- **Sales Tax Item:** Select this item type for the sales tax that you include on the invoice.

- **Sales Tax Group:** This item type is similar to the Group item type, but you use it only for sales taxes that are collected in one transaction and owed to multiple agencies.

4. **Type an item number or name.**

Press the Tab key or use your mouse to click the Item Name/Number text box beneath the Type drop-down list box. Then type a short description of the item.

5. **(Optional) Make the item a subitem.**

If you want to work with *subitems* — items that appear within other items — check the Subitem Of check box and use the corresponding drop-down list box to specify the parent item to which a subitem belongs.

If you set up a parent item for coffee mugs and subitems for blue, yellow, and red mugs, for example, you can produce reports that show parent items (such as mugs) and subitems (such as the differently colored mugs). Subitems are just an extra complexity, so if you're new to this QuickBooks stuff, I suggest that you keep things simple by avoiding them.

6. **Describe the item in more detail.**

Move the cursor to the Description text box and type a description. This description then appears on the invoice. Note that if you specified the item type as Inventory Part in Step 3, you see two description text boxes: Description on Purchase Transactions and Description on Sales

Transactions. The purchase description appears on purchase orders, and the sales description appears on sales invoices.

7. **If the item type is Service, Non-Inventory Part, or Other Charge, tell QuickBooks how much to charge for the item, whether the item is subject to sales tax, and which income account to use for tracking the income that you receive from selling the item.**

   • For a Service type, use the Rate text box to specify the price you charge for one unit of the service. If you charge by the hour, for example, the rate is the charge for an hour of service. If you charge for a job — such as a repair job or the completion of a specific task — the rate is the charge for the job or task.

   • For a Non-Inventory Part type, use the Price text box to specify the amount you charge for the item.

   • For an Other Charge type, use the Amount or % text box, which replaces the Rate text box, to specify the amount you charge for the item. You can type an amount, such as **20** for $20.00, or you can type a percentage. If you type a percentage, QuickBooks calculates the Other Charge Amount as the percentage multiplied by the preceding item shown on the invoice. (You usually put in an Other Charge after using a Subtotal Item — something I talk about in the "Creating other wacky items for invoices" section, later in this chapter.)

   • For all three types, use the Taxable check box to indicate whether the item is taxed. (Note that the Taxable check box only appears if you told QuickBooks in the EasyStep Interview that you charge customers sales tax.)

   • For all three types, use the Account drop-down list to specify which income account you want to use to track the income that you receive from the sale of this item.

8. **If the item type is Inventory Part, tell QuickBooks how much to charge for the inventory part, how much the inventory part costs, and which income account to use for tracking the product sales income.**

   For an Inventory Part item type, QuickBooks displays the New Item window, as shown in Figure 2-4.

   You use the extra fields that this special version of the window displays to record the following information:

   • **Description on Purchase Transactions:** Describe the part. This description appears on the documents (such as purchase orders) used when you buy items for your inventory.

   • **Cost:** Specify the average cost per unit of the items you currently have. This field acts as the default rate when you enter the item on a purchase transaction.

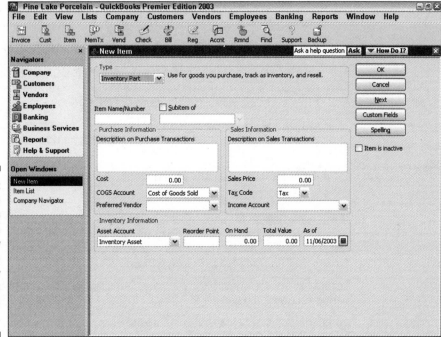

Figure 2-4:
The
QuickBooks
New Item
window
with
Inventory
Part item
type
selected.

- **COGS (Cost of Goods Sold) Account:** Specify the account that you want QuickBooks to use for tracking this item's cost when you sell it. (QuickBooks suggests the Cost of Goods Sold account. If you've created other accounts for your COGS, select the appropriate account.)

- **Preferred Vendor:** Specify your first choice when ordering the item for your business. (If the vendor isn't on your Vendor list, QuickBooks asks you to add it. If you say, "Yeah, I do want to add it," QuickBooks displays the Add Vendor window, which you can then use to describe the vendor.)

- **Description on Sales Transactions:** Type in a description of the item that you want to appear on documents, such as invoices and so on, that your customers see. (QuickBooks suggests the same description you used in the Description on Purchase Transactions text box as a default.)

- **Sales Price:** Enter the amount that you charge for the item.

- **Taxable:** Indicate whether the item is taxed.

- **Income Account:** Specify the account that you want QuickBooks to use for tracking the income from the sale of the part. This is probably the Resale Income or Sales account. You typically use the Resale Income account to track wholesale (nontaxable) sales and the Sales account to track retail (taxable) sales.

- **Asset Account:** Specify the other current asset account that you want QuickBooks to use for tracking this inventory item's value.

- **Reorder Point:** Specify the lowest inventory quantity of this item that can remain before you order more. When the inventory level drops to this quantity, QuickBooks adds a Reminder to the Reminders list, notifying you that you need to reorder the item. (To see the Reminders List, choose Lists⇨Reminders.)

- **On Hand:** Leave this field at zero. To enter a number now is to record an uncategorized transaction, and you don't want to do that.

- **Total Value:** Leave this field at zero, too.

- **As Of:** Enter the current date.

9. **If the item type is Inventory Assembly, tell QuickBooks which cost of goods sold and income account to use for tracking the item, how much to charge for the inventory assembly, and how to build the item from other component inventory items.**

   For an Inventory Assembly item type, QuickBooks displays the New Item window, shown in Figure 2-5.

   You use the extra fields that this special version of the window displays to record the following information:

   - **COGS (Cost of Goods Sold) Account:** Specify the account that you want QuickBooks to use for tracking this item's cost when you sell it. (QuickBooks suggests the Cost of Goods Sold account. If you've created other accounts for your COGS, select the appropriate account.)

   - **Description:** Type in a description of the item that you want to appear on documents, such as invoices and so on, that your customers see. (QuickBooks suggests the same description you used in the Description on Purchase Transactions text box as a default.)

   - **Sales Price:** Enter the amount that you charge for the item.

   - **Tax Code:** Indicate whether the item is taxed.

   - **Income Account:** Specify the account that you want QuickBooks to use for tracking the income from the sale of the part. This is probably the Resale Income or Sales account. You typically use the Resale Income account to track wholesale (nontaxable) sales and the Sales account to track retail (taxable) sales.

   - **Components Needed:** Use the Components Needed list box to identify the component items and the quantities needed to make the inventory assembly.

   - **Asset Account:** Specify the other current asset account that you want QuickBooks to use for tracking this inventory item's value.

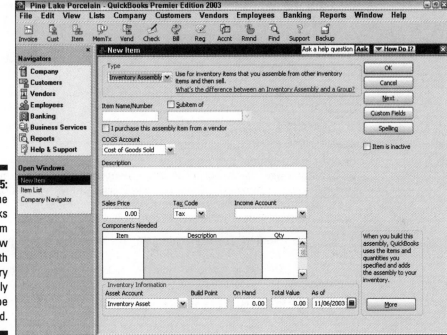

Figure 2-5:
The
QuickBooks
New Item
window
with
Inventory
Assembly
item type
selected.

- **Build Point:** Specify the lowest inventory quantity of this item that can remain before you manufacture more. When the inventory level drops to this quantity, QuickBooks adds a Reminder to the Reminders list, notifying you that you need to make more of the item.

- **On Hand:** Leave this field at zero. To enter a number now is to record an uncategorized transaction, and you don't want to do that.

- **Total Value:** Leave this field at zero, too.

- **As Of:** Enter the current date.

10. **If the item type is Sales Tax Item, tell QuickBooks what sales tax rate to charge and what government agency to pay.**

    Note: The Sales Tax Item version of the New Item window looks a little different than the window shown in Figure 2-5.

    If the item type is Sales Tax Item, you need to tell QuickBooks what the sales tax rate is and which government agency you remit sales taxes to. But this is straightforward stuff. Enter the sales tax rate into the appropriate box and the state (or city or whatever tax agency name) into the appropriate box.

    - **Tax Name and Description:** Specify further details for later identification.

    - **Tax Rate:** Specify the sales tax rate as a percentage.

• **Tax Agency:** Name the state or local tax agency that collects all the loot you remit. If the tax agency isn't on the list, you can add it by picking <Add New> from the drop-down list box.

11. **If the item type is Payment, describe the payment method and how you want QuickBooks to handle the payment.**

    Note: The Payment Item version of the New Item window looks a little different than the window shown in Figure 2-5.

    Use the Payment Method drop-down list to specify the method of payment for a Payment item. QuickBooks provides a starting list of several of the usual payment methods. You can easily add more payment types by choosing <Add New> from the drop-down list box. When you choose this entry, QuickBooks displays the New Payment Method dialog box. In the dialog box's only text box, identify the payment method: cows, beads, shells, or some other what-have-you.

    After you're finished, use the area in the lower-left corner of the New Item window to either group the payment with other undeposited funds or, if you use the drop-down list box, deposit the payment to a specific account.

12. **Click OK or Next when you're finished.**

    When you finish describing one item, click OK to add the item to the list and return to the Item List window. Click Next to add the item to the list and keep the New Item window on-screen so that you can add more items.

13. **If you added a new Inventory item, record the purchase of the item.**

    After you've finished describing any new inventory items, you need to make another transaction in order to categorize the purchase of the items (unless they just showed up one morning on your doorstep). For an explanation of these transactions, turn to Chapter 7.

Creating other wacky items for invoices

In the preceding section, I don't describe all the items that you can add. For example, you can create a *subtotal item* to calculate the subtotal of the items you list on an invoice. (You usually need this subtotal when you want to calculate a sales tax on the invoice's items.) You may want to create other wacky items for your invoices as well, such as discounts. I describe these special types of items in the next few sections.

Creating subtotal items to stick subtotals on invoices

You need to add a subtotal item if you ever want to apply a discount to a series of items on an invoice. To add a subtotal item to your Item list, choose Lists⇨Item List, click the Item button, and choose New from the drop-down menu. This displays the New Item window — the same one you've seen several times already in this chapter. Specify the item type as Subtotal and then provide an item name (such as "Subtotal").

When you want to subtotal items on an invoice, all you do is stick this subtotal item on the invoice after the items you want to subtotal. Keep in mind, though, that QuickBooks doesn't set up a subtotal feature automatically — you have to add a subtotal item; otherwise, you can only apply a discount item that you create to the single item that immediately precedes the discount. A discount item, by the way, calculates a discount on an invoice.

Creating group items to batch stuff you sell together

You can create an item that puts one line on an invoice that's actually a combination of several other items. To add a group item, display the New Item window and specify the item type as Group. QuickBooks displays the New Item window shown in Figure 2-6.

If you purchase three parts — a blue mug, a red mug, and a yellow mug — but sell the items in a set, for example, you can create an item that groups the three items. Note that when you create a group, you continue to track the group member inventories individually and don't track the inventory of the group as a new item.

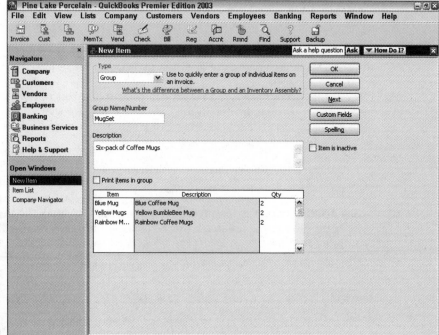

Figure 2-6: The QuickBooks New Item Window with the item type Group selected.

In the New Item window, use the Item/Description/Qty list box to list each item included in the group. When you click an item line in the Item/Description/Qty list box, QuickBooks places a downward-pointing arrow at the right end of the Item column. You click this arrow to open a drop-down list of items. (If the list is longer than can be shown, you can use the scroll bar on the right to move up and down the list.) If you click the Print Items in Group check box, QuickBooks lists all the items in the group on invoices. (In the case of the mugs, invoices list the individual blue, red, and yellow mugs instead of just listing the group name, such as "mug set.")

Creating discount items to add discounts to invoices

You can create an item that calculates a discount and sticks the discount on an invoice as another line item. To add a discount item to the list, display the New Item window, specify the item type as Discount, and provide an item name or number and a description.

Use the Amount or % text box to specify how the discount is calculated. If the discount is a set amount (such as $50.00), type the amount. If the discount is calculated as a percentage, enter the percentage, including the percent symbol. When you enter a percentage, QuickBooks calculates the Discount amount as the percentage multiplied by the preceding item shown on the invoice. (If you want to apply the discount to a group of items, you need to use a subtotal item and follow it with the discount.)

Back in Figure 2-1, I showed an invoice that uses both a Subtotal item and a Discount. If you're interested in how this works, look back there.

Use the Account drop-down list to specify the expense account that you want to use to track the cost of the discounts you offer.

Click Apply Discount Before Taxes if you want to use this option. (This option appears only if you indicated in the EasyStep Interview that you charge sales tax.) If you need to collect sales tax and you didn't set this function up in the EasyStep Interview, follow these steps:

1. **Choose Edit⇨Preferences.**

   The Preferences dialog box appears.

2. **Click the Sales Tax icon from the list on the left, click the Company Preferences tab, and mark the Yes option button in the Do You Charge Sales Tax? area.**

3. **Then add the sales tax item(s) to your Item list.**

Creating Sales Tax Group items to batch sales taxes together

Sales Tax Groups enable you to batch several sales taxes that you're supposed to charge as one sales tax so that they appear as a single sales tax on the invoice. Combining the taxes is necessary — or at least possible — when you're supposed to charge, say, a 6.5 percent state sales tax, a 1.7 percent county sales tax, and a 0.4 percent city sales tax, but you want to show one, all-encompassing 8.6 percent sales tax on the invoice.

To add a Sales Tax Group item, display the New Item window and specify the item type as Sales Tax Group. QuickBooks displays the New Item window, as shown in Figure 2-7. Use the Tax Item/Rate/Tax Agency/Description list box to list the other sales tax items that you want to include in the group. When you click an item line in the list box, QuickBooks places a down arrow at the right end of the Tax Item column. You can click this arrow to open a drop-down list of Sales Tax items.

Editing items

If you make a mistake, you can change any piece of item information by displaying the Item List window and double-clicking the item so that QuickBooks displays the Edit Item window. You then can use the Edit Item window to make changes.

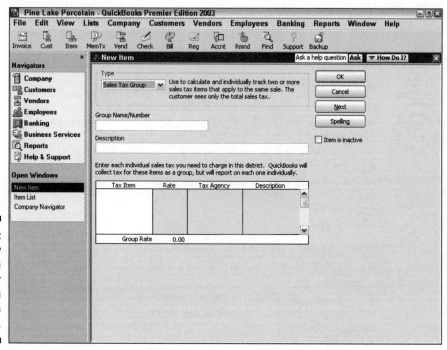

Figure 2-7:
The New Item window for the item type Sales Tax Group.

Adding Employees to Your Employee List

If you do payroll in QuickBooks or if you track sales by employees, you need to describe each employee. Describing employees is pretty dang easy. Choose Lists⇨Employee List to display that window. Then click the Employee button and choose New from the drop-down menu to have QuickBooks display the New Employee window, as shown in Figure 2-8.

See Figure 2-8? It's pretty straightforward, right? You just fill in the fields to describe the employee.

Lesser computer book writers would probably provide step-by-step descriptions of how you move the cursor to the First Name text box and type the person's first name, how you move the cursor to the next text box, type something there, and so on. Not me. No way. I know that you can tell just by looking at this window that all you do is click a text box and type the obvious bit of information. Right?

I'll tell you a couple of important things about the New Employee window, however. When you release an employee, it's important to enter the release date for the employee after you've written that final paycheck on the Employment Info tab. This way, when you process payroll in the future, you can't accidentally pay the former employee. As for the Type field, most employees probably fit the regular category. If you're uncertain whether an employee fits the guidelines for corporate officer, statutory employee, or owner, see the Circular E publication from the IRS. And sleep tight.

The Additional Info tab enables you to create customizable fields, in case you want to keep information that isn't covered by the QuickBooks default fields — favorite color and that type of thing. Note, too, that you can include the information shown in Figure 2-9 by choosing Payroll and Compensation Info from the Change Tabs box. Again, what you need to do in this tab is fairly straightforward. And, by the way, if you've told QuickBooks that you want to do payroll, QuickBooks does prompt you to enter the information it needs to calculate things like federal and state income taxes, payroll taxes, and vacation pay.

After you finish describing an employee, click OK to add the employee to the list and return to the Employee List window. Or click Next to add the employee to the list and add more employees.

You can also inactivate an employee from your list if it starts to get cluttered with names of employees who may no longer work for you. Read about inactivating items, employees, customers, and vendors in the sidebar "Inactivating list items" elsewhere in this chapter.

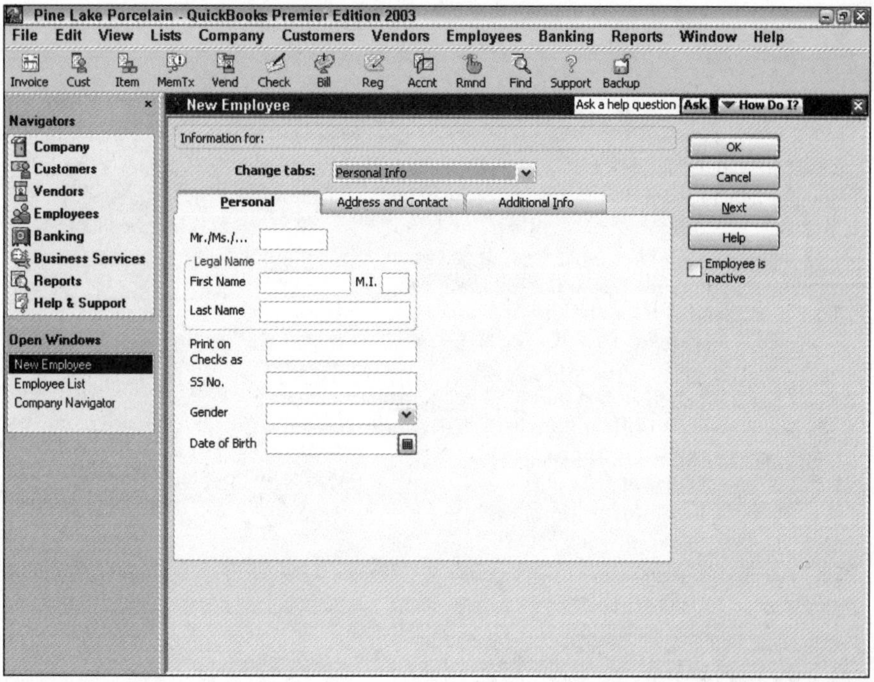

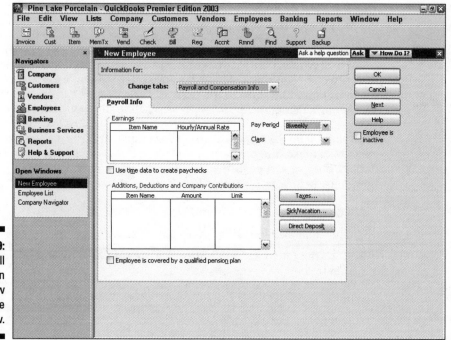

Figure 2-8:
The New
Employee
window.

Figure 2-9:
The Payroll
Info tab in
the New
Employee
window.

Inactivating list items

One of the neat features in QuickBooks is that it enables you to simplify your lists by hiding items that are no longer active, including those that you expect to be active again later. If you have seasonal employees, you can hide them from your Employee list for the times of the year when they don't work. Or if you sell commemorative key chains only every five years, you can keep them from cluttering your Item list in the off years. You can also inactivate customers and vendors from their respective lists.

To inactivate something from a list, all you have to do is open the list and double-click the item.

When QuickBooks opens the item, employee, customer, or vendor that you want to inactivate, check the Item Is Inactive box. (The name of the box changes, depending on what you're trying to inactivate.) Then click OK. QuickBooks hides this member from your list. The next time you display the list, the Show All box appears.

To view and edit hidden members of your list, just click the Show All box. Any inactive members show up with little hand icons beside them. If you want to reactivate a member, all you have to do is click the hand icon, and the member is reactivated.

Customers Are Your Business

This is sort of off the subject of lists, but I read about a survey that some business school had conducted. In the survey, people who wanted to start a business were asked what is the most important thing that a person needs to start a business. Almost all of them answered, "Cash." The same survey also asked a large number of people who had already started businesses — many of whom had been running their businesses successfully for years — what's the most important thing that a person needs to start a business. They all answered, "Customers."

Weird, huh? I do think that those survey results are true, though. You need customers to get into business. Everything else — including cash — is secondary. But I've sort of gotten off the track. I'm supposed to be describing how you add to your Customer List. Here's the blow-by-blow:

1. **Choose Lists⇨Customer:Job List.**

   The Customer:Job List window appears.

2. **Click the Customer:Job button and choose New from the drop-down menu.**

   QuickBooks displays the Address Info tab of the New Customer window, as shown in Figure 2-10. Use this window to describe the customer in as much detail as possible.

3. **Type the customer's name.**

Enter the name of the customer as you want it to appear in the customer list. You can list customers by company name or by the representative's last name.

4. **Give the company name.**

That's right, type the customer's company name.

If you see a Check Credit button in the New Customer window, you can click it to get credit information from Dun & Bradstreet — all the inside dirt on the very customer you're describing. This service isn't free. For a subscription, you'll pay roughly $20 to $40 a month, depending on the level of service; or, if you're not a subscriber, you'll pay roughly $15 for each credit report. Dun & Bradstreet credit reports, in case you haven't seen one before, are pretty interesting. You know who the firm owners are and generally get information both on a firm's revenues and its current payment practices. Two cautions, however. Some of the information is provided by the customer (so you can't know how good the information is). Also, some of the information is often rather, well, out of date. In spite of these problems, however, the information is often very useful for assessing the financial condition of your more important customers.

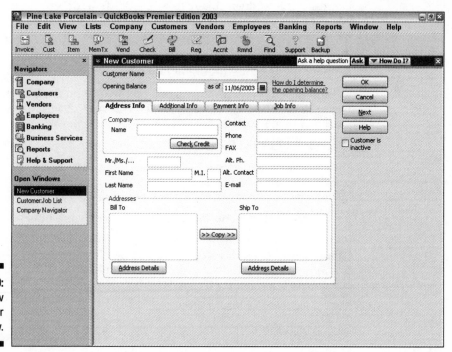

Figure 2-10:
The New
Customer
window.

5. **(Optional) Give the name of your contact, along with other pertinent information.**

   Move the cursor to the Mr./Ms. text box and type the appropriate title. Same with the First Name, M.I., and Last Name text boxes. (QuickBooks automatically types the names into the Contact text box as you type them. Nice touch, eh?)

   Go ahead and fill in the Phone, FAX, Alt. Ph. (alternate phone), and E-mail text boxes while you're at it.

6. **(Really optional) Give the name of your alternate contact.**

   Move the cursor to the Alt. Contact text box and type the name of the alternate contact.

7. **Give the billing address.**

   You can use the Bill To text box to provide the customer's billing address. QuickBooks copies the Company and Contact names to the first lines of the billing address, so you need to enter only the address. To move from the end of one line to the start of the next, press Enter.

8. **Give the shipping address.**

   You can use the Ship To text box to provide the customer's shipping address if this address differs from the Bill To address. (If it's the same, just click Copy.) You enter this information in the same way that you enter the Bill To address. A few deft mouse clicks. Some typing. You're done.

9. **(Optional) Click the Additional Info tab and record some more data.**

   If you want, click the Additional Info tab. When you do, QuickBooks displays the tab shown in Figure 2-11. You can use this tab to describe the customer in more detail.

10. **(Optional) Click the Payment Info tab and record some more data.**

    You can click the Payment Info tab and then use its boxes to record bits of customer information, such as the account number that should be included with any payments. I'm not showing the Payment Info tab here.

11. **(Optional) Click the Job Info tab to add specific job information.**

    Because you're creating a new customer account, not invoicing by jobs, I'll wait and explain this step in the next section. If you're the "can't-wait" type, feel free to take a look. You can add a specific job to the new customer's information.

12. **Save the customer information.**

    When you finish describing a customer, click OK to add the customer to the list and return to the Customer:Job List window. Or click Next to add the customer to the list and keep the New Customer window on-screen so that you can add more customers.

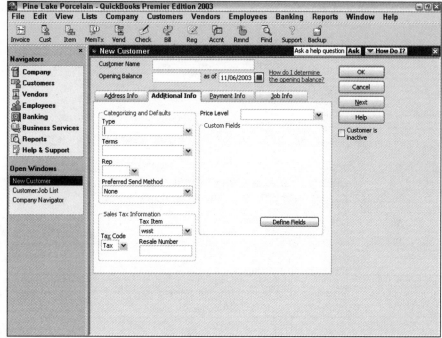

Figure 2-11:
Add more
details in
the
Additional
Info tab.

If you want to change some bit of customer information, display the Customer:Job List window, double-click the customer account you want to change, and then make changes by using the Edit Customer window.

QuickBooks enables you to synchronize the contact information in your name lists with Microsoft Outlook or Symantec Act. To do so, choose Company⇨Synchronize Contacts. Follow the steps of the Synchronization Setup Wizard to set up this feature in QuickBooks. (You only need to do this once.)

It's Just a Job

In QuickBooks, you can track invoices by customer or by customer and job. This may sound kooky, I know; but in some businesses, tracking invoices makes sense, especially businesses that invoice customers, often several times, for specific jobs.

Take the case of a construction subcontractor who does foundation work for a handful of builders of single-family homes. This construction subcontractor invoices his customers by job, and he invoices each customer several times for the same job. For example, he invoices Poverty Rock Realty for the foundation job at 1113 Birch Street when he pours the footing and then again when he lays the block. At 1028 Fairview, the same foundation job takes more than one invoice, too.

To set up jobs for customers, you need to first describe the customers (as I explain in the preceding section). Then follow these steps:

1. **Choose the Lists⇨Customer:Job List command.**

   QuickBooks displays the Customer:Job List window.

2. **Select the customer for which you want to set up a job.**

   This step is simple. Just click the customer name.

3. **Click the Customer:Job button from the bottom of the window and choose Add Job from the drop-down menu.**

   QuickBooks displays the New Job window (as shown in Figure 2-12). You use this window to describe the job. A great deal of the information in this window appears on the invoice.

4. **Give the job name.**

   The cursor is in the Job Name text box. Just type the name of the job or project.

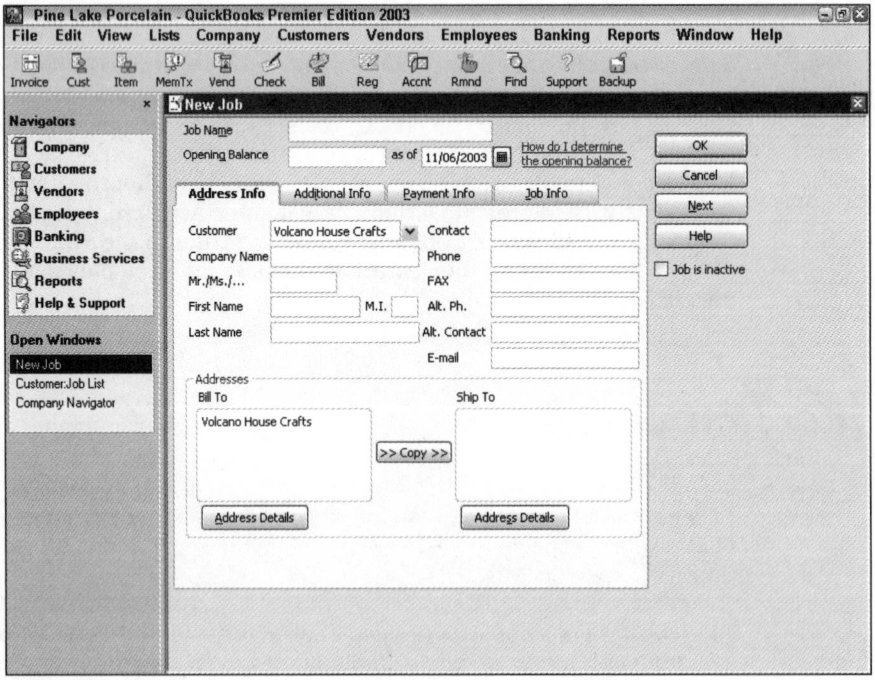

Figure 2-12:
The New
Job
window.

5. **Identify the customer.**

   Just on the off chance that you selected the wrong customer in Step 2, take a peek at the Customer drop-down list box. Does it name the correct customer? If not, activate the drop-down list and click the correct customer.

6. **(Optional) Name your contact and fill in other relevant information.**

   You can enter the name of your contact and alternate contact in the Mr./Ms., First Name, M.I., and Last Name text boxes. QuickBooks fills in the Contact text box for you. You probably don't need to be told this, but fill in the Phone and FAX text boxes just so that you have that information on hand. If you want to get really optional, fill in the Alt. Ph. and Alt. Contact text boxes. Go ahead: Take a walk on the wild side.

7. **Give the job's billing address.**

   You can use the Bill To text box to provide the customer's job billing address. Because chances are good that the job billing address is the same as the customer billing address, QuickBooks copies the billing address from the Customer list. But, if need be, make changes.

8. **Give the Ship To address.**

   You can use the Ship To text box to provide the job's shipping address. Click the Copy button if the shipping address is the same as the Bill To address.

9. **(Massively optional) Click the Additional Info tab to categorize the job.**

   You can use the Customer Type drop-down list box to give the job type. The only initial types in the default list are Corporate and Referral. You can create other types by choosing <Add New> from the Customer Type drop-down list box (so that QuickBooks displays the New Customer Type dialog box) and then filling in the dialog box blanks.

10. **Set the customer's credit limit.**

    That is, enter it if you've set one.

11. **Type 0 (zero) for the Opening Balance.**

    Move the cursor to the Opening Balance text box and type **0** (zero).

12. **Enter the current date.**

    Move the cursor to the As Of text box and enter the current date.

13. **(Optional) Add specific job information.**

    Click the Job Info tab, as shown in Figure 2-13, and fill in the information about the job. You can use the Job Status drop-down list box to choose None, Pending, Awarded, In Progress, Closed, or Not Awarded, whichever is most appropriate. The Start Date is (I know that this one is hard to believe) the day you start the job. As anyone knows, the

The little things do, too, matter

If you're not familiar with how payment terms work, you can get a bird's-eye view here. For the most part, payment terms just tell the customer how quickly you expect to be paid. For example, Net Due Upon Receipt means that you expect to be paid as soon as possible. If Net is followed by some number, as in Net 15 or Net 30, the number indicates the number of days after the invoice date within which the customer is supposed to pay. So Net 15 means that the customer is supposed to pay within 15 days of the invoice date.

Some payment terms, such as 2% 10 Net 30, include early payment discounts. In other words, the customer can deduct 2 percent from the bill if it's paid within 10 days. Either way, the customer must pay the bill within 30 days. For more information on how to make early payment discounts work for you, see Chapter 21.

Projected End and the End Date aren't necessarily the same. Don't fill in the End Date until the job is actually finished. The Job Description field can contain any helpful information you can fit on one line, and the Job Type is an extra field you can use. (If you do use this field, you can add a new job type by choosing <Add New> from the Job Type list box.)

14. **Save the job information.**

    After you finish describing the job, click OK to add the job to the list and return to the Customer:Job List window. Or click Next to add the job to the list and keep the New Job window on-screen so that you can add more jobs.

You can edit job information the same way that you edit customer information. Display the Customer:Job List window by choosing Lists➪Customer:Job List. When QuickBooks displays the list, double-click the job and use the Edit Job window QuickBooks displays to make the changes.

Adding Vendors to Your Vendor List

Adding vendors to your Vendor list works the same basic way as adding customers to your Customer list does. Here's how to get the job done:

1. **Choose the Lists➪Vendor List command.**

   QuickBooks displays the Vendor List window. Along with listing your vendors, it lists any sales tax agencies that you identified as part of setting up Sales Tax items.

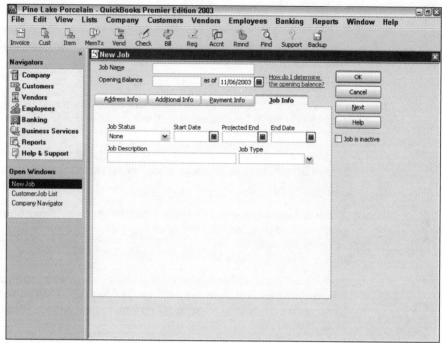

Figure 2-13:
The New
Job tab.

2. Click the Vendor button and choose New from the drop-down menu.

QuickBooks displays the Address Info tab of the New Vendor window, as shown in Figure 2-14. You use this window to describe the vendors and all their little idiosyncrasies.

3. Give the vendor's name.

The cursor is already in the Vendor Name text box. All you have to do is type the vendor's name as you want it to appear on the Vendor list. If you want to list your vendors by company name, enter the company name. To list them by the first or last name of the sales representative, enter one of these names.

4. (Optional) Give the name of your contact.

Fill in the Mr./Ms., First Name, M.I., and Last Name text boxes. QuickBooks fills in the Contact text box for you automatically.

5. Give the address to which you're supposed to mail checks.

You can use the Address text box to provide the vendor's address. QuickBooks copies the Company and Contact names to the first line of the address, so you need to enter only the street address, city, state, and zip code. To move from the end of one line to the start of the next, press Enter.

6. **(Optional) Give the vendor's telephone and fax numbers and, if available, the e-mail address.**

   The window also has an Alt. Ph. text box for a second telephone number. Hey. They thought of everything, didn't they?

7. **Verify the Print On Check As text box.**

   QuickBooks assumes that you want the company name to appear on any checks you write for this vendor. If not, change the text box to whatever you feel is more appropriate.

   At this point, click the Additional Info tab. The window you see on-screen hopefully now bears an uncanny resemblance to Figure 2-15.

8. **(Optional) Give your account number.**

   If the vendor has assigned account numbers or customer numbers to keep track of customers, type your account or customer number in the Account No. text box. You can probably get this piece of information from the vendor's last invoice.

   An account number is required if you want to use QuickBooks' online bill payment feature (which I describe in Chapter 11) to pay the vendor. QuickBooks transfers the account number to the memo field of the payment check.

9. **Categorize the vendor.**

   See that Type drop-down list box? You can use it to assign the vendor a type. If you activate the drop-down list by clicking its arrow, you see the initial QuickBooks list of vendor types. You can pick any of these types, but my suggestion is that you diligently identify any vendor to whom you need to send a 1099 as a *1099 contractor*. (A 1099 contractor is any unincorporated business to which you pay more than $600 during the year.)

   To create a new vendor type, choose <Add New> from the drop-down list and fill in the blanks in the New Vendor Type dialog box that QuickBooks displays. You can create as many new vendor types as you need.

10. **Specify the payment terms that you're supposed to observe.**

    Activate the Terms drop-down list and click one of its terms. QuickBooks has already set up all the usual ones. (If you want to, you can choose <Add New> to set up additional payment terms.)

    If a vendor offers an early payment discount, it's usually too good of a deal to pass up. Interested in more information about early payment discounts? Is yours an inquiring mind that needs to know? See Chapter 21 to find out about the advantages of early payment discounts.

11. **(Optional) Specify your credit limit, if the vendor has set one.**

    This procedure is obvious, right? You click the Credit Limit text box and enter the number.

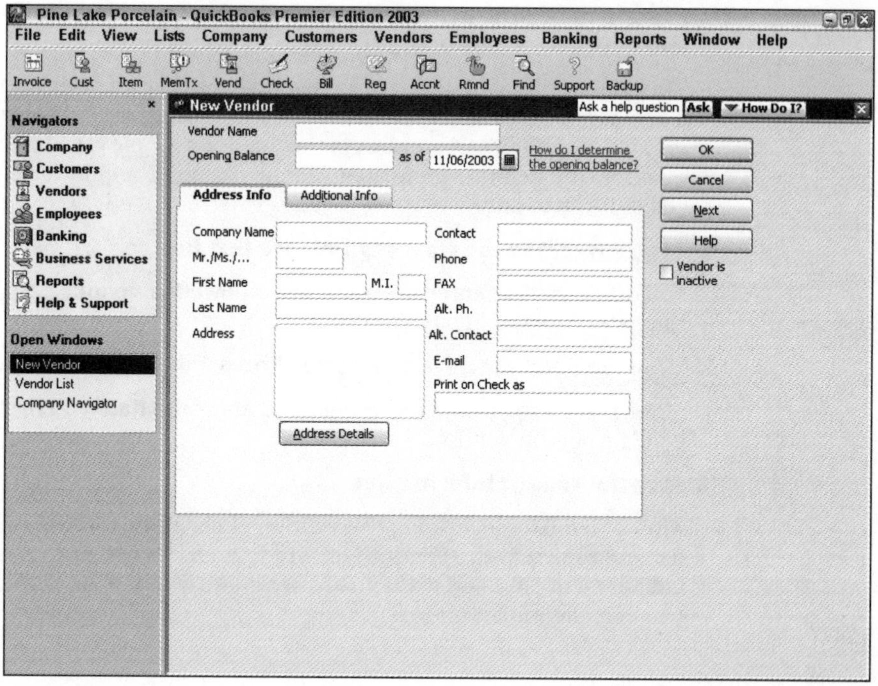

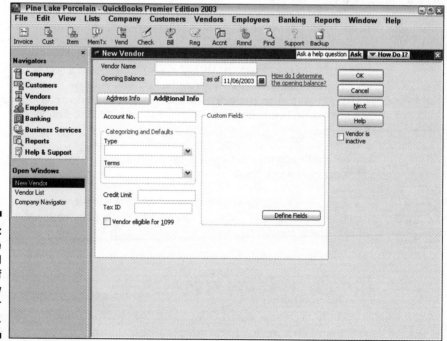

Figure 2-14:
The
Address
Info tab of
the New
Vendor
window.

Figure 2-15:
The
Additional
Info tab of
the New
Vendor
window.

12. **(If applicable) Store the vendor's federal tax identification number and check the Vendor Eligible for 1099 check box.**

    This number may be the vendor's social security number if the vendor is a one-man or one-woman business. If the vendor has employees, the federal tax identification number is the vendor's employer identification number. You need this information only if you're required to prepare a 1099 for the vendor.

13. **Type 0 (zero) in the Opening Balance text box.**

    You don't want to enter the amount you owe the vendor because you do that later, when you pay your bills.

14. **Type the date on which you opened an account with the vendor.**

    Move the cursor to the As Of field and enter the date you first purchased goods from the vendor.

15. **Save the vendor information.**

    After you finish describing the vendor, click OK to add the vendor to the list and return to the Vendor List window. Or click Next to add the vendor to the list and leave the New Vendor window on-screen so that you can add more vendors.

The Other Lists

Throughout the preceding sections, I've covered almost all the most important lists. A few others I haven't talked about yet: Price Level, Classes, Other Names, Sales Rep, Customer Type, Vendor Type, Job Type, Terms, Customer Messages, Payment Method, Ship Via, and Memorized Transactions. I'm not going to give blow-by-blow descriptions of how you use these lists because you don't really need them. The other QuickBooks lists are generally more than adequate. You can usually use the standard lists as is, without building other lists.

Just so I don't leave you stranded, however, I want to give you quick-and-dirty descriptions of these other lists and what they do.

To see some of these lists, you either choose the list from the Lists menu or you choose the Lists⇨Customer & Vendor Profile Lists command and choose the list from the submenu that QuickBooks displays.

The Price Level list

The first time I encountered QuickBooks' *Price Level* feature, I was sorely confused about how the feature worked. I'm still a little confused — not about how the feature works but about who'd really want to use this feature.

But, heck, what do I know. Here's the deal: *Price Levels* enable you to adjust an item price as you're creating an invoice. For example, you can create a price level that increases the price for some item by 20%. And you create a price level that decreases the price for some item by 10%. You adjust a price by selecting a price level from the price field on an invoice. (This may not make much sense until you see the Create Invoices window, which I describe in Chapter 4, but it's fairly straightforward.)

The Class list

Classes enable you to classify transactions by department or location, for example, so that you can track trends and assess performance across parts of your business. Classes are cool, really cool. But they add another dimension to the accounting model that you use in QuickBooks. So I'm not going to describe them here. I urge you — nay, I implore you — to get comfortable with how the rest of QuickBooks works before you begin mucking about with classes. I'll just tell you that you can display the Class list by choosing the Lists⇨Class List command.

You can probably perform basic class tracking activities easier and better with a clever chart of accounts or a Customer:Job List.

You don't see a Class Lists command on the Lists menu if you indicated during the EasyStep Interview that you don't want to use classes.

The Other Names list

QuickBooks provides an Other Names list that works as a watered-down, wimpy Vendor and Employee list combination. You can write checks to people named on this Other Names list, but you can't do anything else. You can't create invoices or purchase orders for them, for example. And you don't get any of the other information that you want to collect for vendors or employees.

You're really better off working with good, accurate, rich Vendor and Employee lists. If you don't like this suggestion, however, just choose Lists⇨Other Names List to display the Other Names List window, click the Other Names button, choose New from the drop-down menu, and then fill in the blanks in the New Name window.

The Sales Rep list

You can create a list of the sales representatives you work with and then indicate which sales rep sells to a customer or generates a sale. To do this, use the Lists⇨Customer & Vendor Profile Lists⇨Sales Rep command. When you choose the command, QuickBooks displays the Sales Rep List window, which lists all the sales representatives. To add sales representatives, click the Sales Rep button, choose New from the drop-down menu, and then fill in the window that QuickBooks displays.

Customer, Vendor, and Job Types list

You can create lists of customer types, vendor types, and job types and then use these to categorize customer, vendor, and job information. This is probably no surprise, but to do this, you need to use the appropriate command:

- ✔ Lists➪Customer & Vendor Profile Lists➪Customer Type List
- ✔ Lists➪Customer & Vendor Profile Lists➪Vendor Type List
- ✔ Lists➪Customer & Vendor Profile Lists➪Job Type List

When you choose one of these commands, QuickBooks displays the appropriate List window, which lists all the customer types, vendor types, or job types. To add types, click the Type button, choose New from the drop-down menu, and then fill in the window that QuickBooks displays.

How you use any of these type lists depends on your business. But in a situation where you want to sort or segregate customers, vendors, or jobs in some way that's unusual, use the Customer Type, Vendor Type, or Job Type list.

The Terms list

QuickBooks maintains a Terms list, which you use to specify what payment terms are available. To add terms, choose Lists➪Customer & Vendor Profile Lists➪Terms List. When you choose this command, QuickBooks displays the Terms List window. To add more terms, click the Terms button, choose New from the drop-down menu, and then fill in the window that QuickBooks displays.

The Customer Message list

This list is another minor player in the QuickBooks drama. You can stick messages at the bottom of invoices if you first type the message in the Customer Message list. QuickBooks provides a handful of boilerplate messages. You can add more messages by choosing Lists➪Customer & Vendor Profile Lists➪Customer Message List. When QuickBooks displays the Customer Message List window, click its Customer Message button and choose New. Then use the New Customer Message window that QuickBooks displays to create a new message.

The Payment Method list

Now this will be a big surprise. (I'm just kidding.) QuickBooks provides descriptions for the usual payment methods. But, of course, you can add to these by using the Lists⇨Customer & Vendor Profile Lists⇨Payment Method command. When you choose the command, QuickBooks displays the lost city of Atlantis. Okay, not really. QuickBooks actually displays the Payment Method window. To add more methods, click the Payment Method button, choose New from the drop-down menu and then fill in the window that QuickBooks displays.

The Ship Via list

QuickBooks provides descriptions for the usual shipping methods. These descriptions are probably entirely adequate. If you need to add more, however, you can do so by using the Lists⇨Customer & Vendor Profile Lists⇨Ship Via command. When you choose the command, QuickBooks displays the Ship Via List window, which lists all the shipping methods that you or QuickBooks has said are available. To add more methods, click the Shipping Method button, choose New from the drop-down menu, and then fill in the window that QuickBooks displays. Friends, it doesn't get much easier than this.

The Memorized Transaction list

The Memorized Transaction list isn't really a list. At least, it's not like the other lists I describe in this chapter. The Memorized Transaction list is a list of accounting transactions — invoices, bills, checks, purchase orders, and so on — that you've asked QuickBooks to memorize. To display the Memorized Transaction list, choose Lists⇨Memorized Transaction List.

You can have QuickBooks memorize transactions so that you can quickly record them later or even put them on a schedule for recurring usage. This feature can save you lots of time, especially for transactions you regularly make.

The Reminders list

Here's a list that's not accessible from the Lists menu. QuickBooks keeps track of a bunch of different stuff that it knows you need to monitor. If you choose Company⇨Reminders, QuickBooks displays the Reminders window. On it you see such entries as invoices and checks that need to be printed, inventory items you should probably reorder, and so on.

Organizing and Printing Lists

To organize a list, you must be in single-user mode if you aren't already. (I describe multi-user mode in Chapter 3.) To move an item and all its subitems, just click the diamond beside the item and drag the item up or down the list to a new location. To make a subitem its own item, click the diamond beside the item and drag it to the left. To make an item a subitem, first move the item so that it's directly beneath the item you want it to fall under. Then click the diamond beside the item and move it to the right. To alphabetize a list, click the button in the lower-left corner of the list window. (The name of this button changes, depending on the list that you're displaying.) Then choose Re-sort List from the pop-up menu. Sensing that you definitely mean business and don't want it fooling around, QuickBooks displays a message box that asks whether you're sure that you want to re-sort your list. Click OK to alphabetize.

You can't reorganize the Vendor list.

Jotting down notes for list items

To enter more information about a name on a list, display the list and select the customer, vendor, employee, or other name. Then click the button in the lower-left corner of the list window. (The name of this button changes, depending on the type of list.) Choose Notepad from the pop-up menu. In the Notepad dialog box that appears for the person, type your notes and click OK. You can also click Date Stamp to stamp the current date on the note.

Printing lists

You can print a list by displaying the list, clicking the button in the lower-left corner of the list window, and choosing Print list. However, the best way to print a list is often to print a list report. You can create, customize, and print a list report by choosing Reports⇨List and then choosing the list that you want to print. You can also create one of a handful of different list reports by clicking the Reports button in the list window and choosing a report from the pop-up menu. For more information on printing reports, see Chapter 14.

Click the Activities button in a list window to quickly access common activities associated with the items on that list. Or, click Reports to quickly access common reports related to the items on the list.

Exporting List Items to Your Word Processor

If you use QuickBooks to store the names and addresses of your customers, vendors, and employees, you can create a text file of the contact information for these people. You can then export this file to another application, like a word processor, to create reports that use this information, for example, or in some cases, even for mass mailings or mailing labels.

The Company menu provides a Print Mailing Labels command, however, for producing mailing labels for customers and vendors.

To export list information to a text file, click the button in the lower-left corner of the list window and choose Print List. When QuickBooks displays the Print dialog box, mark the File option button, click Print, and then provide a filename when prompted.

Chapter 3

Sharing QuickBooks Files

• •

In This Chapter

▶ Understanding how QuickBooks works on a network

▶ Installing QuickBooks for network use

▶ Setting up user permissions

▶ Specifying multi-user mode

▶ Working with a shared QuickBooks file

• •

*O*kay, here's a cool deal: You can use the standard version of QuickBooks to set up user permissions, which lets you specify who has access to which areas of your QuickBooks file. And if you have the Pro or Premier versions of QuickBooks, you can also work with your QuickBooks file on a network and in a multiple-user environment, using a powerful new feature called record locking.

If you work on a network and need to make use of or just want to learn about the QuickBooks network features, you should read this chapter. If your computer isn't connected to a network but you want to designate unique permissions for different people using a QuickBooks file on a single computer, you should still read the section "Setting Up User Permissions" in this chapter. And if you're the only one using QuickBooks, you can skip this chapter.

Sharing a QuickBooks File on a Network

Two important features power the QuickBooks Pro multi-user network capability: *user permissions* and *record locking*. The *user permissions* feature lets multiple users of a QuickBooks file have unique permissions settings to access different areas of QuickBooks. (The standard version of QuickBooks also includes user permissions, which you can use on a standalone computer, but it's especially pertinent for network users of QuickBooks.) *Record locking*, a feature specific to the Pro and Premier versions, allows more than one person to log on to and work with a QuickBooks file at once.

User permissions

QuickBooks lets you set user permissions so that you can give different QuickBooks users different privileges. For example, Jane Owner may be able to do anything she wants because, metaphorically speaking, she's "Da Man." But Joe Clerk may only be able to enter bills. Joe, a lowly clerk of perhaps dubious judgment and discretion, may not have the ability to view the company's profit and loss statement, print checks, or record customer payments. This idea makes sense at a practical level, right? In a situation where a bunch of different people access the QuickBooks file, you want to make sure that confidential information remains confidential.

You also want to make sure that people can't intentionally or unintentionally corrupt your financial records. For example, you don't want someone to enter incorrect data (perhaps because they stumble into some area of the QuickBooks program where they have no business being). And you don't want someone fraudulently recording transactions — like fake checks that they then go cash.

I think that if you reflect on this user permissions stuff, you'll realize, "Hey, yeah, that only makes sense!" So I'm not going to talk a bunch more about it. But let me conclude by throwing out a couple of general observations about how you decide which user permissions are appropriate:

✔ **Data confidentiality:** This issue probably has the most to do with your management philosophy. The more open you are about stuff, the less you probably have to worry about people snooping around for stuff. I want to point out, however, that payroll is always a touchy subject. If everybody knows what everyone else is paid, some interesting discussions occur. But you already know that. . . .

✔ **Data corruption:** Regarding data corruption, you need to know that people usually apply two general rules:

  • Don't give people access to tools they don't know how to use. That's only asking for trouble.

  • Make sure that no one person gets to muck around unsupervised in some area of the accounting system — especially if that person records or handles cash.

If at all possible, employ a "buddy" system where people do stuff together so that people always double-check — even if only indirectly — other people's work. Maybe Joe records a bill, for example, but Jane always cuts the check to pay the bill. Maybe Raul records customer invoices, but Chang sends them out. Maybe Saul records cash receipts, but Britt deposits them. You see the pattern, right? If two people deal with a particular economic event — again, especially one that involves cash — it's a really good idea for Joe and Jane, Raul and Chang, and Saul and Britt to look over each other's shoulders.

Just what is a network, anyway?

A *network* is just a set of computers that some-one has cabled together so that the people who use the computers can share information. Uh, well, er, this is somewhat self-serving, but let me say that if you don't currently use a network, *Networking For Dummies,* 6th Edition, by Doug Lowe, and *Home Networking For Dummies,* by Kathy Ivens (both published by Wiley Publishing, Inc.), explain how to set up a small business network in a couple of hours and live to tell about it.

Record locking

You can most easily understand what record locking is by comparing it to the other variety of locking, *file locking.* Most of the other programs that you use — perhaps even every one but QuickBooks — use file locking. What file locking means is this: If one person on the network has, for instance, a word-processing document open, nobody else on the network can open that docu-ment. Other people may be able to open a copy of the document that they can save on their own computers, but they can't edit the original document. The operating system "locks" the original document, or file, so that only one person can fool around with the file at a time. This locking assures the integrity of the data and the changes that people make to the data. (If this business about assuring integrity seems weird, think about the difficulty of making sure that both people's changes end up in a word-processing docu-ment that both people are simultaneously editing.)

Record locking works differently. With record locking, more than one person on the network can open and edit the same file at once. But only one person can work with a specific record.

A *record* is just a part of a file. For example, in a file of bills you owe to vendors, the file is the entire collection of bills. The individual bills are records within the file. So more than one person can open the file of bills. But individual bills — the individual records that make up the file — are locked when a person grabs a record.

This information sounds like too much confusion, but differentiating between files and the records *within* a file is what makes sharing files possible. In QuickBooks, for example, if Jane is entering one bill for the Alpha Company in a file, Joe can edit a bill for Beta Corporation, because the two bills are different records. However, Jane can't — because of record locking — fool around with the Beta Corporation bill that Joe's editing. And Joe can't — again because of record locking — fool around with the Alpha Company bill that Jane's entering.

Restated more generally, no two people can edit the same record in the file at the same time. Record locking enables employees to use a file in a multi-user environment because it lets more than one person work with a file.

Installing QuickBooks for Network Use

To install QuickBooks Pro for network use, you must first install QuickBooks on all the computers on the network that need to access and work with the QuickBooks file. This task isn't tricky. You don't need to install QuickBooks in any fancy way to be able to share QuickBooks files.

You need to purchase a copy of QuickBooks Pro for each computer that's going to run the program. So if you have five computers on which you want to use QuickBooks, you need to buy five copies of QuickBooks. Or you can buy the special five-license version of QuickBooks. If you attempt to install a single copy of QuickBooks (with a single key code) on multiple computers, QuickBooks won't allow two computers using the same key code to share a file in multi-user mode.

When you create the file that you want to share, however, you need to make sure that you store the file in a location where the other QuickBooks users can access it. You may need to store the file on a server. You can also store the file on a client computer as long as you designate sharing permissions for either the folder or the drive on which you save the QuickBooks file.

Choosing a good password

The administrator has access to all areas of QuickBooks, so picking a good password is especially important. Other users (especially those with higher levels of access permission) also need to select their passwords carefully.

A good password is one that you can easily remember but others can't easily guess. Combinations of letters and numbers are the best way to go. For example, use your grade school nickname plus the number of your favorite basketball player. Or a random number combined with the name of your favorite restaurant (as long as you don't walk around all day muttering, "Number nine, number nine, number nine," and raving about your love of this particular eatery). Avoid using telephone numbers, family names, and family dates (such as the birthday of a family member). And *absolutely do not* use banking PIN numbers or Social Security numbers.

One last tip: QuickBooks lets you create passwords from zero to 16 characters in length. As a general rule, choose a password that's five or more characters in length.

Another important thing: Whoever creates the QuickBooks file automatically becomes the *file administrator*. The file administrator has access to all areas of the file and sets up the other file users. So, you don't want just anybody setting up the QuickBooks file. Either the business owner or the head of accounting is well suited for this job. In any case, the person who sets up the file should be trustworthy, regularly around the office, and easy to reach for any questions or problems that arise. And this person probably should have a strong background in accounting. See the following section for more details.

Designating the QuickBooks Administrator

Before you can begin sharing a QuickBooks file, either over a network or on a single computer, you need to first set up a name and password for the QuickBooks administrator. QuickBooks prompts you to do so when, during the EasyStep Interview (which I describe in Chapter 1), you indicate that you're using QuickBooks in a multi-user setting.

If you didn't indicate in the EasyStep Interview that you wanted to use QuickBooks in a multi-user setting, you can still do so and set up an administrator. Choose Company➪Set Up Users to display the Set Up QuickBooks Administrator dialog box. For security reasons, I can't show up a picture of this dialog box, but just between you and me, all it does is provide text boxes into which you type a user name and password for the administrator.

To make what is probably an obvious point, the business owner usually is the administrator. If the business owner isn't the administrator — for example, because he or she doesn't possess QuickBooks skills — someone else who is deeply trusted and perhaps almost revered by the business owner, such as the firm's C.P.A. or resident goddess, can fulfill this role.

Setting Up User Permissions

After you set up the administrator's password, you're ready to tell QuickBooks who else will use the file and set permissions for these other people. You can provide this information during the EasyStep Interview. You can also give QuickBooks this information later. To do it later, use the User List dialog box shown in Figure 3-1. If you just set up the QuickBooks administrator, the User List dialog box is already on-screen.

Figure 3-1:
The User
List dialog
box.

If the User List dialog box isn't currently open, choose Company⇨Set Up
Users and follow these steps:

1. **Click Add User.**

   Doing so displays the first dialog box of the Set Up User Password and
   Access Wizard, as shown in Figure 3-2. You use this wizard to add new
   users and specify user permissions.

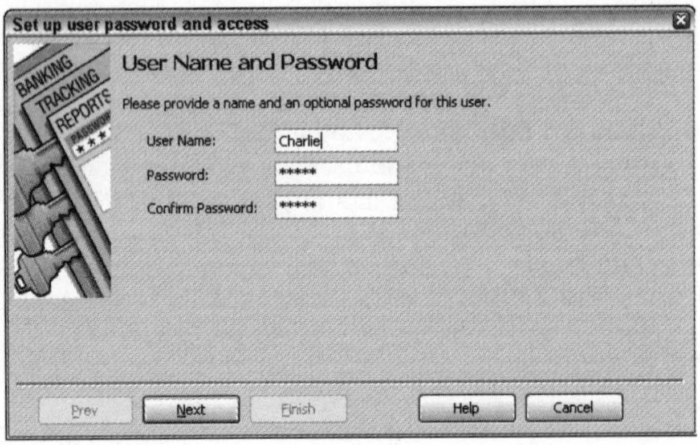

Figure 3-2:
Adding a
new user
and entering
the new
user's
password.

2. **Type a user name and password for the additional person you want
   to be able to use the QuickBooks file; type the password again in the
   Confirm Password box.**

   Re-entering the password confirms that you typed the password correctly
   the first time.

   From this point forward, when someone opens the QuickBooks file,
   QuickBooks asks for a user name and password. So in order for another
   person to access the QuickBooks file, he or she must enter the user
   name and password that you've set.

3. Click Next.

QuickBooks displays a dialog box (not shown here) asking whether you want the person to have access to all areas of the QuickBooks file or only some areas.

4. Click All Areas or click Selected Areas and then click Next.

If you specify that you want to give access to only some areas, QuickBooks displays a series of dialog boxes (starting with the Sales and Accounts Receivable dialog box shown in Figure 3-3) that allow you to set permissions for each area.

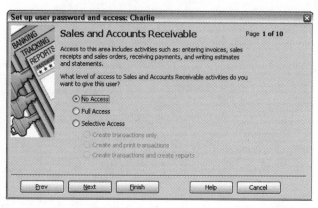

Figure 3-3:
Designating
access
permissions
to each
individual
area.

Can I alert you to a potentially dangerous security flaw in QuickBooks? I don't want to unnecessarily alarm you, but the C.P.A.s I teach QuickBooks to tell me that it's very common for embezzling employees to print something like an invoice but then not save the invoice. (Take a peek at the dialog box shown in Figure 3-3. See how you need to decide whether someone can print invoices?) By printing and then sending an invoice, the embezzler tells some customer of yours that they need to pay your firm money . . . but because QuickBooks doesn't make you save a transaction before you print it, the invoice may never be recorded in the QuickBooks system. That means, sadly, that when the customer sends you payment, the embezzler can just steal the check without your being the wiser. The moral of this little story is: Think carefully about the access permissions you set.

5. Designate the access permission level for each area in the Set Up User Password and Access Wizard.

Click No Access to make the area off-limits for the user. Click Full Access to give the user permission to create and print transactions and reports in the area, or click Selective Access to give partial access to the area. If you click Selective Access, specify the limited access. Click Next after supplying each area's access information to proceed to the next area. The other areas' dialog boxes look and work the same way.

6. **Tell QuickBooks whether you want the user to be able to change or delete existing transactions and those recorded before the closing date you specify.**

   After you go through the access permissions for all the areas, QuickBooks displays the dialog box shown in Figure 3-4. Use the option buttons in this dialog box to restrict user access to existing transactions. By specifying a closing date, you can prevent users — for example, new Quick Books users or new employees — from altering data before a given date.

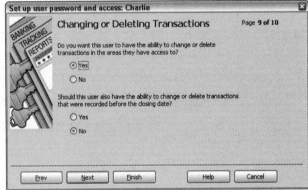

Figure 3-4: Granting permissions to change existing and historical transactions.

To set a closing date, log on to the QuickBooks file as the administrator. Then, make sure that you're working in single-user mode. (If you aren't, choose File⇨Switch to Single-User Mode.) Then choose Company⇨ Set Up Users and click the Closing Date button. In the Set Closing Date dialog box, enter the date on and before which you want to restrict changes to transactions into the Date Through Which Books Are Closed box and click OK.

7. **Click Next.**

   Specify whether you want the user to be able to access QuickBooks data from another application, such as TurboTax.

8. **Review the permissions that you've granted the new user.**

   Figure 3-5 shows a summary of the permissions for a user. Click Prev if you need to go back and change permissions for an area.

9. **Click Finish to finish setting up the new user.**

   QuickBooks displays the User List dialog box again, but with the new user added. Click Add User to add another new user, click Edit User to edit the selected user, or click Close to close the dialog box.

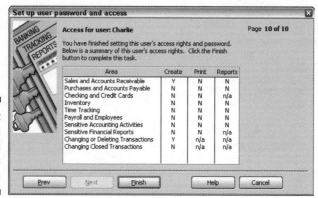

Area	Create	Print	Reports
Sales and Accounts Receivable	Y	N	N
Purchases and Accounts Payable	N	N	N
Checking and Credit Cards	N	N	n/a
Inventory	N	N	N
Time Tracking	N	N	N
Payroll and Employees	N	N	N
Sensitive Accounting Activities	N	N	N
Sensitive Financial Reports	N	N	n/a
Changing or Deleting Transactions	Y	n/a	n/a
Changing Closed Transactions	N	n/a	n/a

Figure 3-5:
Reviewing a
new user's
access
rights.

A user can log on and open a QuickBooks file from any computer on the network, as long as the computer has QuickBooks installed and has network access to the QuickBooks file. If a person attempts to open a restricted area or perform an unauthorized action, QuickBooks displays a message box that indicates that the person lacks the permissions necessary to perform the action.

Individual users can specify and save their own personal preferences for working with QuickBooks. For example, a user can decide to display and even customize the QuickBooks icon bar or set options for graphs, reminders, and warnings. Users can access their individual preference settings by choosing Edit⇨Preferences. Select an area by clicking an icon (such as General) on the left. Click the My Preferences tab if it isn't already selected.

Specifying Multi-User Mode

In order for more than one person to work with the QuickBooks file at once, the users must work with the QuickBooks file in what is called *multi-user mode*. The first person who opens the file needs to specify multi-user mode for others to be able to open the file. To specify multi-user mode, choose File⇨Switch to Multi-User Mode. When you choose this command, QuickBooks displays a dialog box alerting you that you've switched to multi-user mode, as shown in Figure 3-6. Then it redisplays the QuickBooks file. You can tell that you're working in multi-user mode because the QuickBooks title bar indicates so. When other people open the QuickBooks file, it automatically opens in multi-user mode. For another user to work in single-user mode, the other users must close the QuickBooks file.

Figure 3-6:
Switching to
multi-user
mode.

Working in Multi-User Mode

Sharing a QuickBooks file over a network involves a couple of tricks. First, you need to make sure that no one is using the file that you want to open in single-user mode. If someone is and you try to open the file, QuickBooks displays a message that indicates that someone is currently using the company file in single-user mode. Tell the person to switch to multi-user mode and then click Try Again.

As soon as you begin creating or editing a transaction, QuickBooks locks the transaction. This way, no one else can edit the transaction as you work on it. You can tell whether you have a transaction open in edit mode by what QuickBooks indicates in the title bar at the top of the form: QuickBooks puts the phrase, "Editing Transaction" in the title bar. Other users can open the transaction as you edit it in edit mode, but they can't make changes to it until you're through.

For example, if you attempt to edit a transaction that your co-worker Harriet already has open in edit mode, QuickBooks displays a message that says, "Excuse me, Bubba? Harriet is working with that transaction. You need to come back later."

Part II
Daily Chores

In this part . . .

Okay. You've got QuickBooks set up. Or maybe you were lucky enough to have someone else do all the dirty work. But all that doesn't matter now. It's in this part where the rubber really hits the road. You need to start using QuickBooks to do a bunch of stuff on a regular, and maybe daily, basis. Invoice customers. Record customer payments. Pay bills. This part describes how you do all these things.

Chapter 4

Invoices and Credit Memos

. . . .

In This Chapter

▶ Preparing invoices

▶ Fixing invoice mistakes

▶ Preparing credit memos

▶ Fixing credit memo mistakes

▶ Printing invoices and credit memos one at a time

▶ Printing invoices in a batch

▶ Printing credit memos in a batch

. . . .

*I*n this chapter — you may be surprised to hear — I describe how you create and print invoices in QuickBooks, in addition to telling you how to create and print credit memos.

You use the QuickBooks invoice form to bill customers for the goods you sell. You use its credit memos form to handle returns and canceled orders for which you've received payments.

Making Sure That You're Ready to Invoice Customers

I know that you're probably all set to go. But first, you need to check a few things, okay? Good.

You already should have installed QuickBooks, of course. (I describe how in Appendix A.) You should have set up a company, a chart of accounts, and all of your lists in the EasyStep Interview. You also should have entered your starting trial balance or talked your accountant into entering it for you, as I describe in Chapter 1.

As long as you've done all this prerequisite stuff, you're ready to start. If you don't have one of the prerequisites done, you need to complete it before going any further.

Sorry. I don't make the rules. I just tell you what they are.

Preparing an Invoice

After you complete all the preliminary work, preparing an invoice with Quick Books is a snap. If clicking buttons and filling in text boxes are becoming old hat to you, skip the following play-by-play commentary and simply display the Create Invoices window — by choosing Customers⇨Create Invoices, for example — and then fill in this window and click the Print button. If you want more help than a single sentence provides, keep reading for step-by-step instructions.

In the following steps, I describe how to create the most complicated and involved invoice around: a *product invoice.* Some fields on the product invoice don't appear on the *service* or *professional invoice,* but don't worry if your business is a service or professional one. Creating a service or professional invoice works basically the same way as creating a product invoice — you just fill in fewer fields. And keep in mind that you start with Steps 1 and 2 no matter what type of invoice you create. Without further ado, here's how to create an invoice:

1. **Choose Customers⇨Create Invoices.**

   As an alternative to the Customers⇨Create Invoices command, you can also click Customers in the Navigators box and then click the Invoices icon.

   The Create Invoices window appears, as shown in Figure 4-1.

2. **Select the template, or invoice form, that you want to use from the Template drop-down list box.**

   QuickBooks comes with four predefined invoice forms: Product, Professional, Service, and Progress. Which one appears by default depends on which one you told QuickBooks you wanted to use in the EasyStep Interview. You can, however, download additional templates by choosing Download Templates from the drop-down list. Or create your own custom invoice template (or modify an existing one) by clicking the Customize button. I describe customizing invoice forms in the "Customizing Your Invoices and Credit Memos" section, later in this chapter.

3. **Identify the customer and, if necessary, the job.**

   Activate the Customer:Job drop-down list by clicking the down arrow at the right end of the box. Scroll through the Customer:Job list until you see the customer or job name that you need, and then click it.

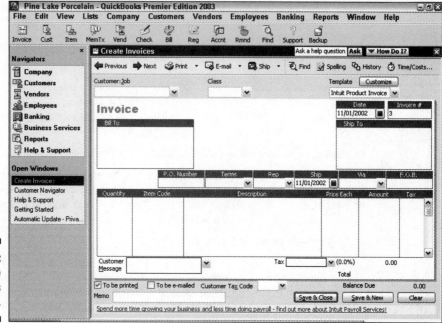

Figure 4-1:
The Create
Invoices
window.

4. (Optional) Assign a class to the invoice.

If you use classes to track expenses and income, activate the Class drop-down list and choose an appropriate class for the invoice. To turn this handy way of categorizing transactions on or off (which is overkill for some businesses), choose Edit⇨Preferences, click Accounting on the left, click the Company Preferences tab, and then select or clear the Use Class Tracking check box.

5. Give the invoice date.

Press Tab several times to move the cursor to the Date text box. Then enter the correct date in MM/DD/YY format. You also can use the following secret codes to change the date:

- **Press** + (the plus symbol) to move the date ahead one day.

- **Press** – (the minus symbol) to move the date back one day.

- **Press T** to change the date to today's date (as specified by the system time that your computer's internal clock provides).

- **Press M** to change the date to the first day of the month (because *M* is the first letter in the word *month*).

- **Press H** to change the date to the last day of the month (because *H* is the last letter in the word *month*).

- **Press Y** to change the date to the first day of the year (because, as you no doubt can guess, *Y* is the first letter in the word *year*).

- **Press R** to change the date to the last day of the year (because *R* is the last letter in the word *year*).

You can also click the button on the right side of the Date field to display a small calendar. To select a date from the calendar, just click the date you want. Or click the arrows on the top-left and top-right sides of the calendar to display the previous or next month.

6. (Optional) Enter an invoice number.

QuickBooks suggests an invoice number by adding 1 to the last invoice number that you used. You can accept this addition, or, if you need to have it your way, you can tab to the Invoice # text box and change the number to whatever you want.

7. Fix the Bill To address, if necessary.

QuickBooks grabs the billing address from the Customer list. You can change the address for the invoice, however, by replacing some portion of the usual billing address. You can, for example, insert another line that says, "Attention: William Bobbins," if that's the name of the person to whom the invoice should go.

8. Fix the Ship To address, if necessary.

I feel like a broken record, but here's the deal: QuickBooks also grabs the shipping address from the Customer list. So, if the shipping address has something unusual about it for just this one invoice, you can change the address by replacing or adding information to the Ship To address block.

9. (Optional . . . sort of) Provide the purchase order number.

If the customer issues purchase orders, enter the number of the purchase order that authorizes this purchase in the P.O. Number text box. (Just for the record, P.O. is pronounced pee-oh. Not poh or poo.)

10. Specify the payment terms.

To specify the payment terms, activate the Terms drop-down list box and select something from it. I have only one request to make: Don't offer a customer an early payment discount without reading the first couple of sections in Chapter 21. Please. I'm only looking out for your welfare. Really.

11. (Optional) Name the sales representative.

Rep doesn't stand for *Reputation,* so don't put three-letter editorial comments in here. (Although I can't, for the life of me, imagine what you could do with three letters.) If you want to track sales by sales representative, use the Rep drop-down list box. Simply activate the list box by clicking its arrow, for example, and then pick a name. Sales representatives can include employees, but they can also include other people you've entered in your other lists. To quickly add a sales rep, choose

<Add New> and then use the handy-dandy dialog boxes QuickBooks displays. To work with the Sales Rep List, choose Lists⇨Customer & Vendor Profile Lists⇨Sales Rep List.

12. Specify the shipping date if it's something other than the invoice date.

To specify the date, simply move the cursor to the Ship text box and then type the date in MM/DD/YY fashion. You can move the cursor by pressing Tab or by clicking the text box.

Oh — one other quick point: Remember all those secret codes I talk about in Step 4 for changing the invoice date? They also work for changing the shipping date.

13. Specify the shipping method.

You can probably guess how you specify the shipping method, but parallel structure and a compulsive personality force me to continue. So, to specify the shipping method, move the cursor to the Via drop-down list, activate the list, and then select a shipping method.

By the way, you can add new shipping methods to the list by choosing <Add New> and then filling out the cute little dialog box that QuickBooks displays. Setting up new shipping methods is really easy. Really easy.

14. Specify the FOB point by using the F.O.B. text box.

FOB stands for *free-on-board*. The FOB point is more important than it first seems — at least in a business sense — because the FOB point determines when the transfer of ownership occurs, who pays freight, and who bears the risks of damage to the goods during shipping.

If a shipment is free-on-board at the *shipping* point, the ownership of the goods being sold transfers to the purchaser as soon as the goods leave the seller's shipping dock. (Remember that you're the seller.) In this case, the purchaser pays the freight and bears the risk of shipping damage. You can specify the FOB shipping point either as FOB Shipping Point or by using the name of the city. If the shipping point is Seattle, for example, FOB Seattle is the same thing as FOB Shipping Point. Most goods are shipped as FOB Shipping Point, by the way.

If a shipment is free-on-board at the *destination* point, the ownership of the goods that are being sold transfers to the purchaser as soon as the goods arrive on the purchaser's shipping dock. The seller pays the freight and bears the risk of shipping damage. You can specify the FOB destination point either as FOB Destination Point or by using the name of the city. If the destination point is Omaha, for example, FOB Omaha is the same thing as FOB Destination Point.

15. Enter each item that you're selling.

Move the cursor to the first row of the Quantity/Item Code/Description/ Price Each/Amount/Tax list box. Okay, I know that isn't a very good name for it, but you know what I mean, right? You need to start filling in the line items that go on the invoice. After you move the cursor to a row in the list box, QuickBooks turns the Item Code field into a drop-down list box. Activate the Item Code drop-down list box of the first empty row in the list box and then select the item.

When you select the item, QuickBooks fills in the Description and Price Each text boxes with whatever sales description and sales price you've entered in the Item list. (You can edit the information for this particular invoice if you need to.) Enter the number of items sold in the Quantity text box. (After you enter this number, QuickBooks calculates the amount by multiplying Quantity by Price Each.) If you need other items on the invoice, use the remaining empty rows of the list box to enter each one. If you checked the Taxable check box when you added the item to the Item list, the word *Tax* appears in the Tax column to indicate that the item will be taxed. If the item is nontaxable (or you feel like being a tax evader for no good reason), click the Tax column and select *Non.*

You can put as many items on an invoice as you want. If you don't have enough room on a single page, QuickBooks just adds as many pages as necessary to the invoice. Information about the invoice total, of course, goes only on the last page.

Click the Time/Costs button at the top of the form to display the Choose Billable Time and Costs dialog box. Use this dialog box to select costs you've assigned to the customer or job. Use the Items tab to select items purchased for the job. Use the Expenses tab to select reimbursable expenses and enter markup information. Use the Time tab to select billable time recorded by the Timer program, the Weekly Timesheet, or in the Time/Enter Single Activity window.

16. Enter any special items that the invoice should include.

If you haven't worked much with the QuickBooks item file, then you have no idea what I'm talking about. (For more information about adding to and working with lists in QuickBooks, cruise through Chapter 2.)

To describe any of the special items, activate the Item Code drop-down list box of the next empty row and then select the special item. After QuickBooks fills in the Description and Price Each text boxes, edit this information (if necessary). Describe each of the other special items — subtotals, discounts, freight, and so on — that you're itemizing on the invoice by filling in the empty rows in the list box.

If you want to include a discount item and have it apply to multiple items, you need to stick a subtotal item on the invoice after the inventory or other items you want to discount. Then stick a discount item directly after the subtotal item. QuickBooks calculates the discount as a percentage of the subtotal.

17. (Optional) Add a customer message.

Click the Customer Message box, activate its drop-down list, and select a clever customer message. To add customer messages to the Customer Message list, choose <Add New> and then fill in the dialog box that

QuickBooks displays. (I know that I talk about the Customer Message box in Chapter 2, but I want to quickly describe how to add a customer message again so that you don't have to flip back a bunch of pages.)

18. Specify the sales tax.

If you specified a tax rate in the Customer List, QuickBooks uses it as a default. If it isn't correct, move the cursor to the Tax list box, activate the drop-down list, and select the correct sales tax.

19. (Truly optional) Add a memo.

You can add a memo description to the invoice if you want to. This memo doesn't print on invoices, but only on the Customer Statement. Memo descriptions give you a way of storing information related to an invoice with that invoice. Figure 4-2 shows a completed Create Invoices window.

20. If you want to delay printing this invoice, unmark the To Be Printed check box that's below the column of buttons in the lower-left area of the Create Invoices window.

I want to postpone talking about what checking the To Be Printed check box does until I finish the discussion of invoice creation. I talk about printing invoices just a little bit later in the chapter. I promise.

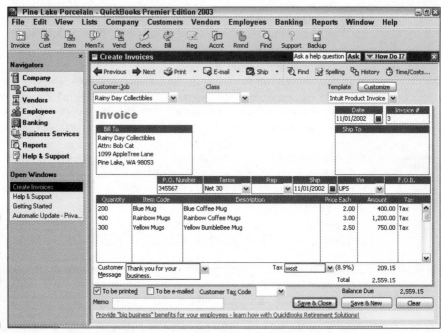

Figure 4-2:
A completed Create Invoices window.

21. **Save the invoice.**

    To save a completed invoice, click either Save & New or Save & Close. QuickBooks saves the invoice that's on-screen. If you clicked Save & New, QuickBooks displays an empty Create Invoices window so that you can create another invoice.

    You can page back and forth through invoices that you created earlier by clicking the Next and Previous buttons.

    When you're done creating invoices, you can click the invoice form's Close button. The Close button, also known as the Close box, is the little box marked with an "X" in the upper right corner of the window.

Fixing Invoice Mistakes

I'm not a perfect person. You're not a perfect person. Heck, very few people are. So everyone makes mistakes. You don't need to get worked up over mistakes that you make while entering information in invoices, though, because in the following sections, I show you how to fix the most common mistakes you might make on your invoices.

If the invoice is still displayed on-screen

If the invoice is still displayed on-screen, you can just move the cursor to the box or button that's wrong and then fix the mistake. Because most of the bits of information that you enter in the Create Invoices window are short and sweet, you can easily replace the contents of some fields by typing over whatever's already there. To start all over again, however, just click the Clear button. To save the invoice after you've made your changes, click Save & New.

If you need to insert a line in the middle of the invoice or change your mind about selling the last of your sparkly-blue widgets, right-click the appropriate line and choose Insert Line or Delete Line from the shortcut menu that appears.

If the invoice isn't displayed on-screen

If the invoice isn't displayed on-screen but you haven't yet printed it, you can use the Next and Previous buttons to page through the invoices. When you get to the one with the error, simply fix the error as I describe in the preceding section. If you make an error fixing the invoice, you can click the Revert button to go back to the saved invoice. The Revert button replaces the Clear button when you're viewing an existing invoice — an invoice you've already saved.

If you've printed the invoice, you also can make the sort of change I describe in the preceding paragraphs. For example, you can page through the invoices until you find the one (now printed) that has the error. And you can change the error and print the invoice again. I'm not so sure that you want to go this route, however, if you've already sent out the invoice. You may want to consider fixing the invoice by issuing either a credit memo (if the original invoice overcharged) or another invoice (if the original invoice undercharged). The reason I suggest issuing a credit memo (which I show you how to do in the appropriately titled section "Preparing a Credit Memo," later in this chapter) or another invoice is that life gets awfully messy if you or your customer has multiple copies of the same invoice floating around and causing confusion.

Deleting an invoice

I hesitate to mention this, but you also can delete invoices. Procedurally, deleting an invoice is easy. You just display the invoice in the Create Invoices window and choose Edit➪Delete Invoice. When QuickBooks asks you to confirm your deletion, click Yes. But read the following paragraph first. You may not want to delete the invoice. . . .

Even though deleting invoices is easy, it isn't something that you should do casually or for fun. Deleting an invoice is okay if you've just created it; only you have seen it, and you haven't yet printed it. In this case, no one needs to know that you've made a mistake. It's your private secret. But the rest of the time — even if you've created an invoice that you don't want later — you should keep a copy of the invoice in the QuickBooks system. By doing so, you have a record that the invoice existed, which usually makes answering later questions easier.

"But how am I to correct my books if I leave the bogus invoice?" you ask.

Good question. To correct your financial records for the invoice that you don't want to count anymore, simply void the invoice. The invoice remains in the QuickBooks system, but QuickBooks doesn't count it (it loses its quantity and amount information). Good news — voiding an invoice is just as simple as deleting one. Just display the invoice in the Create Invoices window and then choose Edit➪Void Invoice.

Preparing a Credit Memo

Credit memos can be a handy way to fix data entry mistakes that you didn't find or correct earlier. Credit memos are also handy ways to handle things such as customer returns and refunds. If you've prepared an invoice or two in your time, you'll find that preparing a QuickBooks credit memo is a lot easier than using old-fashioned methods.

In the following steps, I describe how to create the most complicated and involved kind of credit memo: a *product credit memo*. Creating a *service* or *professional credit memo* works basically the same way, however. You just fill in fewer fields.

1. **Choose Customers⇨Create Credit Memos/Refunds to display the Create Credit Memos/Refunds window.**

   QuickBooks displays the Create Credit Memos/Refunds window, as shown in Figure 4-3.

2. **Identify the customer and, if necessary, the job.**

   Activate the Customer:Job drop-down list. Then select the customer or job by clicking it.

3. **(Optional) Specify a class for the credit memo.**

   If you're using classes to categorize transactions, activate the Class drop-down list and select the appropriate class for the credit memo.

4. **Date the credit memo (going steady is optional).**

   Press Tab to move the cursor to the Date text box. Then enter the correct date in MM/DD/YY format. You also can use the secret date-editing codes that I describe in the section "Preparing an Invoice" earlier in the chapter. Oh, boy.

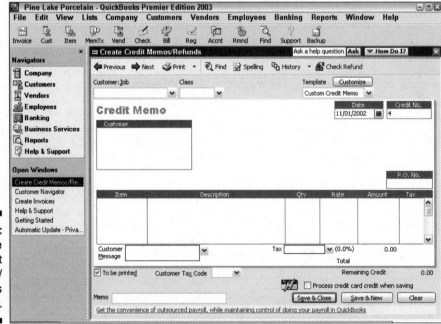

Figure 4-3:
The Create
Credit
Memos/
Refunds
window.

5. (Optional) Enter a credit memo number.

QuickBooks suggests a credit memo number by adding 1 to the last credit memo number you used. You can accept the number or tab to the Credit No. text box to change the number to whatever you want.

6. Fix the Customer address, if necessary.

QuickBooks grabs the billing address from the Customer list. You can change the address for the credit memo, however, by replacing some portion of the usual billing address. Typically, you should use the same address for the credit memo that you used for the original invoice or invoices.

7. (Optional . . . sort of) Provide the purchase order number.

If the credit memo adjusts the total remaining balance on a customer purchase order, you should probably enter the number of the purchase order into the P.O. No. text box.

Here's my logic on this suggestion for those readers who care: If you billed your customer $1,000 on P.O. No. 1984, which authorizes a $1,000 purchase, you've "used up" the entire purchase order — at least according to the customer's accounts payable clerk who processes your invoices. If you make sure that a credit memo for $1,000 is identified as related to P.O. No. 1984, however, you essentially free up the $1,000 purchase balance, which may mean that you can use, or bill on, the purchase order again.

8. If the customer is returning items, describe each item.

Move the cursor to the first row of the Item/Description/Qty/Rate/Amount/Tax text box. In the first empty row of the box, activate the Item drop-down list and then select the item. After you select it, QuickBooks fills in the Description and Rate text boxes with whatever sales description and sales price you entered in the Item list. (You can edit this information if you want, but it's not necessary.) Enter the number of items that the customer is returning (or not paying for) in the Qty text box. (After you enter this number, QuickBooks calculates the amount by multiplying Qty by Rate.) Enter each item that the customer is returning by filling in the empty rows of the list box.

As with invoices, you can put as many items on a credit memo as you want. If you don't have enough room on a single page, QuickBooks just keeps adding pages to the credit memo until you're finished. The total information, of course, goes on the last page.

9. Describe any special items that the credit memo should include.

If you want to issue a credit memo for other items that appear on the original invoice — freight, discounts, other charges, and so on — add descriptions of each item to the Item list.

To add descriptions of these items, activate the Item drop-down list of the next empty row and then select the special item. (You activate the list by clicking the field once to turn it into a drop-down list box and then by clicking the field's down arrow to access the list box.) After QuickBooks fills in the Description and Rate text boxes, edit this information (if necessary). Enter each special item — subtotal, discount, freight, and so on — that you're itemizing on the credit memo.

If you want to include a discount item, you need to stick a subtotal item on the credit memo after the inventory or other items that you've discounted. Then stick a discount item directly after the subtotal item. In this way, QuickBooks calculates the discount as a percentage of the subtotal.

10. **(Optional) Add a customer message.**

    Activate the Customer Message list and select a clever customer message.

11. **Specify the sales tax.**

    Move the cursor to the Tax list box, activate the list box, and select the correct sales tax.

12. **(Optional, but a really good idea. . . .) Add a memo.**

    You can use the Memo text box to add a memo description to the credit memo. I suggest that you use this description to explain your reasons for issuing the credit memo and to cross-reference the original invoice or invoices. Note that the Memo field prints on the Customer Statement, however. Figure 4-4 shows a completed Create Credit Memos/Refunds window.

13. **If you want to delay printing this credit memo, clear the To Be Printed check box.**

    I want to postpone talking about what checking the To Be Printed check box does until I finish the discussion of credit memo creation. Coverage on printing invoices and credit memos comes up in the following section.

14. **Save the credit memo.**

    To save a completed credit memo, click either Save & New or Save & Close. QuickBooks saves the credit memo that's on-screen and then, if you clicked Save & New, displays an empty Create Credit Memos/Refunds window so that you can create another credit memo. (Note that you can page back and forth through credit memos that you created earlier by clicking the Next and Previous buttons.) When you're done creating credit memos, you can click the credit memo form's Close button.

To print a refund check, click the Check/Refund button after you've filled out the Create Credit Memos/Refunds window. QuickBooks displays the Write Checks window and automatically fills out the check, linking it to the memo.

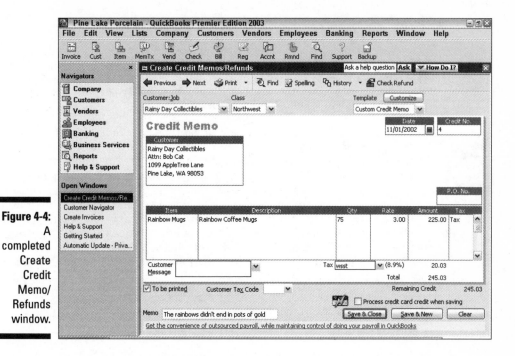

Figure 4-4:
A
completed
Create
Credit
Memo/
Refunds
window.

Fixing Credit Memo Mistakes

Sure, I can repeat the same information that I gave you in the section, "Fixing Invoice Mistakes," and leave you with a strange feeling of déjà vu. But I won't.

Here's everything you need to know about fixing credit memo mistakes: You can fix credit memo mistakes the same way that you fix invoice mistakes. If you need more help, refer to the earlier section of this chapter, "Fixing Invoice Mistakes."

Printing Invoices and Credit Memos

As part of setting up QuickBooks, you selected an invoice type. I assume that you have the raw paper stock for whatever invoice type you chose. If you're going to print on blank letterhead, for example, I assume that you have letterhead lying around. If you decide to use preprinted forms, I assume that you've ordered those forms and have received them.

I also assume that you've already set up your printer. If you've ever printed anything, your printer is already set up. Really.

Loading the forms into the printer

This part is easy. Simply load the invoice forms into the printer the same way you always load paper. Because you have one of about a jillion different printers, I can't give you the precise steps that you need to take, but if you've used a printer a bit, you should have no problem.

Wait a minute. What's that? Your printer is brand-new, and you've never used it before? Okay, here's one of my weird ideas: Use a pencil or something else that's heat-resistant (so that it won't melt and gum up the insides of the printer) to draw an arrow on a piece of paper. (Do not, repeat, do *not* use crayon. And don't let your children watch you do this.) Draw the arrow so that it points toward the top edge of the paper. Load the paper in the printer, with the arrow face up, and note which direction the arrow is pointing. Print something. Anything. When the paper comes out, notice whether the image faces the same direction as the arrow and whether it's on the same side of the paper as the arrow. With this information and a little logic, you should be able to figure out how to load forms correctly.

Setting up the invoice printer

You need to set up the invoice printer only once, but you need to specify a handful of general invoice-printing rules. These rules also apply to credit memos and to purchase orders, by the way.

To set up your printer for invoice printing, follow these steps:

1. **Choose File⇨Printer Setup and, in the Form Name drop-down list box, select Invoice.**

   QuickBooks displays the Printer Setup dialog box, as shown in Figure 4-5.

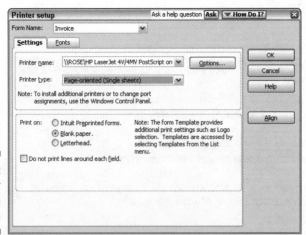

Figure 4-5:
The Printer Setup dialog box.

2. Select the printer that you want to use to print invoices.

Activate the Printer Name drop-down list to see the installed printers. Select the one that you want to use for printing invoices and purchase orders.

3. (Optional) Select the printer type.

The Printer Type drop-down list describes the kind of paper your printer uses. You have two choices: *Continuous* and *Page-Oriented*. Continuous means that your paper comes as one connected ream with perforated edges. Page-Oriented means that your paper is in single sheets.

4. Select the type of invoice form.

Select the option button that describes the type of form that you want to print on: Intuit Preprinted Form, Blank Paper, or Letterhead. Then mark the Do Not Print Lines Around Each Field check box if you don't like the nice little boxes QuickBooks creates to separate each field.

5. (Optional, but a really good idea . . .) Print a test invoice on real invoice paper.

Click the Align button. When QuickBooks displays the Align Printer dialog box, choose the type of invoice you want to print from the list and then click OK. When QuickBooks displays the Fine Alignment dialog box, as shown in Figure 4-6, click Print Sample to tell QuickBooks to print a dummy invoice on whatever paper you've loaded in the invoice printer.

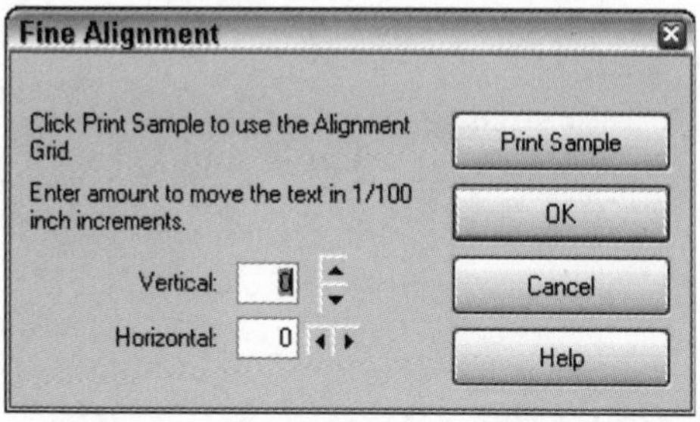

Figure 4-6: The Fine Alignment dialog box.

The dummy invoice that QuickBooks prints gives you a chance to see what your invoices will look like. The invoice also has a set of alignment gridlines that prints over the Bill To text box, which you can use if you need to fine-align your printer.

6. Fix any form-alignment problems.

If you see any alignment problems after you complete Step 5, you need to fix them. (Alignment problems probably occur only with impact printers. With laser printers or inkjet printers, sheets of paper feed into the printer the same way every time, so you almost never need to fiddle with the form alignment.)

To fix any big alignment problems — like stuff printing in completely the wrong place — you need to adjust the way the paper feeds into the printer. When you finally get the paper loaded as best you can, be sure to note exactly how you have it loaded. You need to have the printer and paper set up the same way every time you print.

For minor, but nonetheless still annoying, alignment problems, use the Fine Alignment dialog box's Vertical and Horizontal boxes to adjust the form's alignment. Then print another sample invoice. Go ahead and experiment a bit. You need to fine-tune the printing of the invoice form only once. Click OK in the Fine Alignment dialog box when you finish to have QuickBooks redisplay the Printer Setup dialog box.

Clicking the Options button in the Printer Setup dialog box (refer to Figure 4-5) opens the selected printer's Windows printer setup information, where you can do such things as specify quality settings or print order. Because this information relates to Windows and not to Quick Books, I'm not going to explain it. If you're the curious type or accidentally click it and then have questions about what you see, refer either to your Windows User's Guide or to the printer's user guide.

7. **Save your printer settings stuff.**

   After you finish fiddling with all of the Printer Setup dialog box's boxes and buttons, click OK to save your changes.

   If you want to always print a particular form using some particular settings (maybe you always print two copies of an invoice, for example), see the "Customizing Your Invoices and Credit Memos" section, later in this chapter.

You can print invoices and credit memos either one at a time or in a batch. How you print them makes no difference to QuickBooks or to me, your humble author. Pick whatever way seems to fit your style the best. The following sections show you how.

Printing invoices and credit memos as you create them

If you want to print invoices and credit memos as you create them, follow these steps:

1. **Click the Print button after you create the invoice or credit memo.**

   After you fill in each of the boxes in the Create Invoices window or the Create Credit Memos/Refunds window, click the Print button. Quick Books, ever the faithful servant, displays either the Print One Invoice dialog box (shown in Figure 4-7) or the Print One Credit Memo/Refund dialog box (which looks almost like the Print One Invoice dialog box).

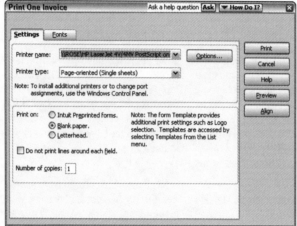

Figure 4-7:
The Print
One Invoice
dialog box.

2. **(Optional) Select the type of invoice or credit memo form.**

    If you're using a different type of invoice or credit memo form than you've described for the invoice printer setup, select the type of form that you want to print on in the Print On box. You can choose Intuit Preprinted Forms, Blank Paper, or Letterhead.

    You shouldn't have to worry about printing test-invoice or credit-memo forms or fiddling with form-alignment problems if you addressed these issues when you set up the invoice printer. So I'm not going to talk about the Align button here. If you want to do this kind of stuff and you need help, refer to the preceding section, "Setting up the invoice printer," in which I describe how to print test forms and fix form-alignment problems.

3. **Print the form.**

    Click the Print button to send the form to the printer. QuickBooks prints the form.

4. **Review the invoice or credit memo and reprint the form, if necessary.**

    Review the invoice or credit memo to see whether QuickBooks printed it correctly. If the form looks wrong, fix whatever caused the problem (perhaps you printed it on the wrong paper, for example) and reprint the form by clicking the Print button again.

Printing invoices in a batch

If you want to print invoices in a batch, you need to check the To Be Printed check box that appears in the lower-left corner of the Create Invoices window. This check mark tells QuickBooks to put a copy of the invoice on a special invoices-to-be-printed list.

What am I printing on?

Sometimes people get confused about the difference between preprinted forms versus letterhead versus plain paper. Here's the scoop: Preprinted forms have your company name, perhaps your logo, and a bunch of other boxes and lines (often in another color of ink) already printed on them. Preprinted forms are often multipart forms. (Examples of preprinted forms come in the QuickBooks box.)

Letterhead is what you usually use for letters that you write. It has your company name and address on it, for example, but nothing else. To save you from having to purchase preprinted forms, QuickBooks enables you to use letterhead to create invoices and forms. (To make the letterhead look a little more bookkeeperish, QuickBooks draws lines and boxes on the letterhead so that it looks sort of like a preprinted invoice.)

Plain paper is, well, plain paper. Nothing is printed on it. So QuickBooks needs to print everything — your company name, all the invoice stuff, and optionally, lines and boxes.

When you later want to print the invoices-to-be-printed list, follow these steps:

1. **Display the Create Invoices window, click the arrow next to the Print button, and choose Print Batch from the drop-down menu.**

   QuickBooks displays the Select Invoices to Print dialog box, as shown in Figure 4-8. This box lists all the invoices you marked as To Be Printed that you haven't yet printed.

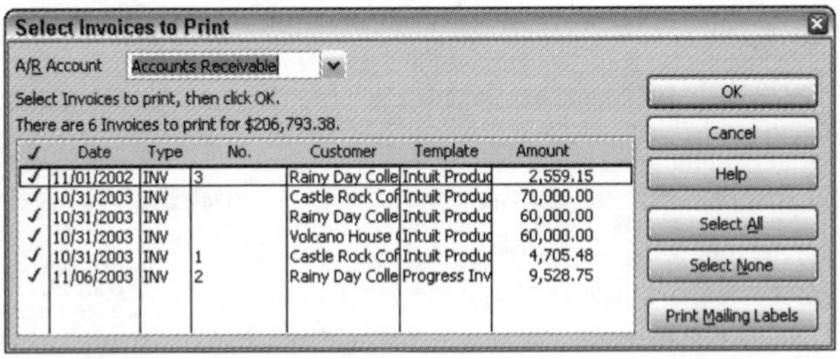

Figure 4-8:
The Select Invoices to Print dialog box.

2. **Select the invoices that you want to print.**

   Initially, QuickBooks marks all the invoices with a check mark, indicating that they will be printed. You can check and uncheck individual invoices on the list by clicking them. You also can use the Select All and the Select None buttons. Click Select All to check all the invoices. Click Select None to uncheck all the invoices.

3. Click OK.

After you correctly mark all the invoices you want to print — and none of the ones you don't want to print — click OK. QuickBooks displays the Print Invoices dialog box, as shown in Figure 4-9.

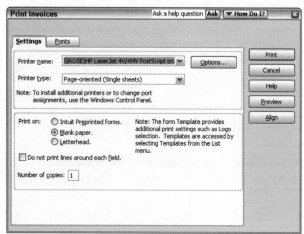

4. (Optional) Select the type of invoice form.

If you use a different type of invoice form than you described during the invoice setup, select the type of form that you want to print on using the Print On options. You can choose Intuit Preprinted Forms, Blank Paper, or Letterhead.

5. Print the forms.

Click the Print button to send the selected invoice forms to the printer. QuickBooks prints the forms and then displays a message box that asks whether the forms printed correctly.

6. Review the invoice forms and reprint them if necessary.

Review the invoices to see whether QuickBooks printed all of them correctly. If all the forms look okay, click OK in the message box. If one or more forms don't look okay, enter the invoice number of the first bad form in the message box. Then fix whatever problem fouled up the form (perhaps you printed it on the wrong paper, for example) and reprint the bad form(s) by clicking the Print button again. (The Print button is in the Print Invoices dialog box.)

Printing credit memos in a batch

If you want to print credit memos in a batch, you need to check the To Be Printed check box that appears in the lower-left corner of the Create Credit Memos/Refunds window. Checking this box tells QuickBooks to put a copy of the credit memo on a special credit-memos-to-be-printed list.

Printing credit memos in a batch works similarly to printing invoices in a batch. Because I describe how to print invoices in a batch in the preceding section, I'm going to speed through the following description of printing credit memos in a batch. If you get lost or have questions, refer to the preceding section.

When you're ready to print the credit memos that are on the to-be-printed list, follow these steps:

1. **Display the Create Credit Memos/Refunds window, click the arrow next to the Print button, and choose Print Batch from the drop-down menu.**

   QuickBooks displays the Select Credit Memos to Print dialog box.

2. **Select the credit memos that you want to print.**

3. **Click OK to display the Print Credit Memos dialog box.**

4. **Use the Print Credit Memos dialog box to describe how you want your credit memos printed.**

5. **Click the Print button to send the selected credit memos to the printer.**

   QuickBooks prints the credit memos.

Sending Invoices and Credit Memos via E-Mail

If you have e-mail already set up on your computer, you can e-mail invoices rather than printing them. To e-mail an invoice or credit memo, click the E-mail button, which appears at the top of the Create Invoices window. Quick Books displays the Edit E-mail Information window, as shown in Figure 4-10.

To send your invoice via e-mail, enter the e-mail address of the business you want to bill or refund money to, edit the message as appropriate (make sure to click that Check Spelling button), and then click the Send Now button.

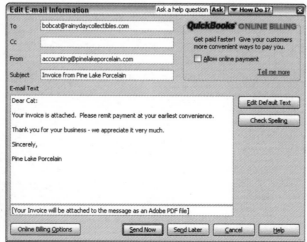

Figure 4-10:
The Edit
E-mail
Information
dialog box.

If you want to wait to send your invoice, click the Send Later button while in the Edit E-mail Information dialog box, or check the To Be Sent box in the lower-left corner of the invoice window; QuickBooks batches your e-mail invoices together. You can send the entire batch later by clicking the arrow next to the Email button and choosing the Send Batch command.

You can also fax invoices and credit memos from inside QuickBooks if you have a modem installed. To do this, click the Print button at the top of the Create Invoices or Create Credit Memos/Refunds window, select your fax/modem from the Printer Name drop-down list box, and then use the wizard that appears to send the fax via your modem (long distance charges may apply — and Carrot Top can't help).

Customizing Your Invoices and Credit Memos

With QuickBooks, you can easily customize the invoice and credit memo templates or create new invoices and credit memos based on one of the existing QuickBooks templates. All you have to do is open the form that you want to customize and click the Customize button. When QuickBooks displays the Customize Template window, select an existing template and click Edit to edit it, or click New to build a new template. If you're creating a new invoice form, QuickBooks displays the Customize Invoice dialog box shown in Figure 4-11.

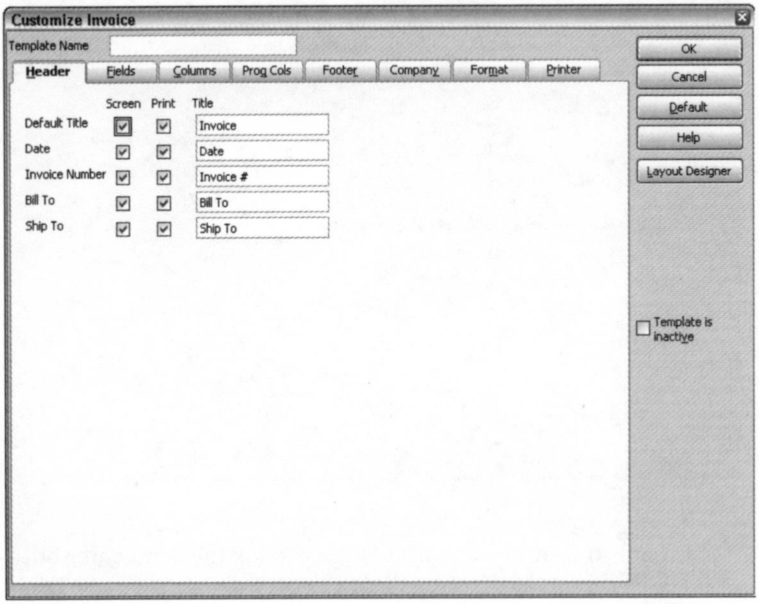

Customize Invoice

Template Name

| Header | Fields | Columns | Prog Cols | Footer | Company | Format | Printer |

OK

Cancel

Default

Help

Layout Designer

	Screen	Print	Title
Default Title	☑	☑	Invoice
Date	☑	☑	Date
Invoice Number	☑	☑	Invoice #
Bill To	☑	☑	Bill To
Ship To	☑	☑	Ship To

☐ Template is inactive

Figure 4-11:
The
Customize
Invoice
dialog box.

You can use the tabs of the Customize Invoice dialog box to customize almost
everything on your invoice. You can choose what you want in the header,
footer, and fields of your invoice and in what order you want the information.
You can choose which information should print and which should appear
on-screen. You can rename the fields and columns. You can also change the
fonts or add a logo to your invoice.

If you want to always print a particular form using some particular settings
(for example, maybe you always print credit memos in landscape mode on
legal paper, just for kicks), click the Printer tab, select the Use Specified
Printers Settings Below For This Invoice option, and then have at it.

If you're creating a new invoice template, click the Layout Designer button
on the Customize Invoice dialog box to start the Layout Designer window, as
shown in Figure 4-12. In this window, you can become a true layout artist and
observe how the overall look of your invoice changes when you move fields
around the page with your mouse.

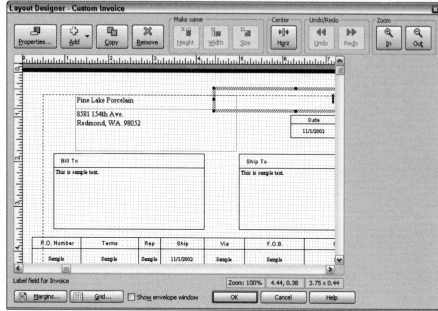

Figure 4-12:
The Layout
Designer
window for
customizing
an invoice.

Chapter 5

Reeling In the Dough

· ·

In This Chapter

▶ Recording and printing sales receipts

▶ Fixing sales receipt mistakes

▶ Recording customer payments

▶ Correcting mistakes in recording customer payments

▶ Tracking customer open invoices and collections

▶ Assessing finance charges

· ·

*Y*ou need to record the amounts customers pay you when they fork over cash, whether at the time of a sale or after you invoice them. In this chapter, I describe how to record these payments and explain how to make bank deposits, track the amounts that customers owe and pay, and assess finance charges.

If you've been using QuickBooks to prepare customer invoices, you're ready to begin recording payments. You'll have no problem. If you haven't been invoicing customers, you need to make sure that you have a couple of things ready to go before you can record cash sales.

First, you need to make sure that your lists are up to date. (I describe updating these lists in Chapter 2.) And second, if you want to print sales receipts, you need to have your printer set up to print them. You do so by choosing File➪Printer Setup and then selecting Sales Receipt from the Form Name drop-down list box. Setting up your printer to print sales receipts works just like setting it up to print invoices and credit memos (as I describe in Chapter 4).

Recording a Sales Receipt

You record a *sales receipt* when a customer pays you in full for the goods at the point of sale. Sales receipts work similarly to regular sales (for which you first invoice a customer and then later receive payment on the invoice). In fact, the big difference between the two types of sales is that sales receipts are recorded in a way that changes your cash balance rather than your accounts receivable balance.

In earlier versions, QuickBooks called *sales receipts* by another name: *cash sales.*

In the following steps, I describe how to record sales receipts for products, which are the most complicated type of cash sale. Recording sales receipts for services works basically the same way, however. You simply fill in fewer fields.

1. **Choose Customers➪Enter Sales Receipt to access the Enter Sales Receipts window.**

   Alternatively, select Customers from the Navigators list and click the Sales Receipt icon.

   The Enter Sales Receipts window appears, as shown in Figure 5-1.

   Your Enter Sales Receipts window may not look exactly like mine for a couple of reasons. The first is that QuickBooks customizes its forms to fit your particular type of business. The second reason is that forms in QuickBooks are really easy to customize. You can customize the Sales Receipt form by clicking the Customize button in the Enter Sales Receipts window.

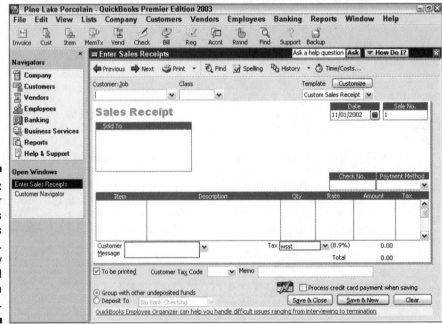

Figure 5-1:
The Enter
Sales
Receipts
window.
Strangely
empty and
perhaps a
bit lonely.

Customizing sales receipt forms works in a similar way to customizing invoices and credit memos, as I describe in Chapter 4. If your Enter Sales Receipts window includes more fields than I describe here, you can also turn to that chapter for help on how to fill out the additional fields or turn them off.

2. Identify the customer and, if necessary, the job.

Activate the Customer:Job drop-down list by clicking the down arrow to the right of the box. Scroll through the Customer:Job list until you see the customer or job name that you want and then click it. Note that unlike with invoices, the Customer:Job field is not required for cash sales.

3. (Optional) Specify a class for the sales receipt.

If you're using classes to categorize transactions, activate the Class drop-down list and select the appropriate class for the sales receipt.

4. Date the sales receipt.

Press Tab to move the cursor to the Date text box. Then type the correct date in MM/DD/YY format. You can change the date by using any of the date-editing codes. (You can find these codes in Chapter 4 and on the Cheat Sheet at the front of the book.)

5. (Optional) Enter a sale number.

QuickBooks suggests a cash sale number by adding 1 to the last cash sale number you used. Use this number, or tab to the Sale No. text box and change the number to whatever you want.

6. Fix the Sold To address, if necessary.

QuickBooks grabs the billing address from the Customer list and uses the billing address as the Sold To address. You can change the address for the cash sale, however, by replacing the appropriate part of the usual billing address.

7. Record the check number.

Enter the customer's check number in the Check No. text box. If the customer is paying you with cold hard cash, you can leave the Check No. text box empty.

8. Specify the payment method.

To specify the payment method, activate the Payment Method drop-down list and select something from it: cash, check, VISA, MasterCard, or whatever. If you don't see the payment method that you want to use, you can add the method to the Payment Method list. Choose <Add New> to display the New Payment Method dialog box. Enter a description of the payment method in the text box and click OK.

9. Describe each item that you're selling.

Move the cursor to the first row of the Item/Description/Qty/Rate/Amount/Tax list box. When you do, QuickBooks turns the Item field into a drop-down list box. Activate the Item drop-down list of the first empty row in the list box and then select the item. When you do, QuickBooks fills in the Description and Rate text boxes with whatever sales description and sales price you entered in the Item list. (You can edit this information if you want, but that probably isn't necessary.) Enter the number of items sold in the Qty text box. (QuickBooks then calculates the amount by multiplying the quantity by the rate.) Describe each of the other items you're selling by filling in the next empty rows of the list box.

If you've already read the chapter on invoicing customers (see Chapter 4), what I'm about to tell you is going to seem very, very familiar: You can put as many items on a sales receipt as you want. If you don't have enough room on a single page, QuickBooks just adds as many pages as you need to the receipt. The sales receipt total, of course, goes on the last page.

10. Describe any special items that the sales receipt should include.

If you didn't set up the QuickBooks item file, you have no idea what I'm talking about. But here's the scoop: QuickBooks thinks that anything that you stick on a receipt (or an invoice, for that matter) is something that you're selling. If you sell blue, yellow, and red thingamajigs, you obviously need to add each of these items to the Item list. But if you add freight charges to your receipt, QuickBooks thinks that these charges are just another thingamajig and requires you to enter another item in the list. The same is true for a volume discount that you want to stick on the receipt. And if you add sales tax to your receipt, well, guess what? QuickBooks thinks that the sales tax is just another item that needs to be included in the Item list. (For more information about working with your Item list and adding new items, refer to Chapter 2.)

To include one of these special items, move the cursor to the next empty row in the Item box, activate the drop-down list by clicking the arrow on the right side of the box, and then select the special item. After Quick Books fills in the Description and Rate text boxes, you may need to edit this information. Enter each special item — subtotals, discounts, freight, and so on — that you're itemizing on the receipt by filling in the next empty rows of the list box.

If you checked the Taxable check box when you added the item to the Item list, the word *Tax* appears in the Tax column to indicate that the item will be taxed.

If you want to include a discount item (so that all the listed items are discounted), you need to stick a subtotal item on the receipt after the inventory items or other items you want to discount. Then stick the discount item directly after the subtotal item. In this way, QuickBooks calculates the discount as a percentage of the subtotal.

11. (Optional) Add a customer message.

Click the Customer Message box, activate its drop-down list, and select a clever customer message. To add customer messages to the customer message list, choose <Add New>. When QuickBooks displays the New Customer Message box, fill it in and click OK.

12. Specify the sales tax.

If you specified tax information when you created your company file during the EasyStep Interview — remember how QuickBooks asked whether you charge sales tax? — QuickBooks fills in the default tax information by adding together the taxable items (which are indicated by the word *Tax* in the Tax column) and multiplying by the percentage you indicated when you created your company file. If the information is okay, move on to Step 13. If not, move the cursor to the Tax box that's to the right of the Customer Message box, activate the drop-down list box, and select the correct sales tax. For more information about setting a default sales tax for a customer on the Customer List, refer to Chapter 2.

13. (Truly optional and probably unnecessary for cash sales) Add a memo in the Memo text box.

You can include a memo description with the cash sale information. This memo isn't for your customer. It doesn't even print on the cash receipt, should you decide to print one. The memo is for your eyes only. Memo descriptions give you a way to store information that's related to a sale with the sales receipt information.

14. Decide how you want to handle the resulting payment.

The option buttons in the lower-left corner enable you to designate whether to group the payment with other undeposited funds or deposit it directly to an account. To decide how to handle the payment, look at a previous bank statement. If your bank lists deposits as a transaction total, you should probably click the Group with Other Undeposited Funds button. If your bank lists deposits individually by check, you should probably click the Deposit To option button and use the drop-down list box to designate the account to which you want to deposit the payment. (I also describe how to handle deposits in the "In the Bank" section, later in this chapter.)

15. Decide whether you're going to print the receipt.

If you're not going to print the receipt, make sure that the To Be Printed check box is empty — if not, click it to remove the check.

Figure 5-2 shows a completed Enter Sales Receipts window.

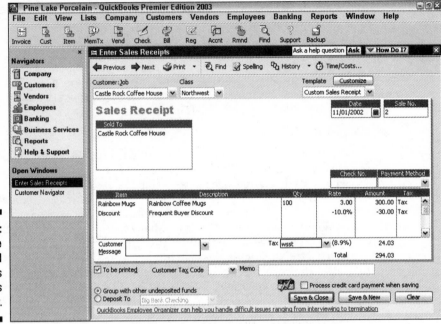

Figure 5-2:
The
completed
Enter Sales
Receipts
window.

16. **Save the sales receipt.**

    To save a completed sales receipt, click either Save & Close or Save & New. QuickBooks saves the sales receipt that's on-screen and then, if you clicked Save & New, displays an empty Enter Sales Receipts window so that you can create another Sales Receipt. (Note that you can page back and forth through receipts that you created earlier by clicking the Next and Previous buttons.) When you're done creating sales receipts, you can click the Enter Sales Receipts window's Close button.

Printing a Sales Receipt

To print a single sales receipt as you're recording the information, click the Print button in the Enter Sales Receipts window. The Print One Sales Receipt dialog box appears, as shown in Figure 5-3. The following steps tell you how to complete this dialog box.

1. **Select the type of sales receipt form.**

    If you're using a different Sales Receipt form type than you described for the invoice/PO printer setup, select the type of form that you want to print on by clicking an option in the Print On box. You can choose Intuit Preprinted Forms, Blank Paper, or Letterhead. (See Chapter 4 for more on these printer options.)

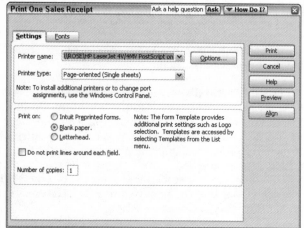

Figure 5-3:
The Print
One Sales
Receipt
dialog box.

You shouldn't have to worry about printing test receipts or fiddling with form alignment problems if you addressed these issues during the invoice/PO printer setup, so I'm not going to talk about the Align button here. If you want to print a test receipt or need to change the alignment, refer to Chapter 4 for information on how to proceed.

2. **Print that puppy!**

Click the Print button to send the form to the printer. QuickBooks prints the sales receipt.

3. **Review the sales receipt and reprint the form, if necessary.**

Review the sales receipt to see whether QuickBooks printed it correctly. If the form doesn't look okay, fix whatever problem fouled up the printing; perhaps you forgot to include the company name and address, for example. Then reprint the form by clicking the Print button (on the Enter Sales Receipts window) again, selecting the form on which you want to print (again) and then clicking the Print button in the Print One Sales Receipt dialog box (you got it — again).

To print a batch of receipts, make sure that you check the To Be Printed box on each receipt that you want to print and then display the Enter Sales Receipts window, click the arrow beside the Print button, and choose Print Batch from the drop-down list. QuickBooks displays the Select Receipts To Print dialog box, which enables you to choose which receipts to print — you choose them by putting a check in the first column and clicking OK — and the Print Sales Receipts dialog box appears. This dialog box resembles the Print One Sales Receipt dialog box in just about every way, and the instructions work in exactly the same manner. For help with this dialog box, refer to the sections on printing invoices and credit memos in batches in Chapter 4.

Correcting Sales Receipt Mistakes

If you make a mistake in entering a cash sale, don't worry. Here's a list of common problems and how to fix them:

✔ **If the sales receipt is still displayed on-screen:** If the sales receipt is still on-screen, you can move the cursor to the box or button that's wrong and then fix the mistake. Most of the bits of information that you enter in the Enter Sales Receipts window are fairly short or are entries that you've selected from a list. You can usually just replace the contents of some field by typing over whatever's already there or by making a couple of quick clicks. If you really messed up and want to start over from scratch, you can click the Clear button. To save a receipt after you've entered it correctly, click Save & Close or Save & New.

If you need to insert a line in the middle of a sales receipt, right-click where you want to insert the line and choose Insert Line from the short-cut menu. To delete a line, right-click it and then choose Delete Line from the shortcut menu.

✔ **If the sales receipt isn't displayed on-screen:** If the sales receipt isn't on-screen and you haven't yet printed it, you can use the Next and Previous buttons to page through the sales receipts. When you get to the one with the error, fix the error as I describe in the preceding section. If you make a mistake while editing a receipt, you can click the Revert button to go back to the saved receipt and not save your changes.

Even if you've printed the customer's receipt, you can make the sort of change that I just described. For example, you can page through the sales receipts by using the Next and Previous buttons until you find the receipt (now printed) with the error. And you can correct the error and print the receipt again. I'm not so sure that you want to go this route, however. Things will be much cleaner if you void the cash sale by displaying the sales receipt and choosing Edit➪Void Sales Receipt. Then enter a new, correct cash sales transaction.

✔ **If you don't want the sales receipt:** You usually won't want to delete sales receipts, but you can delete them. (You'll almost always be in much better shape if you just void the sales receipt.) To delete the receipt, display it in the Enter Sales Receipts window (choose Customers➪Enter Sales Receipt, and then page through the sales receipts by using the Next and Previous buttons until you see the cash sale that you want to delete) and then choose Edit➪Delete Sales Receipt. When QuickBooks asks you to confirm the deletion, click Yes.

If you want to see a list of all your cash sales, choose Edit➪Find Sales Receipts from the menu (if you're already viewing a sales receipt) and then click the Find button. If you're elsewhere in QuickBooks, choose Edit➪Simple Find from the menu, choose Transaction Type from the Filter list box and Sales Receipt from the drop-down list, and then click the Find button. QuickBooks gives you a list of your cash sales.

Recording Customer Payments

If your customers don't always pay you up-front for their purchases, you need to record another type of payment — the ones that customers make to pay off or pay down what you've invoiced them. To record the payments, of course, you need to first record invoices for the customer. If you issue credit memos that customers can use to reduce the amounts they owe, you also need to first record credit memos for the customer. (Check out Chapter 4 for how to record these items.) The rest is easy.

To access a wealth of customer information all on one page, choose Customers⇨ Customer Center. The Customer Center appears, listing outstanding balances, unbilled time and costs, and customers by profitability.

To display the Receive Payments window, simply choose Customers⇨Receive Payments. Or select Customers from the Navigators list and then click the Receive Payments icon. Then describe the customer payment and the invoices paid. If you want the gory details, read through the following steps:

1. **Choose Customers⇨Receive Payments.**

   The Receive Payments window appears, as shown in Figure 5-4. (You may be asked whether your company accepts credit cards — click Yes or No to be done with the dialog box.)

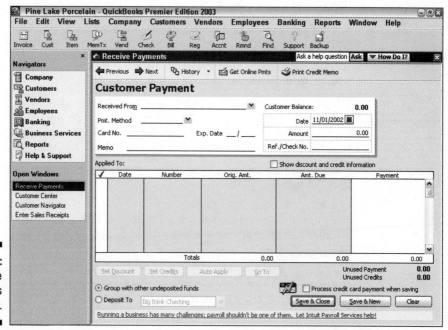

Figure 5-4: The Receive Payments window.

2. **Identify the customer and, if necessary, the job.**

   Activate the Received From drop-down list and select the customer (and job, if necessary) by clicking it. QuickBooks lists the open, or unpaid, invoices for the customer in the big Applied To list box at the bottom of the window.

3. **Specify the payment date.**

   Press Tab to move the cursor to the Date text box and type the correct date in MM/DD/YY format. To edit the date, you can use the secret date-editing codes that I describe in Chapter 4 and on the Cheat Sheet at the front of the book.

4. **Enter the amount of the payment.**

   Move the cursor to the Amount line and type the customer payment amount.

5. **(Optional) Specify the payment method.**

   Activate the Pmt. Method drop-down list and select the payment method.

6. **(Optional) Give the check number.**

   You can guess how this works, right? You move the cursor to the Ref./ Check No. line. Then you type the check number from the customer's check. Do you need to complete this step? Naw. But this bit of information may be useful if you or the customer later have questions about what checks paid for what invoices. So I'd go ahead and enter the check number.

7. **(Optional) Add a memo description.**

   Use the Memo description for storing some bit of information that will help you in some way. Note that this field prints on the Customer Statement.

8. **Decide how you want to handle the payment.**

   The option buttons in the lower left corner of the window should look somewhat familiar because they also appear in the Enter Sales Receipts window. These options enable you to designate whether to group the payment with other undeposited funds or deposit it directly to an account.

9. **If the customer has any outstanding credits, decide whether to apply them in this payment.**

   QuickBooks totals the amounts of any of the customer's existing credits. They could be anything from an overpayment on a previous invoice to a return credit or anything else.

   If you want to apply a credit memo to a specific open invoice, select the invoice and then click the Set Credits button. When QuickBooks displays the Credits tab of the Discount and Credits dialog box, as shown in Figure 5-5, click the credit memo you want to apply and then click Done.

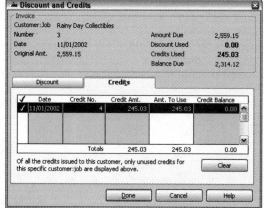

10. Identify which open invoices the customer is paying.

As long as you have the Automatically Apply Payments preference selected, QuickBooks automatically applies the payment to the open invoices, starting with the oldest open invoice. You can change this application by entering amounts in the Payment column. Simply click the open invoice's payment amount and enter the correct amount.

You can leave a portion of the payment unapplied, if you want to. You also can create a credit memo for the unapplied portion of a customer payment by clicking the Print Credit Memo button. (For information on what steps you need to follow next to print a credit memo, refer to Chapter 4.)

If you want to apply the customer payment to the oldest open invoices, click the Auto Apply button. If you want to unapply payments that you've already applied to open invoices, click the Clear Selections button. Clear Selections and Auto Apply are the same button. QuickBooks changes the name of the button, depending on whether you've already applied payments.

11. Adjust the early payment discounts, if necessary.

If you offer payment terms that include an early payment discount, QuickBooks reduces the open invoice original amount (shown in the Orig. Amt. column) by the early payment discount you specify to calculate the adjusted amount due (shown in the Amt. Due column).

To specify the discount, select the open invoice that has the early payment discount that you want to change. Then click the Set Discount button. With little or no hesitation, the Discount tab of the Discount and Credits dialog box appears, as shown in Figure 5-6. Type the dollar amount of the discount in the Amount of Discount text box. Then specify the expense account that you want to use to track early payment discounts by activating the Discount Account drop-down list and selecting one of the accounts. (Interest Expense is probably a good account to use, unless you want to set up a special early discounts expense account called something like Discount Expense or Discounts Given. After all, early payment discounts amount to interest.)

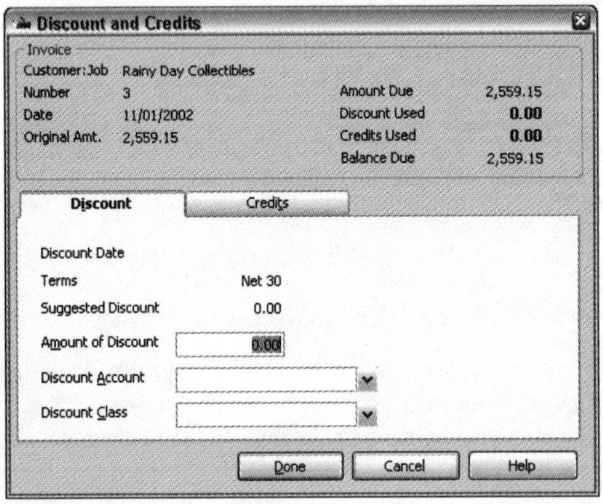

Figure 5-6:
The
Discount tab
of the
Discount
and Credits
dialog box.

When you're finished, click OK to return to the Receive Payments window. (For more information on the costs and benefits of early payment discounts, see Chapter 22.)

12. **Record the customer payment information.**

After you identify which invoices the customer is paying — the unapplied amount should probably show as zero — you're ready to record the customer payment information. You can do so by clicking Save & New or Save & Close. QuickBooks saves the customer payment shown on-screen. If you click Save & New, QuickBooks then displays an empty Receive Payments window so that you can enter another payment.

You can return to customer payments you recorded earlier by clicking the Previous button.

Correcting Mistakes in Customer Payments Entries

You can correct mistakes that you make in entering customer payments in basically the same way that you correct mistakes that you make in entering cash sales.

First, you display the window you used to enter the transaction. In the case of customer payments, you choose Customers⇨Receive Payments to display the Receive Payments window. Then use the Next and Previous buttons to page through the customer payments you entered previously until you see the one that you want to change. And then you make your changes. Then you click Save & Close. Pretty straightforward, right?

In the Bank

Whenever you record a cash sale or a customer payment on an invoice and mark the Group With Other Undeposited Funds options, QuickBooks adds the cash to its list of undeposited funds. These undeposited funds could be a bunch of checks that you haven't yet deposited, or they could consist of currency and coins. (I wanted to use the word *coinage* here because that's what your bank deposit slip probably uses. My long-suffering editor, however, overruled me, saying coinage is a crummy word and overly complex.)

Eventually, though, you'll want to take the money out from under your mattress and deposit it in the bank. To do so, follow these steps:

1. **Choose Banking⇨Make Deposits.**

   Or, alternatively, select Banking from the Navigators list and click the Deposit icon.

   The Payments to Deposit dialog box appears, as shown in Figure 5-7. This dialog box lists all the payments, regardless of the payment method. Amounts from sales receipts are listed as RCPT, and amounts from invoice payments are listed as PMT.

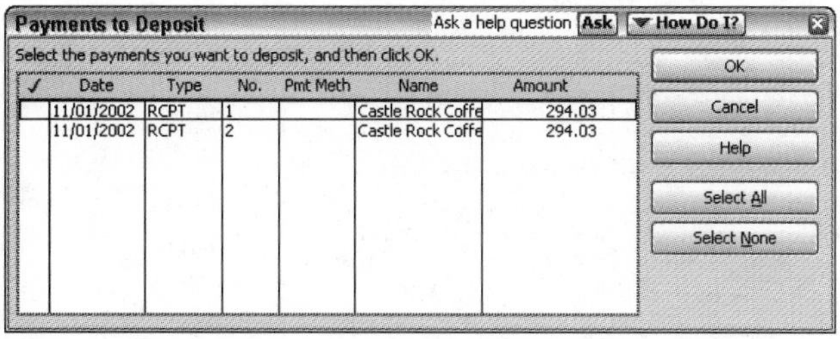

Figure 5-7: The Payments to Deposit dialog box.

2. **Select the payments that you want to deposit.**

   Click a payment or cash receipt to place a check mark in front of it, marking it for deposit. If you want to uncheck a payment, click it again. To uncheck all the payments, click the Select None button. To check all the payments, click the Select All button.

3. Click OK.

After you indicate which payments you want to deposit, click OK. QuickBooks displays the Make Deposits window, as shown in Figure 5-8.

4. Tell QuickBooks into which bank account you want to deposit the money.

Activate the Deposit To drop-down list and select the bank account in which you want to place the funds.

5. Specify the deposit date.

Press Tab to move the cursor to the Date text box and type the correct date in MM/DD/YY format. Use the secret date-editing codes if you need to edit the date. (Get these codes from Chapter 4 or the Cheat Sheet at the front of the book if you don't know them.)

6. (Optional) Add a memo description, if you want.

I don't know what sort of memo description you would add for a deposit. Sorry. A bank deposit is a bank deposit. At least to me.

By the way, if you need to redisplay the Payments to Deposit dialog box — maybe you made a mistake or something, and now you need to go back and fix it — click the Payments button. Note, though, that Quick Books won't display the Payments to Deposit dialog box unless the undeposited funds list has payments on it.

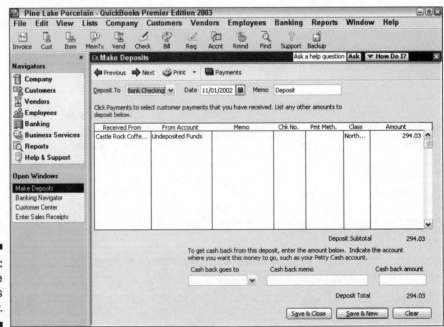

Figure 5-8:
The Make
Deposits
window.

7. **Specify the cash back amount.**

   If you want cash back from the deposit, activate the Cash Back Goes To drop-down list box and select a cash account. Then enter a memo in the Cash Back Memo text box and the amount of cash back you're taking in the Cash Back Amount text box.

8. **Record the deposit.**

   Click Save & Close or Save & New. If you click Save & New, QuickBooks displays a new blank Make Deposits window.

Improving Your Cash Inflow

I'm not going to provide a lengthy discussion on how to go about collecting cash from your customers. I do, however, want to quickly tell you about a couple of other things. You need to know how to monitor what your customers owe you and how to assess finance charges. Don't worry, though. I explain these two things as briefly as I can.

TIP

Using QuickBooks to write a letter

With QuickBooks Pro, you can seamlessly integrate your QuickBooks data to create collection letters in Microsoft Word. You can also use the QuickBooks predesigned business letter templates to speed the process of many of the business letters you write. To have QuickBooks help you write a letter, choose Company➪Write Letters. Then click the option button for the type of letter you want to create or edit and click Next.

If you choose to create a collection letter, you can specify which customers and jobs you want QuickBooks to search for money owed you. You can tell QuickBooks whether you want to create a separate letter for each customer who owes you money or each job on which you're owed money. You can also specify the limit for how overdue an invoice must be to warrant a collection letter. After you set the parameters and

click Next, QuickBooks searches for overdue invoices that fit your criteria.

If you choose to create a type of letter other than a collection letter, QuickBooks offers many choices based on whether you're sending the letter to a customer, a vendor, an employee, or someone else. For example, you can create credit approval, credit denial, or credit request letters. You can create birthday or apology letters. And you can create faxes or bounced check letters, just to name a few.

After you specify the information about the type of letter that you want to create, QuickBooks asks you a few questions about how you want to sign the letter. It then creates the letter and displays it in Microsoft Word so that you can edit the letter as necessary and then print or save it.

Tracking what your customers owe

You can track what a customer owes in a couple of ways. Probably the simplest method is to display the Customer Detail Center for the customer. To do so, choose Customers⇨Customer Detail Center. QuickBooks whips up a page that lists open invoices for the customer and recent payments received from the customer. It also shows the customer's contact information. Figure 5-9 shows the Customer Detail Center for a customer.

You also should be aware that QuickBooks provides several nifty accounts receivable, or A/R, reports. You get to these reports by choosing Reports⇨ Customers & Receivables. QuickBooks then displays a submenu of about half a dozen reports that describe how much money customers owe you. Some reports, for example, organize open invoices into different groups based on how old the invoices are. (These reports are called *agings*.) Some reports summarize only invoices or payments. And some reports show each customer's open, or unpaid, balance.

In Chapter 14, I describe, in general terms, how you go about producing and printing QuickBooks reports. So refer to Chapter 14 if you have questions. Let me also say that you can't hurt anything or foul up your financial records just by printing reports. So go ahead and noodle around.

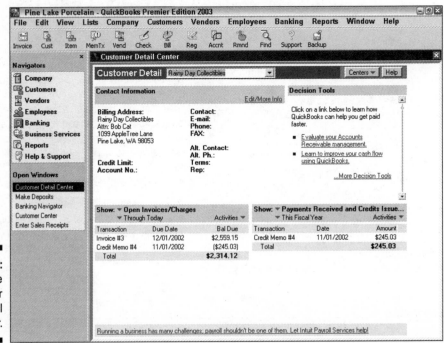

Figure 5-9:
The Customer Detail Center.

You can print a statement to send to a customer by choosing Customers⇨ Create Statements. Use the Select Statements to Print dialog box to describe which customers you want to print statements for and the date ranges you want the statements to show, and then click OK to print the statements.

Assessing finance charges

I wasn't exactly sure where to stick this discussion of finance charges. But finance charges seem to relate to collecting the cash your customers owe, so I figure that I'm okay talking about assessing finance charges here.

To assess finance charges, follow these steps:

1. **Choose Edit⇨Preferences.**

   To be able to assess finance charges, you need to first set them up.

   Only the QuickBooks administrator can change the company finance charge settings, and he or she can do so only in single-user mode.

   To set up finance charges, choose Edit⇨Preferences. Then click the Finance Charge icon in the list on the left and click the Company Preferences tab.

   QuickBooks displays the Preferences dialog box, shown in Figure 5-10. (If you've assessed finance charges before, QuickBooks displays the Assess Finance Charges window. You can display the Preferences dialog box and check or edit your finance charge settings by clicking the Settings button in the Assess Finance Charges window.)

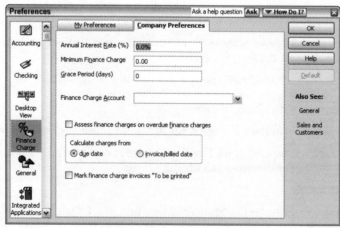

Figure 5-10:
The Preferences dialog box for finance charges.

2. **Enter the annual interest rate that you want to use to calculate finance charges.**

   Move the cursor to the Annual Interest Rate (%) text box and enter the annual interest rate.

3. **(Optional) Enter the minimum finance charge — if one exists.**

   Move the cursor to the Minimum Finance Charge text box and enter the minimum charge. If you always charge at least $2.00 on a past due invoice, for example, type **2**.

4. **Enter the number of days of grace that you give.**

   Days of Grace. That sounds kind of like an artsy movie or serious novel, doesn't it? Basically, this number is how many days of slack you're willing to cut people. If you type **3** in the Grace Period (days) text box, QuickBooks doesn't start assessing finance charges until three days after the invoice is past due.

5. **Specify which account you want to use to track the finance charges.**

   Activate the Finance Charge Account drop-down list and select an account. Finance charges are, essentially, interest that you charge your customers. So unless you have some other account that you want to use, you may just want to use the Interest Income account that appears on most of the standard charts of accounts.

6. **Indicate whether you want to charge finance charges on finance charges.**

   Does this statement make sense? If you charge somebody a finance charge and they don't pay the finance charge, eventually it becomes past due, too. So then what do you do the next time you assess finance charges? Do you calculate a finance charge on the finance charge? If you want to do this — and if state and local laws let you — check the Assess Finance Charges on Overdue Finance Charges check box.

7. **Tell QuickBooks whether it should calculate finance charges from the due date or the invoice date.**

   Select either the Due Date or Invoice/Billed Date option button. As you may guess, you calculate bigger finance charges if you start accruing interest on the invoice date.

8. **Tell QuickBooks whether it should print finance charge invoices.**

   Check the box for Mark Finance Charge Invoices "To Be Printed" if you want to print invoices later for the finance charges that you calculate.

9. **Click OK.**

   After you use the Preferences dialog box to tell QuickBooks how the finance charges should be calculated, click OK.

10. Choose Customers⇨Assess Finance Charges.

Or, alternatively, select Customers from the Navigators list and click the Finance Charges icon. The Assess Finance Charges window appears, as shown in Figure 5-11. This window shows all the finance charges that QuickBooks has calculated, organized by customer.

11. Give the finance charge assessment date.

Move the cursor to the Assessment Date text box and enter the date when you're assessing the finance charges, which I'm willing to bet is the current date. (This date is also the invoice date that will be used on the finance charge invoices, if you create them.)

12. Confirm which customers you want to be assessed finance charges.

QuickBooks initially marks all the finance charges, which means that it sets up a new invoice for each finance charge. (QuickBooks marks finance charges with a little check mark.) If you want to unmark (or later mark) a finance charge, click it. To unmark all the charges, click the Unmark All button. To mark all the charges, click the Mark All button.

You can produce a collections report for any of the customers or jobs listed in the Assess Finance Charges dialog box by selecting the customer name and then clicking the Collection History button.

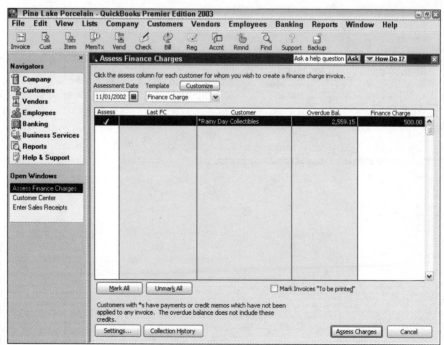

Figure 5-11:
The Assess Finance Charges window.

13. **Indicate whether you want finance charge invoices printed.**

    If you do, check the Mark Invoices "To Be Printed" check box.

14. **Click Assess Charges.**

    When the Assess Finance Charges dialog box correctly describes the finance charges that you want to assess, click Assess Charges. You're finished with the finance charge calculations and assessments.

    I'm not going to describe how to print invoices containing finance charges because I already slogged through invoice printing in painstaking detail in Chapter 4. If you have questions about how to print the invoices, you may want to visit that chapter.

CASE STUDY

A word of advice from an accountant

While I'm on the subject of tracking what your customers owe you, let me share a thought about collecting this money. You should have firm collection procedures that you follow faithfully. For example, as soon as an invoice is a week or so past due, it's very reasonable to place a friendly telephone call to the customer's accounts payable department and verify that the customer has received the invoice and is in the process of paying. You have no reason to be embarrassed because some customer is late in paying you! What's more, you may find out something surprising and essential to your collection. You may discover, for example, that the customer didn't receive the invoice. Or you may

find out that something was wrong with the gizmo you sold or the service you provided.

As soon as an invoice is a month or so past due, you need to crank up the pressure. A firm letter asking that the customer call you to explain the past due amount is very reasonable — especially if the customer assured you only a few weeks ago that payment was forthcoming.

When an invoice is a couple of months past due, you need to get pretty serious. You'll probably want to stop selling the customer anything more because it's unclear whether you'll be paid. And you may want to start a formal collection process. (Ask your attorney about starting such a process.)

Chapter 6

Paying Bills

• •

• •

*Q*uickBooks gives you two ways to pay and record your bills. And you have many options when it comes to deciding when to pay your bills, how to pay your bills, and how to record your bills for the purposes of tracking inventory and expenses.

In this chapter, I explain not only how to pay vendor bills but also how to pay that all-important bill that so many businesses owe to their state and local governments. I'm talking, of course, about sales tax.

Pay Now or Pay Later?

When it comes to paying bills, you have a fundamental choice to make. You can either record and pay your bills simultaneously, or you can record your bills as they come in but then pay them as they're due. The first method is easiest, as you may guess, because you do everything at once. The second method, called the *accounts payable method,* gives you more accurate financial records and makes for more precise management of your cash and outstanding bills.

If you have a small business with little overhead, you may just as well record and pay bills simultaneously. But if you need precise measurement of your expenses and bills — if you want to use what's termed *accrual-basis accounting* — you should use the accounts payable method of paying bills. I should note, too, that using the accounts payable method with QuickBooks is not as difficult as it may seem at first.

And now you're ready to begin. In the next section of this chapter, I describe how to pay bills by writing checks. A little later in the chapter, in the "Recording Your Bills the Accounts Payable Way" section, you find out how to pay bills by using the accounts payable method.

Recording Your Bills by Writing Checks

When you record bills by writing checks, you're doing *cash-basis accounting*. In a nutshell, this means that you count bills as expenses when you write the check to pay the bill.

I talk a little bit about cash-basis accounting in Appendix B. But let me say here that a tradeoff is implicit in the choice to use cash-basis accounting. If you use cash-basis accounting — which is what I do in my little business — you greatly simplify your bookkeeping. But you lose precision in your measurement of your expenses. And you don't keep track of your unpaid bills inside QuickBooks. They just stack up in a pile next to your desk.

As long as you understand this tradeoff and are comfortable with it, you're ready to begin using this method, which you do by following the steps provided in the paragraphs that follow.

The slow way to write checks

You can write checks either from the register or from the Write Checks window. Using the Write Checks window is the slow way, but it enables you to record your expenses and the items (if any) that you purchase. Using the Write Checks window is the best choice in the following situations:

 ✔ You're paying for an inventory item.

 ✔ You're paying for something for which you have a purchase order.

 ✔ You plan to be reimbursed for the bill that you're paying.

 ✔ You want to record what job or class this bill falls under.

To use the Write Checks window to write checks, follow these steps:

1. **Choose Banking⇨Write Checks.**

   Alternatively, select Banking from the Navigators list and then click the Checks icon. The Write Checks window appears, as shown in Figure 6-1. Notice that this window has three parts:

   • The check part on the top, which you no doubt recognize from having written thousands of checks in the past.

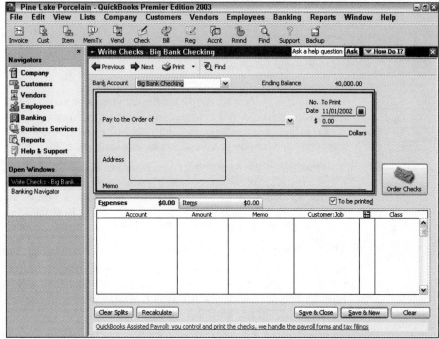

Figure 6-1:
The Write
Checks
window.

- The buttons on the top and bottom.

- The Expenses and Items tabs near the bottom of the window. This part is for recording what the check is for, as I explain in Steps 8, 9, and 10.

2. Click the Bank Account drop-down list and choose the account from which you want to write this check.

This step is very important if you have more than one account. Make sure that you choose the correct account; otherwise, your account balances in QuickBooks will be incorrect.

3. Specify the check date.

Click in the Date box and type the check date. I don't keep reminding you about this, but because I'm still in the early part of this book, remember that you can enter today's date by pressing the *T* key. You can also click the button to the right of the Date box to get a popup calendar. To select a date from the popup calendar, click the calendar day that you want to use.

4. Fill in the Pay to the Order Of line.

If you've written a check to this person or party before, the AutoFill feature fills in the name of the payee in the Pay to the Order Of line for you after you start typing the name. (AutoFill does so by comparing what you type with names shown in the Customer, Vendor, Employee, and

Other Names lists.) AutoFill also puts the payee's address in the Address box. The AutoRecall feature can even fill out the entire check for you, based on the last check that you wrote to this vendor. (You can enable AutoRecall by choosing Edit⇨Preferences, clicking the General icon, and selecting the Automatically Recall Last Transaction For This Name box on the My Preferences tab.)

Does the check look all right? Maybe all you need to do is tab around, adjusting numbers. Otherwise, read the next 12 steps. (Another 12-step program?). In these steps, I explain how to record information about a new vendor and pay a check to that vendor in one fell swoop.

If you've never paid anything to this person before, the program displays a Name Not Found message box after you enter the name on the Pay to the Order Of line. You can either click Quick Add or Set Up to add the payee name to one of your lists. (To find out how to do so, check out the "To Quick Add or to Set Up?" sidebar, elsewhere in this chapter.)

5. Type the amount of the check.

Now comes my favorite part. I've always found it a big bother to write out the amount of checks. I mean, if you write a check for $21,457.00, how do you fit twenty-one thousand, four hundred fifty-seven dollars, and no cents on the line? Where do you put those hyphens, anyway?

All you have to do with QuickBooks is enter the amount next to the dollar sign and press Tab. When you press Tab, QuickBooks writes out the amount for you on the Dollars line. At moments like this, I'm grateful to be alive in the twenty-first century when computer technology can do these marvelous things for me.

6. (Optional) Fill in the Address text box.

You need to fill in this box only if the address isn't there already and you intend to send the check by mail in a window envelope.

7. (Optional) Fill in the Memo line.

You can put a message to the payee on the Memo line — a message such as "Quit bleeding me dry." But you usually put an account number on the Memo line so that the payee can record your account number.

If you try to click Save & New and close the dialog box now, QuickBooks tells you that you can't and tries to bite your leg off. Why? Because you can't write a check unless you fill out the Expenses and Items tabs. You use these tabs to describe what the check pays.

8. Move the cursor down to the Account column of the Expenses tab and enter an expense account name.

Chances are that you want to enter the name of an account that's already on the chart of accounts. If that's the case, move the cursor to a field in the Account column, and QuickBooks turns the field into a drop-down list box. Click the down arrow to see a list of all your accounts. You'll probably have to scroll down the list to get to the expense accounts.

Click the one that this check applies to (most likely it's Supplies or Rent). If you need to create a new expense account category for this check, choose <Add New> from the top of the list to see the New Account dialog box. Fill in the information and click OK.

What if the money that you're paying out with this check can be distributed across two, three, or four expense accounts? Simply click below the account that you just entered. The down arrow shoots down next to the cursor. Click the down arrow and enter another expense account, and another, and another, if you want to.

9. **Tab over to the Amount column, if necessary, and change the numbers around.**

    If you're distributing this check across more than one account, you want to make sure that the numbers in the Amount column correctly distribute the check to the appropriate accounts, as shown in Figure 6-2.

10. **If you want to, enter words of explanation or encouragement in the Memo column.**

    Someday, you may have to go back to this check and try to figure out what these expenses mean. The Memo column may be your only clue. Enter some wise words here: "August rent," "copier repair," or "company party."

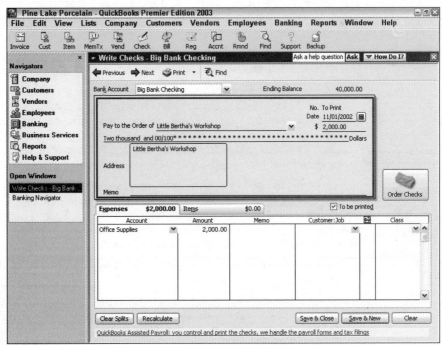

Figure 6-2:
A
completed
check.

To Quick Add or to Set Up?

If you click Quick Add in the Name Not Found message box, you see a Select Name Type message box, asking whether the payee is a Vendor, Customer, Employee, or Other. Most likely, the payee is a vendor, in which case you click Vendor (but you can, of course, click one of the other three options). The address information that you write on the check goes in the Vendor list — or Customer, Employee, or Other Names list, depending on what you clicked. (Refer to Chapter 2 if you're in the dark about adding to your lists.)

Choosing Set Up in the Name Not Found message box is a little more interesting. When you choose this option, you also see the Select Name Type box. Click Vendor, Customer, Employee, or Other. Click OK, and then you see the New whatever window that you may remember from Chapter 2, if you've already added new vendors, customers, or employees to your lists.

By the way, my long-suffering technical editor, Mike, wants me to point out that using the Quick Add method is sort of lazy. With Quick Add, QuickBooks only requires you to collect a minimal amount of information.

11. **(Optional) Assign the expense to the Customer:Job column.**

    If you plan to be reimbursed for these expenses, or if you just want to track your expenses by job, enter the name of the customer who is going to reimburse you. Click the down arrow to find the customer. Enter an amount for each customer or job, if necessary.

12. **(Optional) Assign the expense to a class.**

    You also can track expenses by class by making entries in the Class column. Notice the usual down arrow, which you click to see a list of classes. You won't see the Class column, however, unless you told QuickBooks that you wanted to use classes when you created your company. (You created the company when you worked your way through the EasyStep Interview; see Chapter 1.)

    If you want to have QuickBooks track expenses by class, you have to set it up to do so. To set up QuickBooks to track expenses, choose Edit➪Preferences. When QuickBooks displays the Preferences dialog box, click the Accounting icon, click the Company Preferences tab, and then mark the Use Class Tracking check box.

13. **Use the Items tab to record what you're purchasing.**

    You may be purchasing inventory items or may already have filled out a purchase order for the items for which you're paying. If so, click the Items tab. If you don't have a purchase order for the items, go on to Step 14. If you do have a purchase order for the items, click the Select PO button to see a list of purchases on order with this vendor. Check those for which you're paying and click OK.

QuickBooks doesn't show its purchase order feature unless you told it that you wanted to use purchase orders during the EasyStep Interview. If you now think you want to use them, choose Edit➪Preferences. When QuickBooks displays the Preferences dialog box, click the Purchases & Vendors, click the Company Preferences tab, and then mark the Inventory And Purchase Orders Are Active check box.

14. Move to the Item column and enter a name for the item.

Notice the down arrow in this column. Click the arrow to see the Items list. Does the item that you're paying for appear on this list? If so, click it. If not, choose <Add New> from the top of the list and fill out the New Item window. (Refer to Chapter 2.)

15. Fill in the rest of the rows of items on the Items tab.

You can enter all the items you're purchasing on this tab. Make sure that the Items tab accurately shows the items that you're purchasing, their cost, and the quantity.

When you finish adding items, you may want to use one of the following options that appear in the Write Checks window:

- Click the Print button to print the check in the Write Checks window. This option doesn't print all the checks that you have written and marked as to be printed, however. (I explain how to print more than one check at a time in Chapter 10.)

- The Clear Splits button deletes any individual amounts that you've entered for separate expenses or items on the Expenses and Items tabs. QuickBooks then enters the total amount of the check in the Amount column on the Expenses tab.

- The Recalculate button totals the items and expenses in the window. It also puts the total on both the numeric and text amount lines of the check.

- The To Be Printed check box designates the check for printing. Check this box if you want to print the check with QuickBooks by using your printer and preprinted check forms. Uncheck this box if you're recording a handwritten check.

16. Click Save & New or Save & Close to finish writing the check.

Click Save & Close to tell QuickBooks that you want to save the check and close the check form. Click Save & New to tell QuickBooks that you want to save the check and then display another blank check form. If you don't want to save the check, close the dialog box and then click No when QuickBooks asks if you want to save the check.

You can also use the Next and Previous buttons to move to previously written checks or to a blank check form. If you write check number 101, for example, clicking Next takes you to check 102 so that you can write that one. (Clicking Previous moves you to check 100 in case you need to edit a check you've written earlier.)

Well, that's over with. For a minute there, I thought that it would never end. . . .

The fast way to write checks

If you want to pay a bill that isn't for inventory or that you won't be reimbursed for or that you don't need to track in any way, shape, or form, you can write your check directly from the checking account register. This method is the fast and easy way to go; follow these steps:

1. **Choose Banking⇨Use Register.**

   Or, alternatively, select Banking from the Navigators list and then click the Check Register icon. The checking account register appears, as shown in Figure 6-3. (If you have more than one bank account, you have to select the proper account from the drop-down list and click OK.) The cursor is at the end of the register, ready and waiting for you to enter check information.

2. **Fill in the information for the check.**

   Notice that the entries you make are the same ones that you would make on a check. You need to note a couple of things about the register:

   - If you enter a Payee name that QuickBooks doesn't recognize, you see the Name Not Found message box and you're asked to give information about this new, mysterious vendor. To see what to do next, go back to the preceding set of instructions on writing a check the slow way.

   - You have to choose an account name. Chances are, you can find the right one in the Account drop-down list, but if you can't, enter one of your own. QuickBooks displays the Account Not Found message box and asks you to fill in the information about this new account.

   As you fill out the register, if you decide that you want to be reimbursed for this check or that you want to track expenses and items, click the Edit Transaction button. You see the Write Checks window that you know from Figure 6-1. Follow Steps 3 through 14 in the instructions (in the section "The slow way to write checks" earlier in this chapter) on how to write a check the slow way to fill in the Write Checks window. When you finish filling in the Write Checks window, click Save & New. You're back where you started, in the Register window.

3. **When you finish filling in the check information, click Record.**

   You click Record, of course, to record the check.

   By the way, if you realize that you've made a mistake and haven't yet clicked Record to record the check, you can click that Restore button to go back to square one. Clicking Restore blanks out what you just entered so that you can start all over again.

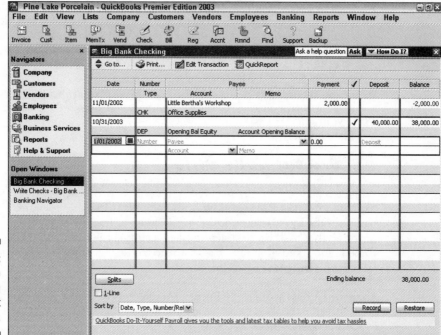

Figure 6-3:
The
checking
account
register.

If you want to print the check (or checks) that you've just entered, you need to flip to Chapter 10 for details. In the meantime, I give you the lowdown on keeping your checkbook in Chapter 8 — so turn there if this discussion of checks has you really excited.

Recording Your Bills the Accounts Payable Way

The accounts payable, or A/P, way of paying bills involves two steps. The first is a trifle on the difficult side, and the second step is as easy as pie. First, you record your bills. If you've read the section earlier in this chapter on writing checks the slow way, you're already familiar with using the Expenses tab and the Items tab to record bills. You need to fill out those tabs for the A/P method as well if you want to distribute a bill to accounts, customers, jobs, classes, and items. If you've read the first half of this chapter, some of what follows will be old hat.

After you record your bills, you can go on to the second step. All you have to do is tell QuickBooks which bills to pay. QuickBooks then writes the checks. You print them. You mail them.

To make the A/P method work, you have to record your bills as they come in. That doesn't mean that you have to pay them right away. By recording your bills, you can keep track of how much money you owe and how much money your business really has. QuickBooks reminds you when your bills are due so that you don't have to worry about forgetting to pay a bill.

When you record bills the accounts payable way, you're using accrual-basis accounting. I explain accrual-basis accounting in Appendix B.

Recording your bills

When a bill comes in, the first thing to do is record it. You can record bills through the Enter Bills window or the Accounts Payable register. If you plan to track bills by expense and item, you need to use the Enter Bills window. I describe that method first. If you have a simple bill to pay that doesn't need to be reimbursed or tracked, skip ahead to the "Paying Your Bills" section, later in this chapter.

To record a bill through the Enter Bills dialog box, follow these steps:

1. **Choose Vendors⇨Enter Bills.**

   Or, alternatively, select Vendors from the Navigators list and then click the Enter Bills icon. Figure 6-4 shows the Enter Bills window. You no doubt notice that the top half of this window looks a great deal like a check — that's because much of the information that you put here ends up on the check that you write to pay your bill. (If you see the word Credit at the top of the form rather than Bill, click the Bill option button in the top-left corner. You also can use this screen to enter credit from vendors.)

2. **Select the name of the vendor you're paying.**

   If you want to pay this bill to a vendor who's already on the Vendor list, simply click the down arrow at the end of the Vendor line and choose the vendor. (QuickBooks then automatically fills the Enter Bills window with as much information as it can remember.) But if this vendor is new, QuickBooks asks you to Quick Add or Set Up some information about the vendor — the address, credit limit, payment terms, and so on. You provide this information in the New Vendor window. If you're not familiar with this window from Chapter 2, make a brief visit to that chapter.

   If you have one or more unfilled purchase orders with the vendor you select, QuickBooks asks you whether you want to receive against a purchase order. Click Yes if you do or No if you don't. If you choose to receive against a purchase order, QuickBooks displays the Open Purchase Orders dialog box, as shown in Figure 6-5. It simply lists the open purchase orders you've recorded. When you select one or more purchase orders to receive against, QuickBooks fills in the items and amounts from these orders for you, which you can modify as necessary.

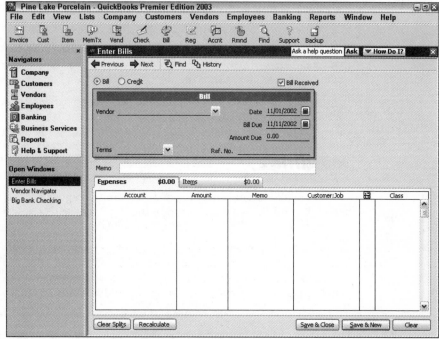

Figure 6-4:
The Enter
Bills
window.

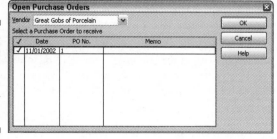

Figure 6-5:
Paying a bill
against a
purchase
order
window.

Hey, you know what? I don't talk about purchase orders until Chapter 7. But here's the *CliffsNotes* version: To create a purchase order, which is just a record of items you order from vendors, choose Vendors➪Create Purchase Orders. When QuickBooks displays the Create Purchase Orders window, describe your order. You print and edit purchase orders, by the way, in the same manner as you print invoices and credit memos.

3. Select the payment terms that describe when the bill is due.

In the Terms line, open the drop-down list and select the payment terms (if the information isn't already there from when you set up the vendor).

4. (Optional) Enter a memo to describe the bill.

You can enter a note in the Memo box. The note that you enter appears on the A/P register.

5. Move the cursor down to the Account column of the Expenses tab and enter an expense account name.

Chances are that you want to enter the name of an expense account that's already on the chart of accounts. If that's the case, click the down arrow to see a list of all your accounts. You probably have to scroll down the list to get to the expense accounts (a fast way to move down the list is to start typing the account name — you go straight down the list). Click the account that this bill represents (most likely it's Supplies or something like that).

If you need to create a new expense account category for this bill, choose <Add New> from the top of the list. You see the New Account dialog box. Fill in the information and click OK.

What if the money that you're paying out because of this bill can be split among two, three, or four expense accounts? Simply click below the account that you just entered. The down arrow appears. Click it to enter another expense account, and another, and another, if you want to.

6. Tab over to the Amount column, if necessary, and change the numbers.

If you're splitting this bill among several accounts, make sure that the numbers in the Amount column add up to the total of the bill.

7. (Optional) Enter words of explanation or wisdom in the Memo column.

8. (Optional) Assign the expense to a Customer:Job.

If you plan to be reimbursed for these expenses, or if you just want to track your expenses by job, enter the customer who is going to reimburse you. Enter an amount for each account, if necessary. You can use the down arrow to find customers and then click them.

9. (Optional) Assign the expense to a Class.

You also can track expenses by class by making entries in the Class column. Notice the usual down arrow and click it to see a list of classes. (You don't see a Class column unless you've told QuickBooks that you want to use classes.)

If you want to have QuickBooks track expenses by class, you can set it up to do so. To set up QuickBooks to track expenses, choose Edit➪ Preferences. When QuickBooks displays the Preferences dialog box, click the Accounting icon, click the Company Preferences tab, and then mark the Use Class Tracking check box.

If you want, click the Recalculate button to total the expenses.

10. Use the Items tab to record the various items that the bill represents.

Click the Items tab. Enter the items you purchased and the prices you paid for them.

If you realize after partially completing the bill that the bill does indeed pay a purchase order, click the Select PO button, which appears on the Items tab of the Enter Bill window.

From the Vendor drop-down list, click the name of the vendor who sent you the bill. In the list of open purchase orders, click in the column on the left to put a check next to the purchase order (or orders) for which you're paying. Easy enough? Click OK when you're done, and QuickBooks fills out the Items tab for you automatically.

11. Move to the Item column and enter a name for the item.

Notice the down arrow in this column. Click it to see the Item list. Does the item that you're paying for appear on this list? If so, click that item. If not, choose <Add New> from the top of the list and fill out the New Item window (refer to Chapter 2).

12. Fill in the rest of the rows of items on the Items tab.

You can enter all the items you're purchasing here. Make sure that the Items tab accurately shows the items that you're purchasing, their costs, and their quantities. If you want to, click the Recalculate button to total the items.

13. Save the bill.

Click Save & New to save your record of the bill and then enter another bill. Or click Save & Close to record your bill but not enter another bill.

Entering your bills the fast way

You also can enter bills directly in the Accounts Payable register. This method is faster, but it makes tracking expenses and items more difficult.

If you want to enter bills directly in the Accounts Payable register, follow these steps:

1. Choose Lists⇨Chart of Accounts.

The chart of accounts opens.

2. Open the Accounts Payable account.

When QuickBooks displays your chart of accounts, double-click the Accounts Payable account in the chart of accounts' list of accounts. You see the Accounts Payable register window, as shown in Figure 6-6. The cursor is at the end of the register, ready and waiting for you to enter the next bill.

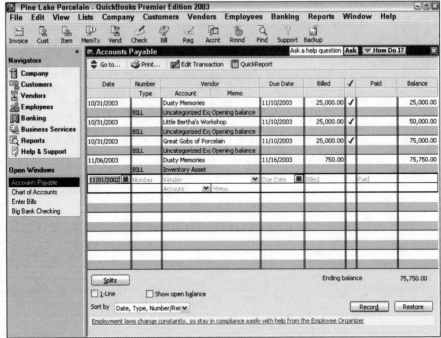

Figure 6-6:
The
Accounts
Payable
register
window.

3. Fill in the information for your bill.

Enter the same information that you would if you were filling in the Enter Bills window that I describe at the beginning of this chapter. In the Vendor text box, click the down arrow and choose a name from the Vendor list.

If you enter a vendor name that QuickBooks doesn't recognize, you see the Vendor Not Found message box, and QuickBooks asks you to give information about this new, mysterious vendor. Either click Quick Add to have the program collect the information from the register as you fill it out or click Set Up to see the New Vendor dialog box. (I describe the choice between Quick Add and Set Up in the "To Quick Add or to Set Up?" sidebar, elsewhere in this chapter. I explain how to set up new vendors in Chapter 2.)

You have to choose an account name. You can probably find the right one in the Account drop-down list, but if you can't, then enter one of your own. You see the Account Not Found message box, and QuickBooks asks you to fill in information about this new account.

If you decide as you fill out the register that you want to be reimbursed for this check or that you want to track expenses and items, choose the Edit Transaction button to see the Enter Bills window. (Refer to Figure 6-4.) Follow Steps 2 through 12 in the "Recording your bills" section (earlier

Using the Find dialog box

When you can't quite remember the information you need in order to find a particular entry or transaction, you can search for the information by using the Find dialog box. For example, if you can't recall when you entered the bill, choose Edit➪Advanced Find to open the Find dialog box. Choose a filter (the category to search by). The box to the right changes to include drop-down list boxes or text boxes that you can use to specify what you'd like to search for.

Choose as many filters as you like, but be careful to enter information accurately, or Quick Books looks for the wrong information. Also, try to strike a balance, choosing only as many filters as you really need to find your information. The more filters you choose, the more searching QuickBooks does, and the longer the search takes.

After you finish choosing filters, click the Find button, and the transactions that match all your filters appear in the list at the bottom of the window. Click the transaction that you want to examine more closely and then click Go To. QuickBooks opens the appropriate window and takes you right to the transaction. Very snazzy, I do believe.

in this chapter) to fill in the Enter Bills window. When you finish filling in the window, click Save & New. You're back where you started — in the Accounts Payable window.

4. **When you fill in all the information, click Record.**

    The Restore button, located just right of Record, is there in case you fill out the register but decide that you want to begin all over again before you've recorded the transaction. Click Restore to clear the information on-screen, and you have a clean slate.

Deleting a bill

Suppose that you accidentally enter the same bill twice or enter a bill that was really meant for the business next door. (Just because you're tracking bills by computer doesn't mean that you don't have to look over the things carefully anymore.) Here's how to delete a bill that you entered in the Accounts Payable register:

1. **Locate the bill in the Accounts Payable register by using one of the following methods:**

    • If you know roughly what day you entered the bill, you can scroll through the list to find it. The entries are listed in date order. (Click the 1-Line check box to display each bill on one line rather than on two lines to make the scrolling go faster.)

- If you don't remember the date, use the Edit menu's Simple Find command.

And now, back to the Accounts Payable register window that you have in progress. . . .

2. **Select the bill that you want to delete by putting the cursor anywhere in the bill.**

3. **Choose Edit⇨Delete Bill.**

QuickBooks confirms that you really, truly want to delete the transaction, and if you click OK, it dutifully deletes the bill from the A/P register.

Remind me to pay that bill, will you?

You can tie a string around your finger, but the best way to make sure that you pay bills on time is to have QuickBooks remind you. In fact, you can make the Reminders message box the first thing that comes on-screen when you start QuickBooks.

To adjust the QuickBooks reminder options, you must be logged on as the administrator in single-user mode. Then choose the Edit⇨Preferences command. When QuickBooks displays the Preferences dialog box, click the Reminders icon from the list on the left and then click the Company Preferences tab to access the dialog box shown in Figure 6-7. See the ninth item on the list: Bills to Pay.

Make sure that its Show Summary or Show List option button is marked, and then give yourself several days' notice before you need to pay bills by typing a number (10 is the default and usually works well) in the Days Before Due Date text box, in the Remind Me column.

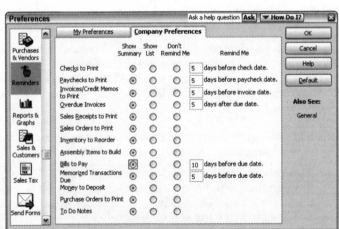

Figure 6-7:
The
Preferences
dialog box.

If you click the Show Summary option (the first button to the right of each option), you get a summary of the bills you owe each time you start QuickBooks. If you choose Show List (the second button to the right of each option), you get the details about each bill.

Which reminds me: Be sure to review the Reminders window when you start QuickBooks or open a new company file. The window lists reminders (like forms you need to print and payments you need to transmit) pops up whenever you start QuickBooks and tells you which unpaid bills you're supposed to pay. You can also see this list by choosing Company⇨Reminders.

Paying Your Bills

If you've done everything right and recorded your bills correctly, writing checks is a snap. Just follow these steps:

1. **Choose Vendors⇨Pay Bills.**

   Or, alternatively, select Vendors from the Navigators list and then click the Pay Bills icon. You see the Pay Bills window, as shown in Figure 6-8.

2. **Change the Payment Date to the date that you want to appear on the checks.**

   By default, this box shows today's date. If you want another date on the payment check — for example, if you're postdating the check — change this date. (See the Cheat Sheet at the beginning of this book for some secret date-editing codes.)

3. **Set a cutoff date for showing bills.**

   In the Show Bills Due On or Before date box, tell QuickBooks which bills to show by entering a date. If you want to see all the bills, click the Show All Bills option button.

4. **Use the Sort Bills By drop-down list box to tell QuickBooks how to sort the bills.**

   You can arrange bills by due date with the oldest bills listed first, arrange them alphabetically by vendor, or arrange them from largest to smallest.

5. **Identify which bills to pay.**

   If you want to pay all the bills in the dialog box, click the Select All Bills button. If you want to clear all of the bills you've marked, click the Clear All Bills button. If you want to pick and choose, click to the left of the bill's due date to pay the bill. A check mark appears where you click. Note that after you apply a payment, the Clear All Bills button replaces the Select All Bills button.

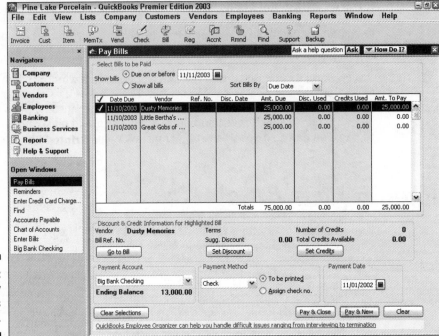

Figure 6-8:
The Pay
Bills
window.

6. **Change the Amt. To Pay figure if you want to pay only part of a bill.**

That's right, you can pay only part of a bill by changing the number in the Amt. To Pay column. (Of course, they can always just send you another bill. . . .)

7. **Get the early payment discount rate on your bills, if any.**

You may be eligible for an early payment discount on some bills. To find out how much of a discount you get, click the Amt. To Pay field and then click the Set Discount button to see the Discount tab of the Discounts & Credits dialog box. Use the Discount tab's Amount of Discount box to give the dollar amount of the discount. Use the Discount tab's Discount Account box for specifying which account should be used for recording the money saved through the discount.

8. **Get a list of credit memos that you can apply to the payment.**

Click the Set Credits button to see the Credits tab of the Discount & Credits dialog box. If you want to use one of the credits listed to reduce the amount of the bill, click it and then click Done.

9. **Choose a payment method.**

   Use the Payment Method drop-down list box to select the payment method you want to use: Check or Credit Card. If you have more than one checking or credit card account, click the down arrow next to the drop-down list box and choose the account that you want to use. If you've subscribed to and set up the QuickBooks online bill payment feature, you have another payment method choice, online payment. I describe making online payments in Chapter 11.

10. **If you plan to print the check, click the To Be Printed button.**

    Many businesses use QuickBooks to keep track of checks, but instead of printing the checks, they write them by hand. If your business uses this method, select the Assign Check No. option. Then, when QuickBooks asks how it should number the check, either give the number by typing it into the appropriate box or tell QuickBooks to just automatically number the check.

11. **Click Pay & Close to pay the bills and close the Pay Bills window.**

    Or, alternatively, click Pay & New to enter more bills. Regardless, QuickBooks goes into the Accounts Payable register and notes that you paid these bills; it then goes into the Checking register and "writes" the checks. Figures 6-9 and 6-10 show you exactly what I mean.

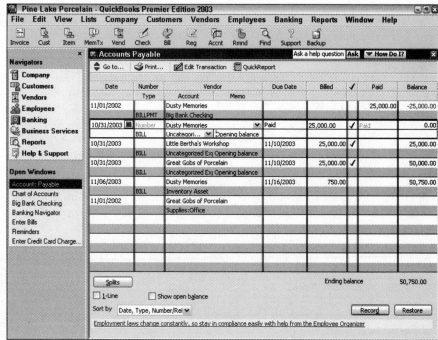

Figure 6-9:
How a paid
bill looks
in the
Accounts
Payable
register.
Oooh. Cool.

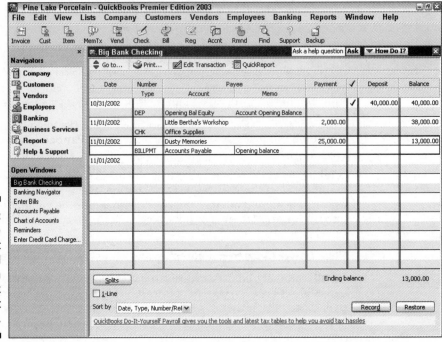

Figure 6-10:
How the
check that
pays a bill
looks in
the bank
account
register.

QuickBooks shows the original bill amount as the amount that's paid, not the original bill amount minus the early payment discount. It needs to use this method to completely pay off the bill.

In the Accounts Payable register, you see BILLPMT in the Type column and the amount paid in the Paid column. The Due Date and Billed columns are now empty.

In the Checking register, you again see BILLPMT in the Type column.

But don't kid yourself — these bills aren't really paid yet. Sure, they're paid in the mind of QuickBooks, but the mind of QuickBooks extends only as far as the metal (or trendy plastic) box that holds your computer. You still have to write or print the checks and deliver them to the payees.

If you're going to write the checks by hand, enter the check numbers from your own checkbook into the QuickBooks Checking register's Number column. You want these numbers to jibe, not jive. (I know, a pun is the lowest form of humor.)

If you plan to print the checks, see Chapter 10.

Paying the Sales Tax

In order to ingratiate itself with you retailers, QuickBooks includes a special dialog box for paying sales tax. However, to make use of this dialog box, you have to have sales tax items or a sales tax group already set up. See Chapter 2 for a thorough explanation of items and groups.

To see how much sales tax you owe and to write checks to government agencies in one fell swoop, choose Vendors⇨Sales Tax⇨Pay Sales Tax to access the Pay Sales Tax dialog box, as shown in Figure 6-11. Or, alternatively, select Vendors from the Navigators list and then click the Pay Sales Tax icon.

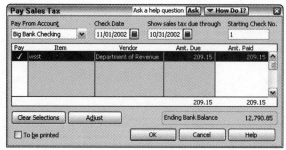

Figure 6-11:
The Pay
Sales Tax
dialog box.

The box is similar to the Pay Bills window. (Refer to Figure 6-8.) The buttons basically work the same way.

Put a check mark in the Pay column next to all the items that you want to pay by clicking in the Pay column. Checks are written automatically in the Checking register. Your payments are likewise recorded in the Sales Tax Payable register.

A Quick Word on the Vendor Details Window

If you choose Vendor⇨Vendor Detail Center, QuickBooks displays a window that summarizes a bunch of information about the vendor in question. This feature doesn't actually provide you with new information. But — and this is noteworthy — it does give you a slick way to essentially get all the information you have regarding a particular vendor. Note that you can select which vendor's information appears in the Vendor Detail window by selecting the vendor from the drop-down list box that appears at the top of the window.

Chapter 7

Inventory Magic

· ·

In This Chapter

▶ Using the Item list to track inventory

▶ Keeping inventory as you purchase items

▶ Keeping inventory as you sell items

▶ Using purchase orders to help track inventory

▶ Adjusting inventory records to reflect what's really in stock

▶ Dealing with Multiple Inventory Locations

· ·

For small and growing businesses, inventory is one of the toughest assets to manage. First, of course, you need to physically care for stuff. Second, you've got to make sure that you don't run out of some item or have too much of some other item.

QuickBooks isn't, unfortunately, all that sophisticated in its inventory management features. But it is easy to use. And with a little jiggering, you can probably get it to work in any simple case. (The one tricky part that I talk about a little later in the chapter is what you can do when you keep inventory in multiple locations. But I'm going to hold off on that discussion for a bit. That'd be like jumping off the deep end of the dock before you've learned to swim.)

Setting Up Inventory Items

Before you can track your inventory, you need to do two things. First, you need to tell QuickBooks that you want to track inventory. To do this, choose Edit⇨Preferences. When QuickBooks displays the Preferences dialog box, click the Purchases & Vendors icon from the list on the left. Your screen should look remarkably similar to the one in Figure 7-1. (You may have to click the Company Preferences tab first.) Make sure that both the Inventory and Purchase Orders Are Active box the Warn If Not Enough Inventory Quantity on Hand (QOH) To Sell boxes are checked.

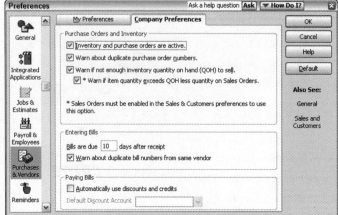

Figure 7-1:
The
Preferences
dialog box
for
Purchases
and
Vendors.

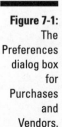

To make changes to company preferences, you must open the QuickBooks file in single-user mode as the administrator.

Here's the second thing you need: an Item list. This list is simply a description of all items that you may conceivably put on an invoice. In other words, all items that you order and sell belong on the Item list.

You should have set up your initial Item list in the EasyStep Interview. If you need to add an item to your list, choose Lists⇨Item List. Then click the Item button, choose New from the drop-down menu, and fill in the New Item window. If you want the blow-by-blow, go to Chapter 2 and get it straight from the horse's mouth. (Wait a second — did I just say that?)

After the inventory stuff is turned on and your Item list is set up and is up to date, you can track your inventory.

When You Buy Stuff

As you unload items from a truck, receive them in the mail, or buy them from a street peddler, you have to record the items so that QuickBooks can track your inventory. How you record the items and pay for them depends on whether you pay cash on the barrelhead, receive a bill along with the items, or receive the items without a bill (in which case you'll pay for the items later).

And you may have filled out a purchase order for the items that you're receiving. If that's the case, receiving the items gets a little easier. If you receive items for which you've already filled out a purchase order, see the section "How Purchase Orders Work," later in this chapter. I strongly recommend filling out a purchase order when you order items that you're going to receive and pay for later.

Recording items that you pay for up front

Okay, you just bought three porcelain chickens in the bazaar at Marrakech, and now you want to add them to your inventory and record the purchase. How do you record inventory you paid for over the counter? By using the Write Checks window, of course — the same way you record any other bills you pay for up front. Just make sure that you fill out the Items column as I describe in Chapter 6.

Recording items that don't come with a bill

What happens if the items come before the invoice? Lucky you, you have the stuff, and you don't have to pay for it yet. However, you do have to record the inventory you just received so that you know you have it on hand. You can't do that in the Write Checks window because you won't be writing a check to pay for the stuff — at least not for a while. How do you record items that you receive before paying for them? Read on:

1. **Choose Vendors⇨Receive Items.**

   Or select Vendors from the Navigators list and click the Receive Items icon. You see the Create Item Receipts window, as shown in Figure 7-2. This window is similar to the Enter Bills window. (See Chapter 6.) (You see the Enter Bills window again when you receive the bill for items.)

2. **Fill in the top part of the window.**

   If you want to record items from a vendor who's already on the Vendor list, just click the down arrow and choose the vendor. If the vendor is a new vendor, choose <Add New> and click Set Up to set up information about the vendor — the address, credit limit, payment terms, and so on. You enter the information in the New Vendor dialog box.

3. **Click the Items tab.**

   You need to click the Items tab only if it isn't already displayed. It probably is. But the computer book writers' code of honor and a compulsive personality require me to tell you that there's another tab — the Expenses tab — and it could possibly be displayed instead.

4. **Move to the Item column and type a name for the item.**

   Notice the down arrow in the Item column. Click it to see the Item list. Does the item that you're paying for appear on this list? If so, click it. If not, enter a new item name. You see the Item Not Found message box. Click Set Up and fill out the New Item dialog box. (See Chapter 2 for help with describing new items.)

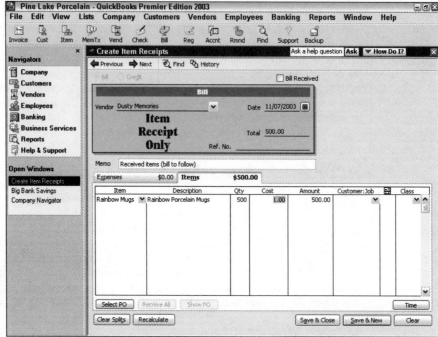

Figure 7-2:
The Create
Item
Receipts
window.

You may just as well go down the packing slip, entering the items in the Items tab. Make sure that the Items tab accurately shows what's on the packing slip. And put a brief description of the items in the Memo field because that description may prove useful later when you want to match up your item receipt with the bill. When you finish, the Create Item Receipts window should look something like what you see in Figure 7-2, earlier in this chapter.

5. **Click Save & New or Save & Close to record the items you just received.**

   Now the items are officially part of your inventory. The item receipt has been entered on the Accounts Payable register. And not only that, but you're all ready for when the bill comes.

Paying for items when you get the bill

The items arrive, and you fill out an item receipt. Three weeks pass. What's this in your mailbox? Why, it's the bill, of course! Now you have to enter a bill for the items that you received three weeks ago. This job is easy:

1. **Choose Vendors⇨Enter Bill for Received Items.**

   Or select Vendors from the Navigators list and click the Receive Bill icon. The Select Item Receipt dialog box appears, as shown in Figure 7-3.

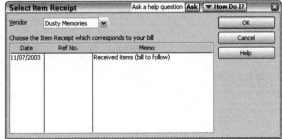

Figure 7-3:
The Select
Item
Receipt
dialog box.

2. **Click the Vendor drop-down list and choose the name of the vendor who sent you the bill.**

   You see one or more item receipts in the box, with the date you put on the receipt, its reference number, and the memo that you wrote on the receipt.

3. **Select the item receipt for which you want to enter a bill and click OK.**

   The Enter Bills window, shown in Figure 7-4, appears. Does this information look familiar? It should — it's the same information that you put in the Create Item Receipts window, only now you're working with a bill, not a receipt.

4. **Compare the Items tab in the window with the bill.**

   Are you paying for what you received earlier? Shipping charges and sales tax may have been added to your bill. You may also need to adjust the price because you may have been guessing when you recorded receiving the items. If so, add and adjust the original receipt information using the Items tab. (You can click the Recalculate button to add the new items.)

   How many days do you have to pay this bill? Is it due now? Take a look at the Terms line to see what this vendor's payment terms are. Change the payment terms if they're incorrect by selecting a different entry from the drop-down list. Remember, you want to pay your bills at the best possible time, but to do so, the terms in the Enter Bills window must match the vendor's payment terms.

5. **Click Save & New or Save & Close to record the bill.**

   Of course, you still need to pay the vendor's bill. Fair enough. Take a look at Chapter 6 if you need help.

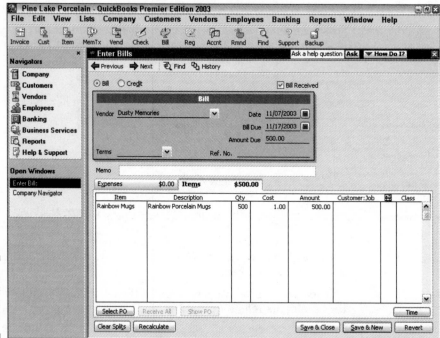

Figure 7-4:
The Enter
Bills
window.

Recording items and paying the bill all at once

Suppose that you receive the bill when you receive the goods. The items are unloaded from the elephant's back, and the elephant driver takes a bow and hands you the bill.

1. **Choose Vendors⇨Receive Items and Enter Bill.**

   Or select Vendors from the Navigators list and click the Receive Items with Bill icon. You see the Enter Bills window. (Refer to Figure 7-4.) If you've been reading this chapter from its beginning, you're familiar with this window and you know exactly what it is and what it does. If you landed cold turkey on this page by way of the index, you need to know, for inventory purposes, how to record the items you're paying for.

2. **Fill out the top part of the window.**

   This stuff is pretty basic. Choose a vendor from the drop-down list and make sure that the vendor's terms for paying this bill are shown correctly. If this vendor is new, choose <Add New>. QuickBooks asks you to fill in an information dialog box about the vendor. Do it. See that you fill out the Bill Due line correctly.

3. **Click the Items tab and list all the items that you're paying for.**

   To see the Item list, move the cursor to the Item column and click the down arrow that appears. Make sure that the quantity and cost of the items are listed correctly on the Items tab.

4. **Click Save & New or Save & Close.**

   QuickBooks adds the items you listed to the Item list and makes them an official part of your inventory.

When You Sell Stuff

In Chapter 4, I tell you how to list the items on the invoice. Maybe you noticed the similarities between the Items tab in the Enter Bills window and the Quantity/Item Code/Description/Price Each/Amount box at the bottom of an invoice. QuickBooks uses both for keeping inventory.

When you sell stuff, QuickBooks automatically adjusts your inventory. In other words, if you buy 400 porcelain chickens and sell 350 of them, you have only 50 on hand. QuickBooks updates records for this change. No muss, no fuss. Gosh, isn't this great? No more lying awake at night, wondering whether you have enough chickens or wombats or whatever. The same thing happens when you make cash sales. When you list the items on the sales receipt, QuickBooks assumes that they're leaving your hands and subtracts them from your inventory.

The moral of this story is "Keep a good, descriptive Item list." And the other moral is "Enter items carefully on the Items tab of checks and bills and in the Item/Description/Qty/Rate/Amount box of sales receipts and invoices."

How Purchase Orders Work

If you have to order stuff for your business, consider using purchase orders. Create QuickBooks purchase orders even if you order goods by phone or by telegraph or even via the World Wide Web — that is, whenever you don't request goods in writing. Filling out purchase orders enables you to tell what items you have on order and when the items will arrive. All you'll have to do is ask QuickBooks, "What's on order, and when's it coming, anyway?" Never again will you have to rack your brain to remember whether you've ordered those thingamajigs and doohickeys.

And when the bill comes, you'll already have it itemized on the purchase order form. Guess what? Having written out all the items on your purchase order, you won't have to fill out an Items tab on your check when you pay the bill. Or, if you're paying bills with the accounts payable method, you won't have to fill out the Items tab in the Enter Bills window. (Look at Chapter 6 if you don't know what I'm talking about here.) When the items arrive, all you have to do is let QuickBooks know — the items are added immediately to your inventory list.

Use purchase orders for items that you order — that is, for items that you'll receive and pay for in the future. If you buy items over the counter or receive items that you didn't order, you obviously don't need a purchase order. What you need to do is just pay the bill and inventory the items you just bought, as I explain in the first half of this chapter.

Choosing a purchase order form for you

The first thing to do when you use purchase orders is to design a purchase order form for your business. (Thankfully, you only have to do this once.) Choose Vendors➪Create Purchase Orders. Or select Vendors from the Navigators list and click the Purchase Orders icon. When QuickBooks displays the Create Purchase Orders window, choose Customize from the Form Template drop-down list box in the upper-right corner of the window. When QuickBooks displays the Customize Template dialog box, choose to either edit the QuickBooks Purchase Order template for your business or create a new template based on the QuickBooks template. If you're like me and enjoy being able to experiment with things as much as you want, click the New button. This way, you always have a fresh, clean template to start from if you ever want to create more customized purchase orders.

QuickBooks displays the Customize Purchase Order dialog box, as shown in Figure 7-5. This dialog box has six tabs for determining what your purchase order looks like.

Click the different tabs to see what you can customize. Some options that are listed on the left side apply to the purchase orders for your business; some don't. If you want to use an option that you see on-screen, click the Screen check box next to that option. Likewise, do the same for printed purchase orders. Click the Print check box if you want an option to appear on the order when you print it. In the Title text boxes, type the word or words that you want to see on purchase orders. The Other options on the Fields and Columns tabs are for putting a field or column of your own on the purchase order.

Play around with this window for a while until your purchase order comes out just right. To see how your choices look on a purchase order, click the Layout Designer button. Here you can use the mouse to drag and drop fields around the page to make it look just the way you want. Click OK to return to the Customize Purchase Order dialog box. If your purchase order doesn't look right, click Cancel and start all over again. And if your purchase order gets too wacky, you can always click the Default button in the Customize

Purchase Order window to go back to the default headers, fields, columns, and footers.

When your purchase order looks magnificent, click OK in the Customize Purchase Order dialog box. If you created a brand-new template, you also have to give it a name.

QuickBooks returns you to the Create Purchase Orders window. If you later decide that you want to change one of your templates, all you have to do is choose Customize again from the Custom Template drop-down list box and then select the template you want to edit from the list and click the Edit button.

Filling out a purchase order

Perhaps you're running low on gizmos, or doohickeys, or some other item on your Item list, and you're ready to reorder these things — whatever they are.

1. **Choose Vendors⇨Create Purchase Orders.**

   Or select Vendors from the Navigators list and click the Purchase Orders icon. You see the Create Purchase Orders window, which is similar to what's shown in Figure 7-6. Note that the exact details of this window depend on how you customize your purchase order form.

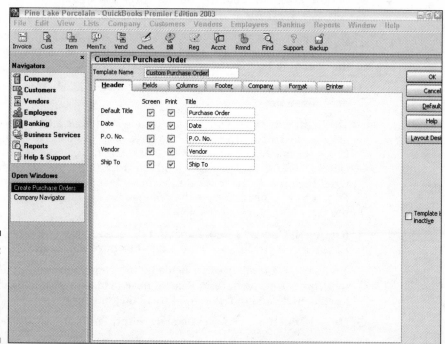

Figure 7-5:
The Customize Purchase Order dialog box.

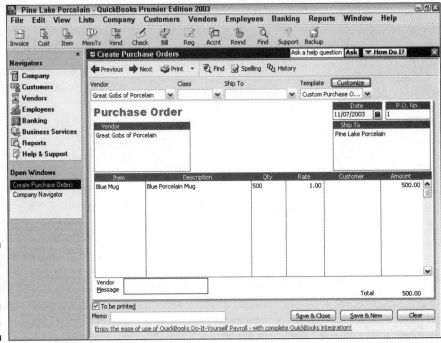

Figure 7-6:
The Create
Purchase
Orders
window.

2. **Choose a vendor from the Vendor drop-down list.**

   Click the down arrow to see a list of your vendors. Click a vendor to see its name and address in the Vendor box. If you can't find the name of the vendor on your list, click <Add New> and fill in the information about the vendor in the New Vendor dialog box.

3. **If you track your inventory by class, choose a class from the Class drop-down list.**

   The Create Purchase Orders window may not have a Class drop-down list. If it doesn't and you want it to have one, you have to set up QuickBooks to track expenses by class. To do so, first open the QuickBooks file in single-user mode as the administrator. Then choose Edit➪Preferences and click the Accounting icon from the list on the left. (You may also need to click the Company Preferences tab.) Finally, mark the Use Class Tracking check box.

4. **(Optional) Choose a Rep, Expected Date, and FOB (which I describe in Chapter 4) if you're using them on your purchase order.**

   You may have to fill in other fields before you get to the item-by-item descriptions at the bottom. Again, these fields may not appear if you haven't indicated that you want them on your form.

5. **Move to the Item column and start entering the items you're ordering.**

Entering the items is the most important part of creating a purchase order. When you move into the Item column, it turns into a drop-down list box. Click its down arrow to see the Item list. You may need to scroll to the item that you want to enter. A fast way to scroll to the item is to type the first couple of letters in the item name. If you type the name of an item that isn't on the Item list, QuickBooks asks whether you want to set up this item. Click Set Up and fill in the New Item dialog box.

Enter as many items as you want in the Item column. QuickBooks will fill in an item description for you, but you can edit whatever it puts into the Description column if need be. In the Qty column, indicate how many of each item you need.

6. **If you want to, fill in the Vendor Message field — and definitely fill in the Memo field.**

   The Message field is where you put a message to the party receiving your order. You could write, "Get me this stuff pronto!"

   No matter what you do, be sure to fill in the Memo field. What you write in this field appears in the Open Purchase Orders dialog box and is the surest way for you to identify what this purchase order is for. Write something meaningful that you can understand two weeks, three weeks, or a month from now when you pay for the items that you're ordering.

   At the bottom of the Create Purchase Orders window is the To Be Printed check box, which tells you whether you've printed this purchase order. If you want to print the purchase order, make sure that this box is checked. After you print the purchase order, the check disappears from the box.

7. **Print the purchase order.**

   Click Print to print the purchase order. If this purchase order is one of many that you've been filling out and you want to print several at once, click the arrow beside the Print button and choose Print Batch from the drop-down menu. Before you print the purchase order, however, you may want to click the arrow beside the Print button and choose Preview to see what the purchase order will look like when you print it. QuickBooks shows you an on-screen replica of the purchase order. I hope it looks okay.

   You use the History button after you receive the items you're so carefully listing on the purchase order. After you receive the items and record their receipt, clicking this button tells QuickBooks to give you the entire history of an item — when you ordered it and when you received it.

   As for the other top four buttons, I think that you know what those are, and if you don't, go to Step 8.

8. **Click Save & New or Save & Close to record the purchase order.**

   QuickBooks saves the purchase order and displays a new, blank purchase order window where you can enter another order.

Checking up on purchase orders

You record the purchase orders. A couple of weeks go by, and you ask yourself, "Did I order those doohickeys from Acme?" Choose Vendors⇨Purchase Orders List to see the Purchase Orders window with a list of outstanding purchase orders. (See Figure 7-7.) Or select Vendors from the Navigators list and click the PO List Items icon. Double-click one of the orders on the list, and it magically appears on-screen.

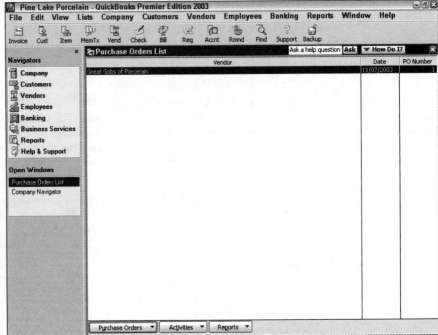

Figure 7-7:
The
Purchase
Orders
window.

You can then change any information you need to. Click Save & New to go back to the Purchase Orders List. You can also enter a new purchase order from this list by clicking the Purchase Orders button and choosing New.

Do you want to delete a purchase order? Just keep the Purchase Orders window open, highlight the purchase order that you want to delete, click the Purchase Orders button, and choose Delete.

Receiving purchase order items

Now that the doohickeys and gizmos have arrived by camel train, you need to record the receipt of the items and add them to your Item list.

The first thing to do is note whether the stuff came with a bill and decide how you want to pay for it. These decisions are the same ones that you have to make if you received the goods without having first filled out a purchase order.

You record purchase order items you receive the same way you record other items you receive:

- ✔ If you pay for purchase order items with a check, you use the Write Checks window.

- ✔ If you receive the purchase order items without a bill, you use the Create Item Receipts window.

- ✔ If you receive the purchase order items with a bill, you use the Enter Bills window.

Regardless of the window you're using, when you select the vendor who sold you the purchase order items, QuickBooks alerts you that open purchase orders exist for the vendor and asks you if you want to receive against a purchase order. Of course you do. (*Receive against* simply means to compare what you ordered to what you received.) When you click Yes, QuickBooks displays the Open Purchase Orders dialog box, as shown in Figure 7-8. Select the purchase order(s) you're receiving against and click OK. QuickBooks fills out the Items tab to show all the stuff you ordered. If what QuickBooks shows is not what you received, you may have to make adjustments.

Figure 7-8:
The Open
Purchase
Orders
dialog box.

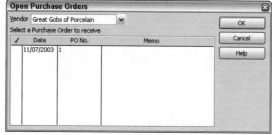

Assembling a Product

QuickBooks 2003 includes, as a new feature, a tool for accounting for the manufacture of items. For example, suppose that Pine Lake Porcelain, the example business used in this book, mostly just buys and resells coffee mugs and other porcelain doodads. But also suppose that, once a year, Pine Lake Porcelain assembles a collection of red coffee mugs into a boxed St. Valentine's Day gift set. In this case, QuickBooks can record the assembly of a boxed gift set that combines, for example, four red coffee mugs, a cardboard box, and some tissue wrapping paper.

Identifying the components

Each of the components that makes up the assembly — in our example, the St. Valentine's Day boxed gift set — needs to be an item on your Item list. Chapter 2 describes how to add items to the Item list. So I won't repeat that information here. Figure 7-9, however, shows something that you don't see every day: The New Item window filled out to describe how a St. Valentine's Day boxed gift set is assembled: four red coffee mugs, a cardboard gift box, and some tissue paper that loved ones can use when they become emotionally overwhelmed with the generosity of this thoughtful gift.

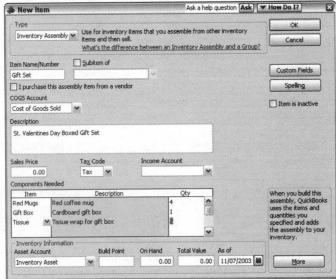

Figure 7-9:
The New
Item
window.

Building the assembly

To build some assemblies, choose the Vendor⇨Inventory Activities⇨Build Assemblies command. QuickBooks displays the Build Assemblies window (see Figure 7-10), which looks complicated but really isn't. All you do is choose the thing you want to build from the Assembly Item drop-down list box and then the quantity you (or some hapless co-worker) has built in the Quantity to Build box. Then you click either Build & Close or Build & New. (Click Build & New if you want to record the assembly of some other items.)

Because I'm on the subject, let me make a handful of observations about the Build Assemblies window and the Build Assemblies command:

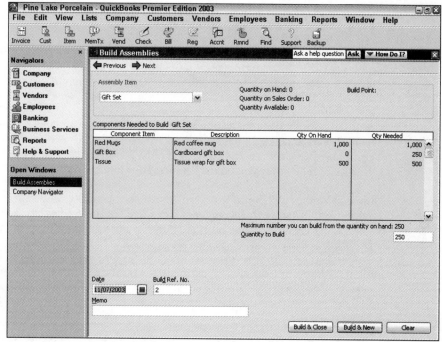

Figure 7-10:
The Build
Assemblies
window.

✔ In the top right corner (roughly) of the window, QuickBooks shows the quantities of the assembly you have on hand and for which customers have placed orders. That's pretty useful information to have, so, hey, remember it's there.

✔ The main part of the Build Assemblies window shows you what goes into your product. Not that you care, but this is called a *bill of materials*.

✔ At the bottom of the bill of materials list, QuickBooks shows you the maximum number of assemblies you can make, given your current inventory holdings.

✔ When you build an item, QuickBooks adjusts the inventory item counts. For example, in the case where you make boxed gift sets, each with four red coffee mugs and two wrapping tissues, QuickBooks reduces the item counts of red coffee mugs and wrapping tissues and increases the item counts of the boxed gift sets when you record building the assembly.

✔ Some of the components used in an assembly may not be inventory items. Take a look back at Figure 7-10, for example. See that cardboard gift box component? QuickBooks doesn't give a rat's butt about the item counts of the cardboard gift boxes because that item is set up as a non-inventory part.

Time for a Reality Check

QuickBooks does a pretty good job of tracking inventory, but you're still going to have to make that complete annual inventory of what you have in stock. What I'm saying here is that you're going to have to go over everything and count it. Sorry. You just can't avoid that chore.

And after you make your count, what happens if your inventory figures differ from those QuickBooks has? First, you have to decide who's right — you or a computer program. You're right, probably. Products get dropped. They break. And that means that you have to adjust the QuickBooks inventory numbers.

Choose Vendors➪Inventory Activities➪Adjust Quantity/Value On Hand. Or select Vendors from the Navigators list and click the Adjust Qty on Hand icon. The Adjust Quantity/Value on Hand window appears, as shown in Figure 7-11.

The first thing to do is choose an account for storing your inventory adjustments. Choose it from the Adjustment Account drop-down list. You also can select a class from the Class drop-down list.

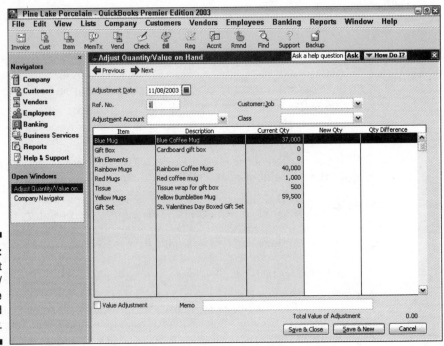

Figure 7-11:
The Adjust
Quantity/
Value
on Hand
window.

For what it's worth, if it were me, I'd set up and use a special inventory adjustments expense account. (This way, I'd have an easy way to see the total inventory adjustments over the year.)

Go down the Item column, entering numbers in the New Qty column where your count differs from the QuickBooks totals. Click Save & Close when you're done.

Dealing with Multiple Inventory Locations

Okay, you've seen now how QuickBooks handles your inventory. It's not fancy. But for many businesses, it gets the job done.

Unfortunately, I've encountered a real headache when using QuickBooks for my inventory. I store inventory in multiple locations: in a Michigan warehouse and in a Chicago distribution facility.

The problem is that QuickBooks is really only set up to deal with a single inventory location. So although I know how much inventory I have in total, if I'm not careful, I don't know how much is in Michigan and how much is in Chicago. And I can't even really check on inventory shrinkage because QuickBooks' records don't tie to location-specific inventory counts.

Now I need to tell you right up front that you don't have any *good way* to deal with this in QuickBooks. But, throughout the following subsections, I explain a couple of sloppy fixes that you can do.

Manually keep separate inventory-by-location counts

This is what I do. I only have a couple of dozen items in my little business, so it's pretty easy for me to just keep a simple manual running tab on what I've got in the Michigan warehouse and what's in the Chicago distribution facility.

My little system is very, er, crude. It's really just a couple of those sticky notes taped to my computer monitor. No kidding. But it lets me know how much inventory I've got (roughly) and where it's stored. And for my purposes, that works okay.

Use different item numbers for different locations

My little system that I've described in the preceding section doesn't work if you've really got a lot of items — it won't work for a multiple location retailer. So if you have a large number of items, I'm sorry, but I think you probably need to set up sets of item numbers for each inventory location. This means a lot more work for you, of course. But it's really the only practical way to handle your inventory if you've got more than a handful of items.

One more thought

I have one more thought for you. I think that we should start a letter-writing campaign. I'm serious. I think that we should all start writing letters to Intuit, asking that a multiple-stores or multiple-inventory locations feature be added to some upcoming version of the program.

Chapter 8

Keeping Your Checkbook

. . . .

In This Chapter

▶ Writing checks from the Write Checks window

▶ Writing checks from the Checking register

▶ Recording deposits

▶ Recording transfers

▶ Voiding and deleting transactions

▶ Searching for transactions

. . . .

This is it. You're finally going to do those everyday QuickBooks things: entering checks, deposits, and transfers. Along the way, you also find out about some neat tools that QuickBooks provides for making these tasks easier, faster, and more precise.

Writing Checks

Chapter 6 shows you the two ways to write checks: from the Write Checks window and from the Checking register. In case you were asleep in the back row of the class, here's the short version of the instructions for writing checks.

Writing checks from the Write Checks window

You can record handwritten checks and other checks that you want to print with QuickBooks by describing the checks in the Write Checks window.

To write a check from the Write Checks window, follow these steps:

1. Choose Banking⇨Write Checks.

Or select Banking in the Navigators list and click the Checks icon. QuickBooks displays the Write Checks window. (See Figure 8-1.)

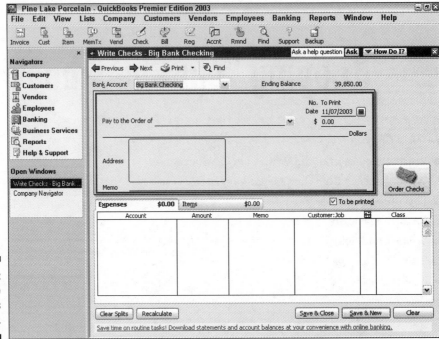

Figure 8-1:
The Write
Checks
window.

2. **Click the Bank Account drop-down list at the top of the window and choose the account from which you want to write this check.**

   This step is really important and is something you should always check before you write a check.

3. **Enter a check number or mark the check for printing.**

   Check the To Be Printed box if you plan on printing the check with QuickBooks, using your printer and pre-printed check forms that you've purchased. (I describe this process in Chapter 10.) If you're recording a check you wrote by hand, enter the check number you used for the check in the No. box.

4. **Fill in the check.**

   If you've written a check to this person or party before, the AutoFill feature fills in the name of the payee in the Pay to the Order Of line for you after you start typing the name. How QuickBooks manages this feat may seem akin to magic, but it's really not that tough. QuickBooks just compares what you've typed so far with names on your lists of customers, employees, and other names. As soon as QuickBooks can match the letters you've typed with a name on one of these lists, it grabs the name.

If you haven't written a check to this person or party before, by the way, QuickBooks asks you to add the payee name. Do that. (If you're not sure whether you want to add a payee or how to add a payee, refer to Chapter 6.)

Enter the amount of the check next to the dollar sign and press Tab. QuickBooks writes out the amount for you on the Dollars line. It also writes out the address.

5. Fill in the Expenses and Items tabs, if necessary.

Don't know what these are? Chapter 6 explains them in minute detail.

6. Click Save & Close or Save & New to finish writing the check.

There you have it. Your check is written, is entered in the Checking register, and is ready to be printed and mailed.

Writing checks from the Checking register

People who've grown accustomed to Quicken, a cousin of QuickBooks, may want to use the Checking register window to write checks. (Quicken users like the register metaphor better, I guess.)

To write a check from the Checking register, follow these steps:

1. Open the Checking register.

Choose Banking⇨Use Register. Or select Banking from the Navigators list and click the Check Register icon. If you have more than one bank account, QuickBooks displays the Use Register dialog box. From the drop-down list, choose the checking account against which you want to write the check and click OK. You see the Checking register window. (See Figure 8-2.) The cursor is at the end of the register, ready and waiting for you to enter check information. (QuickBooks automatically fills in today's date.)

QuickBooks uses the account name in the window title. This is why Figure 8-2 refers to "Big Bank Checking." That's the name of the fictitious bank account I set up.

2. Fill in the information for your check.

Notice that the entries you make in this register are the same ones that you would make in the Write Checks window. If you're more comfortable entering checks in that window, you can click the Edit Transaction button, which is at the top of the Checking register window, to see the Write Checks window in all its glory and write a check there. In fact, if you want to enter expenses or itemize what you're paying for with the check, you have to click the Edit Transaction button and get into the Write Checks window.

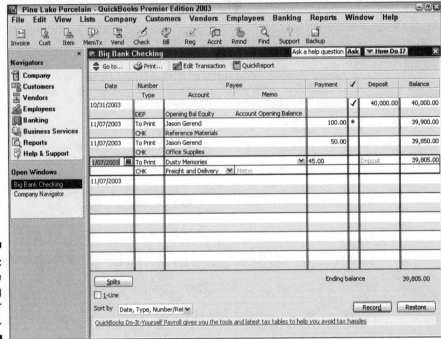

Figure 8-2:
The
Checking
register
window.

Otherwise, just go from field to field and enter the information in the register. Once again, use the drop-down lists to enter the Payee and Account names. If you enter a Payee or Account name that QuickBooks doesn't recognize, the program asks you to give more information.

3. **When you finish filling in the check information, click Record.**

Or click the Clear button if you decide that you want to go back to start all over again. Clicking Clear blanks out what you just entered.

If you write checks by hand as opposed to printing them with QuickBooks, make sure that the check numbers in the Checking register and the check numbers in your checkbook match up. You may need to go into the QuickBooks Checking register and change numbers in the Number column. When your bank statement comes, reconciling your bank statement and your checkbook is much easier if you entered check numbers correctly.

Changing a check that you've written

What if you need to change a check after you've already entered it? Perhaps you made a terrible mistake, such as recording a $52.50 check as $25.20. Can you fix it? Sure. Just go into the Checking register and find the check that you want to change. Go to the Payment or Deposit field and make the change.

If you have more extensive changes to make (for instance, if the check is a split transaction), put the cursor where the check is and click Edit Transaction. QuickBooks displays the Write Checks window with the original check in it. Make the changes. (Don't forget to make changes on the Items and Expenses tabs, too, if necessary.)

When you finish, click Save & Close. You go back to the Checking register, where you see the changes to the check.

If you have the Write Checks window displayed, you can also use the Next and Previous buttons to page through your checks and make any changes.

Packing more checks into the register

Usually, QuickBooks displays two rows of information about each check you enter. It also displays two rows of information about each type of transaction that you enter. If you want to pack more checks into a visible portion of the register, check the 1-Line check box at the bottom of the Checking register window. When you check this box, QuickBooks uses a single-line format to display all the information in the register except the Memo field.

Compare Figure 8-2 with Figure 8-3 to see what the 1-Line display looks like. Checking registers can get awfully long, and the 1-Line display is helpful when you're looking through a long register for a check or transaction.

Depositing Money into a Checking Account

You can't write checks unless you deposit some money in your checking account. You didn't know that? Well, the next time you're taking your exercise in the prison yard, give it some serious thought. From time to time, you must deposit money in your checking account and record those deposits in the Checking register.

You can record deposits in two ways. Find out about those ways in the following sections.

Recording simple deposits

If you have a simple deposit to make — a sum of money that didn't come from one of your customers — just make the deposit directly in the Checking register.

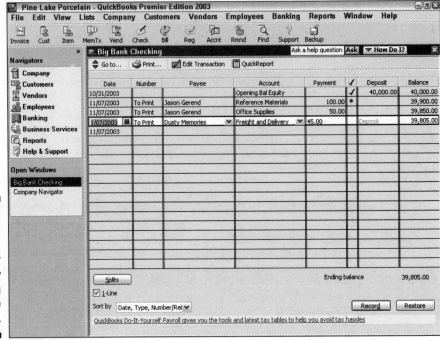

Figure 8-3:
The
Checking
register
window
when using
1-line
display.

For example, suppose that your elderly Aunt Iris sends you $100 with a note explaining how, more than 80 years ago, Great-Uncle Bert started his hammock manufacturing business with only $100, and for good luck she's sending you $100 to help you along.

Recording a simple deposit is, well, pretty simple. Follow these steps:

1. **Open the Checking register.**

   Choose Banking➪Use Register. Or select Banking from the Navigators list and click the Check Register icon. If you have more than one bank account, QuickBooks displays the Use Register dialog box. Select the checking account into which you want to make the deposit and click OK. QuickBooks displays the Checking register window. (Refer to Figure 8-2.)

2. **Enter the date on which you made the deposit in the Date column.**

3. **In the Payee column, enter the name of person or business that sent you money.**

   Don't worry if QuickBooks adds a check number in the Number field when you move to the Payee column. When you enter a deposit amount, QuickBooks changes the Number field to DEP (for deposit, of course).

4. **Enter the amount that you're depositing.**

   Move the cursor to the Deposit column and enter the amount.

Paying for items with cash

To track petty cash purchases, you need a petty cash account. You can set up a petty cash account (which works just like a bank account) by following the steps in "Setting up a second bank account" later in this chapter. To record purchases you make from the money in that coffee can beside your desk, use the petty cash register. You can record cash purchases just as you record checks. (Of course, you don't need to worry about using the correct check numbers when you record cash purchases — you can just use the numbers 1, 2, 3, and so on.) To record cash withdrawals to be used for petty cash in the office, just record the withdrawal as a transfer to your petty cash account, as I describe later in the chapter.

5. **Enter an account for this deposit.**

   Move to the Account field, click the down arrow, and choose an account from the list. Most likely, you'll choose an account such as Uncategorized Income.

6. **Click the Record button.**

   Your deposit is entered, and your checking account's balance is fattened accordingly. Note that all entries in the Checking register are made in chronological order, with deposits first and checks next.

Depositing income from customers

Depositing income from customers is a little more complicated because it involves the Payments to Deposit dialog box. Have you been recording customer payments as they come in? (You do so by choosing Customers⇨ Receive Payments or Customers⇨Enter Sales Receipt, as I describe in Chapter 5.) If you've been recording customer payments and have told QuickBooks to group them with your other undeposited funds, QuickBooks places these payments in your Undeposited Funds account. Now all you have to do is transfer the undeposited funds to your checking account.

1. **Choose Banking⇨Make Deposits.**

   Or select Banking from the Navigators list and click the Deposits icon. Because you have undeposited funds, you see the Payments to Deposit dialog box (see Figure 8-4). This dialog box lists the checks that you've received but haven't put in a checking account or other bank account yet.

2. **Select the checks that you want to deposit.**

   Place a check mark next to the checks that you want to deposit by clicking in the column next to them. Or, if you want to deposit all the checks, click the Select All button. Click OK.

Figure 8-4:
The
Payments to
Deposit
dialog box.

Payments to Deposit

Select the payments you want to deposit, and then click OK.

✓	Date	Type	No.	Pmt Meth	Name	Amount
	11/07/2003	PMT			Castle Rock Coffe	4,705.48

OK
Cancel
Help
Select All
Select None

The Make Deposits window appears (see Figure 8-5). Do you recognize the information in the middle of the window? It describes the checks you just selected to be deposited.

3. **Select the checking account to receive these deposits.**

Select the account from the Deposit To drop-down list at the top of the window. And while you're at it, check the Date text box to make sure that it shows the date you'll deposit these checks in your checking account. In other words, if you're not going to make it to the bank or the ATM machine until tomorrow, put tomorrow's date in the Date text box.

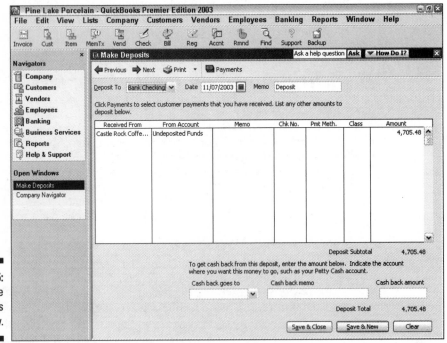

Figure 8-5:
The Make
Deposits
window.

4. **Add any other noncustomer deposits to include on the deposit slip.**

   If your grandma, bless her heart, gave you 1,000 pennies in ten rolls, for example, that's ten extra dollars that you can record on this deposit slip. At the bottom of the list of payments, enter the name of the person who gave you the cash, the account, a memo, check number, the payment method (cash in this case), a class if you're using classes, and the amount.

5. **Write a note to yourself in the Memo box to describe this deposit, if you want to, and click the Print button to get a hard copy of the deposit slip.**

   Many banks accept this deposit slip, so you can print it and put it in the envelope with your ATM deposit or hand it to the bank clerk. Whatever you write on the memo appears on the Checking register. (You should probably write a memo to yourself in case you need to know what this deposit is years from now when you're old and dotty.)

6. **Record any cash back that you plan to get with the deposit.**

   If you need to get cash to replenish your petty cash account, select the account from the Cash Back Goes To drop-down list box, write a memo, and then record the amount of cash you want to get back from the deposit.

7. **Click the Save & Close button at the bottom of the Make Deposits window.**

   Now the deposit is recorded in QuickBooks. It appears in your Checking register next to the letters DEP, which stand for Deposit.

Transferring Money between Accounts

Account transfers occur when you move money from one account to another — for example, from your savings account to your checking account. But, jeepers, why am I telling you this? If you have one of those combined savings and checking accounts, you probably do this sort of thing all the time.

Oh, now I remember why I brought this up — QuickBooks makes quick work of account transfers as long as you've already set up both accounts.

Setting up a second bank account

If you haven't set up a second account, you need to set one up. To do so, open the chart of accounts by choosing Lists⇨Chart of Accounts. Then click the Account button and choose New. Fill in the name of the account and, if you want to, the account number or a description of the account. Then fill in the As Of box with the date that you opened the account. Enter the opening balance as zero so that you can record your initial deposit or transfer of money into the account. You record initial deposits the way I describe earlier in this chapter (either as simple deposits or as customer deposits, whatever the case may be). You record an initial transfer by completing the following steps:

1. **Choose Banking⇨Transfer Funds.**

   Or select Banking in the Navigators list and click the Transfer Funds icon. You see the Transfer Funds Between Accounts window, shown in Figure 8-6.

2. **Select the bank account from which you're going to transfer the money.**

   In the Transfer Funds From box at the top of the window, choose the account from the drop-down list.

3. **Select the bank account to which you want to transfer the money.**

   In the Transfer Funds To drop-down list, select the account that receives the funds.

4. **Enter the amount that you want to transfer and fill in the Memo box.**

   Someday, you may go into the register for the account you're writing this check in and wonder where you transferred this money and why. Filling in the Memo box solves this little mystery beforehand.

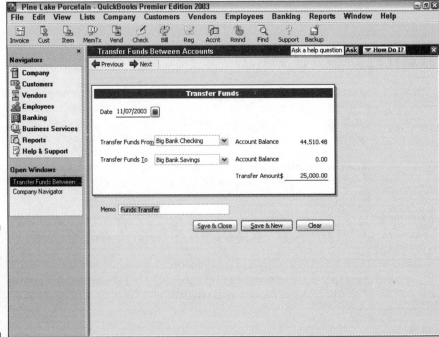

Figure 8-6:
The Transfer Funds Between Accounts window.

5. Click the Save & New or Save & Close button.

QuickBooks records the transfer, which you can confirm by opening your Checking register. You see that the transfer has the letters TRANSFR in the Type column and the name of the account to which you transferred the money in the Account column. The amount you transferred shows up in the Payment column (because you transferred the funds out of this account). Figure 8-7 shows a $25,000 transfer — in the figure the selected transaction is the one I'm talking about — from a checking account called Big Bank Checking to an account called Big Bank Savings. You can tell this transaction is a transfer because the other account name shows up in the Account box. Note that I clicked the Splits button to show the Splits area, which provides extra information.

About the other half of the transfer

Here's the cool thing about transfer transactions. QuickBooks automatically records the other half of the transfer for you. Figure 8-8 shows the other half of the transfer from Figure 8-7. This register is for a savings account called Big Bank Savings. The $25,000 transfer from your checking account actually made it into your savings account. The transfer once again shows up as a TRANSFR.

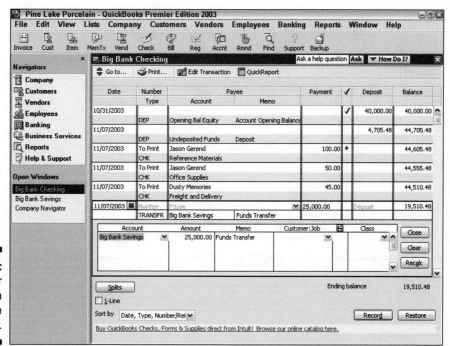

Figure 8-7:
A transfer transaction in the register.

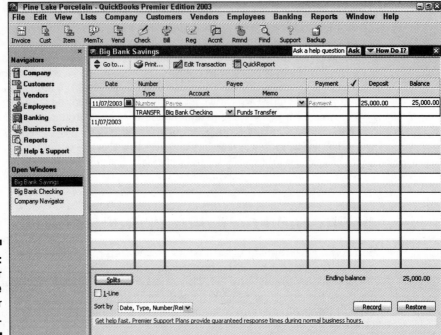

Figure 8-8:
The other
half of the
transfer
transaction.

Changing a transfer that you've already entered

Big surprise here, but changing a transfer that you've already entered works just like changing a check. First, you find the transfer in the account register, and then you click Edit Transaction. You see the Transfer Funds Between Accounts window with the Transfer check you wrote. Make changes to the check and click Save & New or Save & Close. You return to the register, where your deposit is adjusted accordingly.

To Delete or to Void?

What happens if you put a transaction — a deposit, a check, or a transfer payment — in a Checking register and later decide that it shouldn't be there? You have two ways of handling this situation. If you want to keep a record of the transaction but render it moot, meaningless, or nada, then you void the transaction. But if you want to obliterate the transaction from the face of the earth as though it never happened in the first place, then you delete it.

Decide whether you want to void or delete the transaction and then follow these steps:

1. **Find the transaction in the register.**

   In the next section ("The Big Register Phenomenon"), I tell you some quick ways to find transactions.

2. **Choose either Edit⇨Delete Check or Edit⇨Void Check and click the Record button.**

   There, the deed is done. Figure 8-9 shows a Checking register window with a voided check. The voided transaction is the one selected. Notice the word VOID in the Memo column. If this check had been deleted, it wouldn't even show up in the register.

The Edit menu changes depending on what kind of transaction shows or is selected in the open window (that is, Void Deposit, Void Check, and so on).

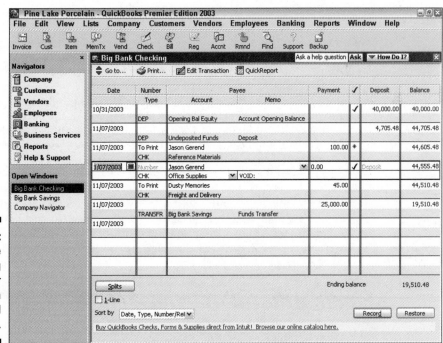

Figure 8-9:
The Checking register shows a voided check.

The Big Register Phenomenon

If you start entering checks, deposits, and transfers into your registers, you soon find yourself with registers that contain hundreds, and even thousands, of transactions. You can still work with one of these big registers by using the tools and techniques that I talk about in the preceding paragraphs. Nevertheless, let me give you some more help for dealing with . . . (drumroll, please) . . . the big register phenomenon.

Moving through a big register

You can use the Page Up and Page Down keys to page up and down through your register, a screen full of transactions at a time. Some people call this activity *scrolling*. You can call it whatever you want.

You can also use the Home key to move through the register. Press the Home key once to move to the front of the field you're currently in. Press the Home key twice to move to the first field of the transaction you're on (the Date field), or press it three times to move to the first transaction in the register.

The End key works in a similar fashion. Bet you can guess how this works. Press the End key once to move to the end of the field you're in, press it twice to move to the last field of the transaction you're on (the Memo field), or press it three times to move to the last transaction in the register.

Of course, you can use the vertical scroll bar along the right edge of the Checking register, too. Click the arrows at either end of the vertical scroll bar to select the next or previous transaction. Click either above or below the square scroll box to page back and forth through the register. Or, if you have no qualms about dragging the mouse around, you can drag the scroll box up and down the scroll bar.

QuickBooks lets you sort your register in different ways, which makes scrolling through and finding transactions much easier. To sort your register the way you prefer, choose an option from the Sort By drop-down list box in the lower-left corner of the Checking register window.

Finding that darn transaction

Want to find that one check, deposit, or transfer? No problem. I discuss this technique earlier in the book, but it's appropriate here, too. The Edit menu's Find command provides a handy way for doing just such a thing. Here's what you do:

1. Choose Edit⇨Advanced Find.

QuickBooks, with restrained but obvious enthusiasm, displays the Advanced tab of the Find window (see Figure 8-10). You use this window to describe — in as much detail as possible — the transaction that you want to find.

Choose the Edit⇨Simple Find command to display the Simple tab of the Find window. The Simple tab enables you to search for transactions by using the transaction type, customer or job name, date, number, and amount. You can easily switch to an advanced search by clicking the Advanced tab.

2. Choose a filter that describes the information that you already have.

In the figure, the Name filter has been chosen. As you click different filters, the Find window changes.

3. Enter the text or number that identifies the transaction that you want to locate.

In the upper-right box, which is set to Name in Figure 8-10, choose the text or number that describes the subject of your search from the drop-down list. Or just type the information in the box. If more than one field is in the box, use as many as you think will help.

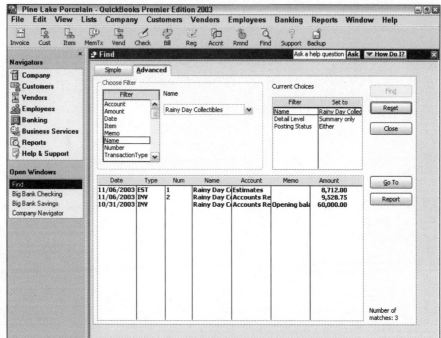

Figure 8-10:
The Advanced tab of the Find window.

By the way, the case of the text doesn't matter. If you type rainy, for example, QuickBooks finds *RAINY* as well as *Rainy*.

4. Repeat Steps 2 and 3 as necessary.

Yes, you can filter through as many fields as you want. In fact, you can filter so much that nothing matches your specification.

5. Click the Find button to begin looking.

If QuickBooks finds transactions that match the one you described, QuickBooks lists them in the bottom half of the window.

Chapter 9

Paying with Plastic

. . . .

In This Chapter

▶ Setting up and selecting credit card accounts

▶ Entering credit card charges

▶ Changing charges that you've already entered

▶ Reconciling credit card statements

▶ Paying the monthly credit card bill

▶ Handling debit cards

. . . .

You can use QuickBooks to track your credit cards in much the same way that you use it to keep a checkbook. The process is almost the same but with a few wrinkles.

Tracking Business Credit Cards

If you want to track credit card spending and balances with QuickBooks, you need to set up a credit card account — if you didn't already do so in the EasyStep Interview. (In comparison, you use bank accounts to track things such as the money that flows into and out of a checking, savings, or petty cash account.)

Setting up a credit card account

To set up a credit card account, you follow roughly the same steps that you use to set up a bank account:

1. **Choose Lists⇨Chart of Accounts.**

   Or select Company in the Navigators list and then click the Chart of Accounts icon. QuickBooks displays the Chart of Accounts window, shown in Figure 9-1.

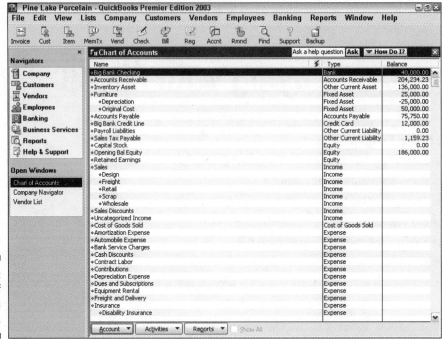

Figure 9-1:
The Chart of
Accounts
window.

2. **Click the Account button in the Chart of Accounts window and then choose New.**

   QuickBooks displays the New Account window, shown in Figure 9-2.

3. **Choose Credit Card from the Type drop-down list.**

   Choosing Credit Card tells QuickBooks that you want to set up a credit card account. I'm sure that you're surprised.

4. **Type a name for the account in the Name text box.**

   Why not do it right? Move the cursor to the Name text box and enter the name of your credit card.

5. **Type the card number in the Card No. text box.**

   If you're creating a general Credit Card account for more than one card, leave the Card No. text box empty. While you're at it, you can describe the card, too. You may want to type **Usury!** in the Description text box, depending on your card's interest rate.

6. **Ignore the Tax Line list box.**

7. **In the Opening Balance text box, enter the balance that you owed at the end of the last credit card billing period after you made your payment.**

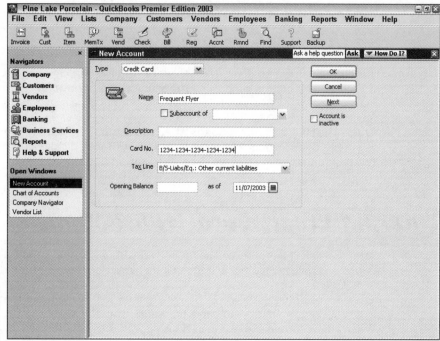

Figure 9-2:
The New
Account
window.

Move the cursor to the Opening Balance text box and use the number keys to enter the balance value. If you just got this credit card and you haven't bought anything with it, leave the box empty. Otherwise, enter the balance that you currently owe. You enter the balance as a positive number, by the way, even though you owe money.

The only time you should enter a credit card account balance equal to something other than zero is at the time that you start using QuickBooks and are entering your trial balance as of the conversion date. Otherwise, you'll foul up your owner's equity. (Refer to Chapter 1 if you have questions about entering the trial balance or about the conversion date.)

8. **Enter the As Of date on which you'll start keeping records for the credit card account.**

   You should probably use the date when you made your most recent payment.

9. **Click OK.**

   QuickBooks redisplays the Chart of Accounts window (refer to Figure 9-1), except this time the window lists an additional account — the credit card account that you just created.

Selecting a credit card account so that you can use it

To tell QuickBooks that you want to work with a credit card account, you use the Chart of Accounts window — the same window shown in Figure 9-1. Go figure!

Choose Lists⇨Chart of Accounts. After you display the window, double-click the credit card account you want to use. QuickBooks displays the Credit Card register so that you can begin recording transactions.

Entering Credit Card Transactions

After you select a credit card account, QuickBooks displays the Credit Card register, shown in Figure 9-3. It looks a lot like a Checking register, doesn't it?

The Credit Card register works like the regular register window that you use for a checking account. You enter transactions in the rows of the register. When you record a charge, QuickBooks updates the credit card balance and the remaining credit limit.

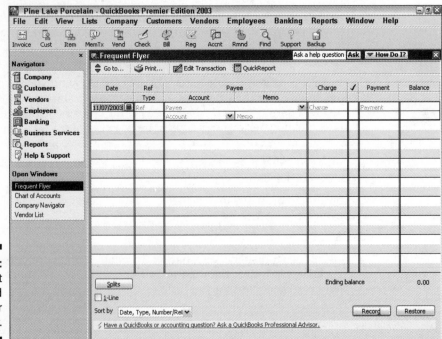

Figure 9-3:
The Credit
Card
Register
window.

Recording a credit card charge

Recording a credit card charge is similar to recording a check or bank account withdrawal. For the sake of illustration, suppose that you charged $50.00 for a business lunch at your favorite Mexican restaurant, La Cantina. Here's how you record this charge:

1. **Choose Banking➪Enter Credit Card Charges.**

   Or select Banking in the Navigators list and then click the Credit Card Charges icon. The Enter Credit Card Charges window appears, as shown in Figure 9-4.

2. **In the Credit Card list box, choose the credit card that you charged the expense against.**

   Click the down arrow next to the Credit Card box and choose a card from the drop-down list.

3. **In the Purchased From field, record the name of the business that you paid with a credit card.**

   Move the cursor to the Purchased From line and click the down arrow. You see a list of names. Choose one from the list.

   If you've never dined at this fine restaurant before, choose <Add new>. Then add the business name.

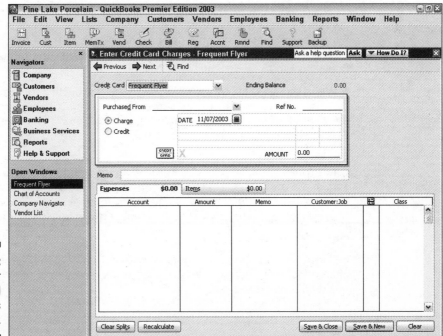

Figure 9-4:
The Enter Credit Card Charges window.

4. **Choose the appropriate option button to indicate whether the transaction is a purchase or a credit.**

    Select the Charge option button if you want to record a purchase (which is what you do most of the time and what this example shows you). Select the Credit option button if you want to record a credit on your account (if you returned something, for example).

5. **Enter the charge date in the Date field.**

    Move the cursor to the Date line (if the cursor isn't already there) and type the date, using the MM/DD/YY format. For example, type either **091603** or **9/16/03** for September 16, 2003. If you're entering this charge two or three days after the fact, don't enter today's date. Enter the date that the charge was made. Using that date makes reconciling your records with your credit card company's records easier when you get the monthly statement.

6. **Type the charge amount in the Amount field.**

    Move the cursor to the Amount line and enter the total charge amount — **50.00** in this example. Don't type a dollar sign, but do type the period to indicate the decimal place.

7. **(Optional) Enter a memo description in the Memo text box.**

    Move the cursor to the Memo text box and type the specific reason that you're charging the item. In this case, you could type **Important Business Lunch** or something like that.

8. **Fill in the Expenses tab.**

    I'm hoping that you read Chapters 6 and 8, that you know all about the Expenses tab, and that you're thoroughly bored by the topic. However, for those of you who opened the book right to this page, you use the Expenses tab to record business expenses.

    Move to the Account column of the Expenses tab, click the down arrow, and choose an Expense account from the list (most likely Travel & Ent:Meals, if this was a business lunch). If you enter a name here that QuickBooks doesn't already know, it asks you to set up an expense account.

    QuickBooks automatically fills in the Amount column when you enter a sum in the Amount line. Type something in the Memo column and assign this expense to a Customer:Job and Class, if you want to. You need to turn on class tracking if you want to assign the expense to a class.

9. **Fill in the Items tab.**

    Because this charge is for a meal at a restaurant, you don't itemize the charge. However, if you were charging lumber, paper supplies, and so on, you'd fill in the Items tab.

If you have a purchase order on file with the vendor that you entered in the Purchased From line, QuickBooks tells you so. Click the Select PO button to see a list of your outstanding purchase orders with the vendor. If you don't know how to handle purchase orders, see Chapter 7.

10. **Record the charge by clicking the Save & New or the Save & Close button.**

    The charge is recorded in the Credit Card register. Figure 9-5 shows what the Credit Card register looks like after I entered a handful of charges.

Changing charges that you've already entered

Perhaps you record a credit card charge and then realize that you recorded it incorrectly. Or perhaps you shouldn't have recorded it at all because you didn't pay for the business lunch. (Someone else paid for it after one of those friendly arguments over who should pay the bill. You know the type of argument I mean: "No, I insist." "On the contrary, I insist." You get the picture.)

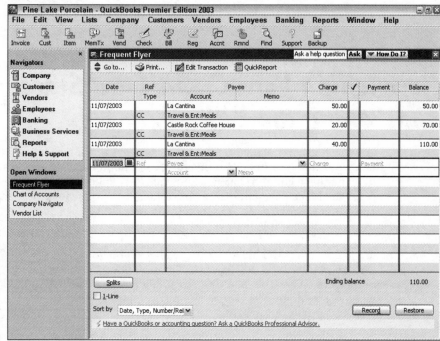

Figure 9-5:
The Credit
Card
Register
window
with some
trans-
actions.

You have to go into the Credit Card register and either edit or delete the charge by following these steps:

1. **Choose Lists⇨Chart of Accounts.**

   You see the Chart of Accounts window.

2. **Double-click the credit card account where the faulty charge is.**

   Like magic, the Credit Card register appears on-screen.

3. **Select the credit card transaction that you want to delete or change.**

   That's easy. Just move the cursor to the transaction.

4. **Void, delete, or edit the transaction:**

   • To void the credit card transaction, choose Edit⇨Void Credit Card Charge and click OK.

   • To delete it, choose Edit⇨Delete Credit Card Charge. QuickBooks displays a message box that asks whether you really want to delete the transaction. Click OK.

   • To edit the transaction, click the Edit Transaction button at the top of the window. You return to the Enter Credit Card Charges window. Make your changes there and click Save & New or Save & Close. You also can make changes inside the Credit Card register and click Record when you're done.

Reconciling Your Credit Card Statement and Paying the Bill

You *reconcile,* or balance, a credit card account the same way you balance a bank account. (For help with this task, see Chapter 13.) After you successfully get the account to balance and click Reconcile Now, QuickBooks displays the Make Payment dialog box, asking how you want to pay the bill. You can either pay by check or enter a bill to be paid later. (The second option is the accounts payable method, remember?)

If you opt to pay the bill by writing a check, you go straight to the Write Checks window, and the Expenses tab is all filled out for you. Fill in the name of the card issuer, the date, and so on. Click Save & New or Save & Close when you're done. The payment is recorded in both the Checking register and the Credit Card register.

If you opt to enter the payment as a bill to be paid at a later date, you go to the Enter Bills window. Fill everything out just as you would if you were in the Write Checks window. When you click Save & New, the transaction is recorded in the Accounts Payable register and the Credit Card register.

See Chapter 6 if you need to know more about either the Enter Bills or Write Checks window.

So, What About Debit Cards?

Debit cards, when you get right down to it, aren't really credit cards at all. Using a debit card is more akin to writing a check than anything else. Rather than withdrawing money by writing a check, however, you withdraw money by using a debit card.

Although a debit card transaction looks (at least to your friends and the merchants you shop with) like a credit card transaction, you should treat a debit card transaction as you treat a check. In a nutshell, here's what you need to do:

✔ When you charge something to a debit card, record the transaction just as you record a regular check. You may want to enter the transaction number as the check number or in the memo line so that you can keep track of the transaction.

✔ When you withdraw cash by using the debit card, record the transaction as a regular withdrawal (or transfer to a petty cash account), as if you'd gone in to the bank with a withdrawal slip.

✔ When you make a deposit through a cash machine by using the debit card, record the transaction just as you record a regular deposit.

Part III
Stuff You Do Every So Often

The 5th Wave   By Rich Tennant

"And tell David to come in out of the hall. I found a way to adjust our project budget estimate."

In this part . . .

After you start using QuickBooks, you need to complete some tasks at the end of every week, month, or year. This part describes these tasks: printing payroll checks, backing up files, printing reports, filing quarterly and annual tax returns. . . . The list goes on and on. Fortunately, QuickBooks comes with some nifty online features to help you get the job done.

Chapter 10

Check Printing 101

*T*his chapter covers the reductivity of the postcolonial implications in Joseph Conrad's *Heart of Darkness*. Just kidding. I'm going to cover how to print checks and checking registers.

Printing checks in QuickBooks is quick — well, it's quick after you set up your printer correctly. If you have a continuous-feed printer, you know by now that these printers have problems printing anything on a form. The alignment always gets messed up.

QuickBooks has check forms that you can buy, and I recommend using them if you print checks. After all, the QuickBooks checks were made to work with this program. And all banks accept these checks.

If you want help printing reports, refer to Chapter 14, where I cover this topic in almost too much detail.

Getting the Printer Ready

Before you can start printing checks, you have to make sure that your printer is set up to print them. You also have to tell QuickBooks what to put on the checks — your company name, address, logo, and so on. And you may try running a few sample checks through the wringer to see whether they come out all right. Follow these steps to set up the printer:

1. **Choose File⇨Printer Setup.**

   After you choose this command, you see the Printer Setup dialog box, shown in Figure 10-1.

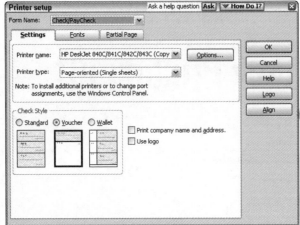

Figure 10-1:
The Printer
Setup
dialog box.

2. Select Check/PayCheck from the Form Name drop-down list box.

QuickBooks sets your printing options differently depending on which
form you want to print. For printing out checks, you want to choose the
Check/PayCheck form from the Form Name drop-down list box at the
top of the dialog box.

**3. In the Printer Name drop-down list box, select the printer that you
have.**

In the Printer Name drop-down list box, click the down arrow and look at
the printer names. When you installed QuickBooks, it had a frank, soft-
ware-to-software talk with Windows to find out what kind of printer you
have, among other things. Your printer is probably already selected, but
if it's not, select the correct printer.

4. Set the correct Printer Type option, if necessary.

This box is probably already filled in, too, thanks to that frank discussion I mention in Step 3. But if it isn't, click the down arrow and choose
Continuous or Page-Oriented. (The former is generally for dot-matrix
printers and the latter for laser and inkjet printers, but it really just
depends on what kind of paper you use for your printer.)

5. Select the appropriate Check Style.

Now you're cooking. This step is where you get to make a real choice.
Standard Checks are sized to fit in legal envelopes. Voucher Checks are
the same width as standard checks, but they're much longer. When you
choose the Voucher Checks option, QuickBooks prints voucher information as well — the items and expenses tabulations from the bottom of
the Write Checks window. QuickBooks also provides information about
the checking account that you're writing this check on. The Wallet
Checks option is for printing checks that are small enough to fit in —
you guessed it — a wallet.

6. **(Optional) Click the Options button and then adjust your printer options. When you're finished, click OK to return to the Printer Setup dialog box.**

   After you click the Options button, QuickBooks displays your printer's Properties dialog box. Use this dialog box to specify print quality, number of copies, and other options specific to your printer.

7. **Click the Fonts tab of the Printer Setup dialog box and then the Fonts button on that tab to customize the fonts on your checks.**

   When you click either the Font button or the Address Font button on this tab, you see the Select Font dialog box (shown in Figure 10-2) or the Select Address Font dialog box. You use the Address Font button to designate how your company's name and address look and the Font button to designate what all other print on your checks looks like. Here's your chance to spruce up your checks and make your company's name stand out.

Figure 10-2:
The Select
Font
dialog box.

Experiment for a while with the font, font style, and type size settings. For example, if you have a bookstore, choose the Bookman font (maybe using bold for your company's name and address); if you run a messenger service, choose Courier; Italian mathematicians can use Times Roman (just kidding). You can see what your choices look like in the Sample box.

When you finish fooling around, click the OK button to go back to the Printer Setup dialog box.

8. **Click the Partial Page tab of the Printer Setup dialog box and then choose a Partial Page Printing Style.**

   Fortunately, some graphics appear; otherwise, you wouldn't have a clue what these options are, would you? These options are for the environmentally friendly among you. Suppose that you feed two checks to the printer, but the check sheets have three checks each. You have a leftover check.

Thanks to this option, you can use the extra check. Click one of the options to tell QuickBooks how you plan to feed the check to the printer — vertically on the left (the Left option), vertically in the middle (the Centered option), or horizontally (the Portrait option). You feed checks to the printer the same way that you feed envelopes to it.

9. **(Optional) Click the Logo button and then enter a company logo or some clip art.**

   In the Logo dialog box, click File and find the directory and BMP (bitmapped) graphic file that you want to load. Click OK. Only graphics files that are in BMP format can be used on your checks.

10. **Click OK when you finish.**

That setup was no Sunday picnic, was it? But your checks are all ready to be printed, and you'll probably never have to go through that ordeal again.

Printing a Check

For some reason, when I get to this part of the discussion, my pulse quickens. Actually writing a check for real money seems terribly serious. I get the same feeling whenever I mail someone cash — even if the amount is nominal.

I think that the best way to lower my heart rate (and yours, if you're like me) is to just print the darn check and be done with it. QuickBooks can print checks in two ways: as you write them and in bunches.

First things first, however. Before you can print checks, you have to load some blank checks into your printer. This process works the same way as loading any paper into your printer. If you have questions, refer to your printer's documentation. (Sorry I can't help more on this process, but a million different printers exist, and I can't tell which one you even have when I look into my crystal ball.)

A few words about printing checks

Check printing is kind of complicated, isn't it? For the record, I'm with you on this one. I really wish it weren't so much work. But you'll find that printing checks gets easier after the first few times.

Pretty soon, you'll be running instead of walking through the steps. Pretty soon, you'll just skate around roadblocks such as check-form alignment problems. Pretty soon, in fact, you'll know all this stuff and never have to read pretty soon again.

Printing a check as you write it

If you're in the Write Checks window and you've just finished filling out a check, you can print it. The only drawback is that you have to print checks one at a time with this method. Here's how:

1. **Fill out your check.**

   Yes, I strongly recommend filling out the check before printing it. Turn to Chapter 6 for help with writing checks using QuickBooks.

2. **Click the Print button in the Write Checks window.**

   You'll see the Print Check dialog box, as shown in Figure 10-3.

3. **Enter a check number in the Printed Check Number text box and click OK.**

   After you click OK, you see the similarly named Print Checks dialog box, shown in Figure 10-4. The settings that you see in this dialog box are the ones that you chose when you first told QuickBooks how to print checks. If you change the settings in the Print Checks dialog box, the changes affect only this particular check. The next time you print a check, you'll see your original settings again.

4. **Either click Print to accept the default settings, or make changes in the dialog box and then click Print.**

   In the Printer Name box, specify which printer you want to print to. In the Check Style area, indicate whether you want to print a Standard, Voucher, or Wallet-sized check.

   If you're printing a partial page of forms on a laser printer, use the Partial Page tab to indicate both the number of check forms on the partial page and how you'll feed them through your printer.

   If you want your company's name and address to appear on the check, select the Print Company Name and Address check box.

   See how the Number of Copies text box is grayed out? If you want to change this setting, you need to go back to the Printer Setup dialog box (choose File➪Printer Setup).

   After you click Print, QuickBooks prints the check, and you see the Did Check(s) Print OK? dialog box (not shown).

Figure 10-3:
The Print
Check
dialog box.

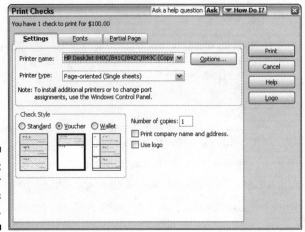

Figure 10-4:
The other
Print Checks
dialog box.

5. **If the check didn't come out right, type the number of the incorrectly printed check in the Did Check(s) Print OK? dialog box and click OK. Then click the Print button again, enter the new check number, and click Print again.**

For example, if check number 1005 printed incorrectly, type **1005**. Then click the Print button again, enter the new check number, and click Print again. If pre-printed check form 1005 is still usable (say, because you accidentally printed check 1005 on blank paper instead of on the form), you can reprint the check on check form 1005 by typing **1005** in the Print Check dialog box (refer to Figure 10-3). If the incorrectly printed check ruined check form 1005 (say, because you loaded the form upside-down), load your printer with a fresh check form and verify the new check number, in this case probably 1006.

QuickBooks doesn't automatically keep track of incorrectly printed check forms, so you have to. If you botch a check form, be sure to write the word *VOID* in large letters and permanent ink across the face of the check. Then file the check away for your reference. Don't throw the check away.

If you still have questions about how to check any mistakes, see the section "What if I make a mistake?" later in this chapter.

6. **If your check looks good, click OK.**

You return to the Write Checks window. Don't forget to sign the check.

Printing checks by the bushel

What if you write a mess of checks and then decide to print them? That's how the process is usually done. Here's how to print a bushel of checks:

1. **Go into the Checking register and make sure that the checks that you want to print are marked To Print.**

   The quickest way to get into the Checking register is to choose the Banking⇨Use Register command. If you have more than one bank account, select the checking account register you want to open and click OK. Do the checks that you want to print have `To Print` in the Number line? If not, place the cursor in the Number line, press *T,* and then click the Record button. QuickBooks automatically fills the Number field with `To Print` and then moves on. (If the check you want to print already has a number, you need to replace the number with T.)

2. **Choose File⇨Print Forms⇨Checks.**

   You see the Select Checks to Print dialog box, in which you select what checks to print (see Figure 10-5).

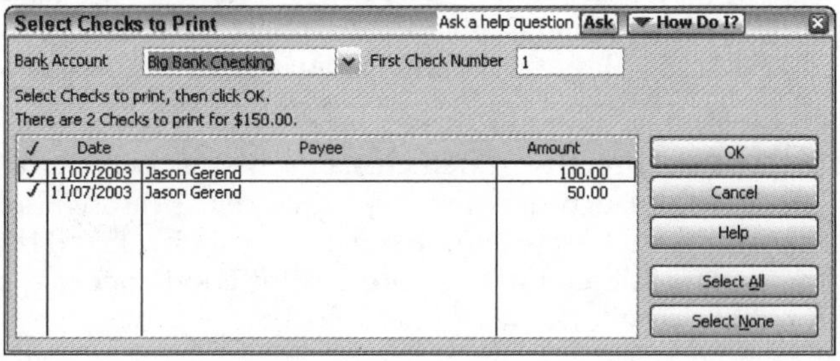

Figure 10-5:
The Select
Checks
to Print
dialog box.

Select Checks to Print		Ask a help question [Ask] [▼ How Do I?]	✕
Bank Account	Big Bank Checking ✕	First Check Number 1	

Select Checks to print, then click OK.
There are 2 Checks to print for $150.00.

✓	Date	Payee	Amount	
✓	11/07/2003	Jason Gerend	100.00	OK
✓	11/07/2003	Jason Gerend	50.00	Cancel
				Help
				Select All
				Select None

3. **Click the check marks next to the checks that you don't want to print and then click OK.**

   All the checks are selected at first. If you want to print them all, fine. If not, click the check marks next to the checks that you don't want to print so that QuickBooks removes the check marks. Or, if you want to print only a few of the checks, click the Select None button and then click next to the checks that you want to print so that QuickBooks places a check in the column.

   When only the checks that you want to print are marked with a check mark, click OK to continue with this crazy little thing called check printing. QuickBooks, happy with your progress, displays the Print Checks dialog box (refer to Figure 10-4). Here you see the settings that you chose when you first told QuickBooks how to print checks.

4. **Either click Print to accept the default settings or make changes in the dialog box and then click Print.**

   You can change the settings in this dialog box if you want them to be different. Any changes that you make for a particular batch of checks don't affect the default settings. The next time you print a check, your original settings appear again.

In the Check Style box, indicate whether you want to print Standard, Voucher, or Wallet-sized checks. If you're printing a partial page of checks, enter the number of checks on the first page in the Number of Checks on First Page text box.

If you want your company's name and address to appear on the checks, select the Print Company Name and Address check box.

Note that the Number of Copies text box is grayed out. If you want to change these settings, you need to choose File⇨Printer Setup.

QuickBooks prints the checks, and then you see the Did Check(s) Print OK? dialog box.

5. **Review the checks that QuickBooks printed. Then do one of the following:**

   • If QuickBooks printed the checks correctly, answer the Did Check(s) Print OK? message box by clicking OK. (QuickBooks, apparently thinking that you now want to do nothing but print checks, redisplays the nearly exhausted Write Checks window.)

   • If QuickBooks didn't print a check correctly, type the number of the first incorrectly printed check in the text box and then click OK. In this case, repeat the steps for check printing. Note, though, that you need to reprint only the first bad check and the checks that follow it. You don't need to reprint good checks that precede the first bad check.

   Don't forget to write the word *VOID* in large letters and permanent ink across the front of incorrectly printed check forms. Then file the checks for safekeeping. (Don't throw them away.) To record the voided check in QuickBooks, see the section "What if I make a mistake?" later in this chapter.

If the numbers of the checks you need to reprint aren't sequential and are, in fact, spread all over creation, make it easy on yourself. Click OK to clear the list of checks to be printed, go into the Checking register, and press *T* in the Number line of the checks you need to reprint. QuickBooks automatically fills these with To Print. Then choose File⇨Print Forms⇨Checks, as in Step 2, and continue from there.

If your checks came out all right, take the rest of the day off. Give yourself a raise while you're at it.

6. **Sign the printed checks.**

   Then — and I guess you probably don't need my help here — put the checks in the mail.

A big bad warning concerning check voiding

In general, you shouldn't void checks from a previous year (you would do this by using the Void command in the Edit menu). If you do, you'll adjust the previous year's expenses, which sounds okay, but you don't want to do this because (a) it means you can no longer prepare income statements and balance sheets that correspond to your financial statements and tax returns and (b) because you've already presumably included the check in your deductions for the previous year. If you do have a check that should be voided — say it's outstanding and has never been cashed or was a mistake in the first place — record a journal entry into the current year that undoes the effect of the check.

What if I make a mistake?

If you discover a mistake after you print a check, the problem may not be as big as you think.

If you've already mailed the check, however, you can't do much. You can try to get the check back (if the person you paid hasn't cashed it already) and replace it with a check that's correct. (Good luck on this one.)

If the person has cashed the check, you can't get the check back. If you overpaid the person by writing the check for more than you should have, you need to get the person to pay you the overpayment amount. If you underpaid the person, you need to write another check for the amount of the underpayment.

If you printed the check but haven't mailed it, void the printed check. This operation has two parts. First, write *VOID* in large letters across the face of the check form. (Use a ballpoint pen if you're using multipart forms so that the second and third parts also show as VOID.) Second, display the Checking register, highlight the check, and then choose Edit↩Void Check. (This option marks the check as one that has been voided in the system so that QuickBooks doesn't use the check in calculating the account balance.) If you're voiding an incorrectly printed check, you need to first create a transaction for the check number that printed incorrectly and then void that transaction.

Of course, if you want to reissue a voided check, just enter the check all over again — only this time, try to be more careful.

If you notice only after clicking OK in the Did Checks Print OK? dialog box that a check printed incorrectly, you can tell QuickBooks you want to reprint the check in one of two ways. If you have the register window displayed, you can change the check's number from 007, for example, to To Print. If you have the Write Checks window displayed, you can select the To Be Printed box.

Oh where, oh where do unprinted checks go?

Unprinted checks — those that you entered by using the Write Checks window but haven't yet printed — are stored in the Checking register. To identify them as unprinted checks, QuickBooks puts To Print in the Number line. What's more, when you tell QuickBooks to print the unprinted checks, what it really does is print the checks in the register that have To Print in the Number line. All this knowledge is of little practical value in most instances, but it results in several interesting possibilities.

For example, you can enter the checks that you want to print directly into the register — all you need to do is type **To Print** in the Number line.

Printing a Checking Register

You can print a Checking register or a register for any other account, too. Follow these steps to print a register:

1. **Open the account register you want to print.**

   Choose Banking⇨Use Register. If you have more than one bank account, select the account register you want to print from the drop-down list box and click OK.

2. **Choose File⇨Print Register.**

   You see the Print Register dialog box, as shown in Figure 10-6.

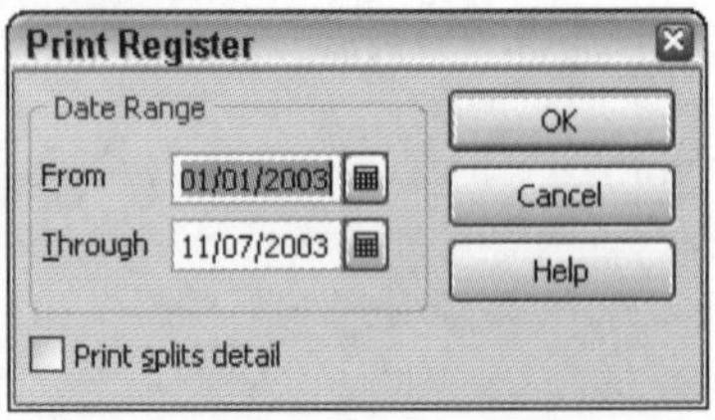

Figure 10-6:
The Print
Register
dialog box.

Print Register

Date Range

From 01/01/2003

Through 11/07/2003

OK

Cancel

Help

☐ Print splits detail

3. **Fill in the Date Range text boxes.**

To print a register of something other than the current year-to-date transactions, use the From and Through text boxes. This step is pretty darn obvious, isn't it? You just move the cursor to the From and Through text boxes and type the range of months that the register should include.

4. **If you want, select the Print Splits Detail check box.**

As you know, a register doesn't show all the messy details, such as the Items and Expenses tab information. But you can select this check box to include all this stuff on your printed register.

5. **Click OK.**

You see the Print Lists dialog box, as shown in Figure 10-7.

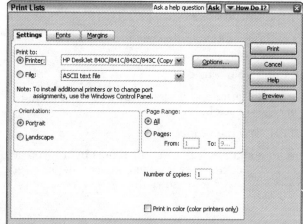

Figure 10-7:
The Print
Lists
dialog box.

6. **If everything is cool, click the Print button and skip the remaining steps. If you want to change options in the Print Lists dialog box, proceed to the next step.**

You don't have to fool around with the Print Lists dialog box. If you want to print a register pronto, just click Print, and QuickBooks sends the register on its merry way to your printer. Then again, if you're the sort of person who likes to fool around with this kind of stuff, carry on with the rest of these steps.

If you want to see the effect that the different settings in this dialog box have, just experiment. You can't hurt anything or anybody.

7. **(Optional) Print the report to disk.**

   To print the report to disk as a text file, select the File option button and choose one of the following Print To options:

   - Choose ASCII Text File if you want to create a text file (for example, when you want to import the register into a word-processing program).
   - Choose Comma Delimited File to import the register into Microsoft Excel or Lotus 1-2-3.
   - Choose Tab Delimited File to, for example, import the register into a database program. (Oooh . . . fancy. . . .)

8. **Choose the paper orientation.**

   Which direction do you want the report to be printed — Portrait (regular) or Landscape (sideways)? Just click the appropriate option button.

9. **(Optional) Tell QuickBooks which pages to print.**

   Use the Print Range option buttons and text boxes to limit the pages for QuickBooks to print.

10. **(Optional) Color your world — print your report in color.**

    If you have a color printer and want to print the register in color, select the Print In Color check box.

11. **(Optional) Preview the report.**

    To see how your settings will affect the report before you actually print it, click Preview. QuickBooks shows you the results on-screen. This feature has probably saved more trees than you can imagine.

12. **Click Print.**

    After you have the report exactly the way you want it (and not one moment before!), click Print, and QuickBooks finally prints the register.

Chapter 11

Online with QuickBooks

*I*n this chapter, I start by discussing QuickBooks' online banking and bill payment — which are pretty cool tools for some businesses. At the end of the chapter, I also very briefly discuss the online payroll services that, finally, I have enough practical experience with to talk about intelligently and authoritatively.

One important Web-related feature that isn't described in this chapter is the QuickBooks Web Site Builder. Refer to Chapter 17 for information about how to work with that tool — and for some down-to-earth advice on Web publishing in general.

Doing the Electronic Banking Thing

Before I discuss using the QuickBooks online banking and payment services, you need to consider whether these features even make sense for you and your business. Online banking does make sense for some people — maybe even you. But then again, it may be more like the fins on a '62 Cadillac: cool, but not that cool.

So what's the commotion about?

For QuickBooks, online banking includes two parts: online banking itself and online bill payment. Basically, online banking enables you to transmit account transfer instructions to your bank and *download*, or retrieve, account information electronically by using your computer and modem. Online bill payment allows you to transmit payment instructions electronically. (You basically tell your bank to write, stamp, and mail a check so that you don't have to.)

And that, my friend, is about all there is to online banking.

A thousand reasons not to bank online

I don't know whether you should bank online, really. But I'll share some thoughts with you.

On its face, online banking sounds pretty neat. And I guess it is neat — in its own little way. I do use the service. And I save time. But online banking does have some problems:

- ✔ To use the full-blown service, you need to use a bank that has signed up for Intuit's service. Many, many big banks have signed up. More banks sign up all the time, of course, but some haven't yet. So if your bank hasn't jumped on the bandwagon — that is, the Intuit bandwagon — you can't really jump on the bandwagon either. Or at least not as a full-fledged member of the band. (I talk more about Intuit's other online services later in the chapter.)

- ✔ To find out whether your bank provides online banking, choose Banking⇨ Set Up Online Financial Services⇨Online Financial Institutions List. After you're connected to the Internet, QuickBooks displays a list of the banks that support Intuit's flavor of online banking.

- ✔ Although a totally electronic system sounds really efficient and very slick, you need to realize that online bill payment (a key component of online banking) often isn't that efficient or slick because, to be quite honest, the system isn't totally electronic.

"What the . . ." you're saying. "I thought that was the point." Let me explain: For better or worse, most businesses are still set up to — and still expect to — receive paper checks with remittance advices. So what often happens when you transmit payment instructions is that the bank or online payment service simply writes (and prints) a check for you. Think about that for a minute. If the bank is printing your check, you still have all the disadvantages of a printed check:

- • You still need to allow extra time for mailing.

- • You still have the possibility that the check will get lost.

- • You still have the possibility that the check will be misapplied. (In other words, the check to pay your power bill may instead be applied to your neighbor's account.)

✔ What's more, you also have the extra complication of having your bank mucking all this stuff up instead of you.

✔ Best of all, the bank charges for this service. (Remember that banks and software companies think that online banking is an exciting new way for them to make money.)

✔ Receiving payments from your bank, as opposed to directly from you, also may confuse your vendors. The confusion occurs because the checks they receive come all bundled up in these cute little envelopes that must be torn along the perforation on just about all sides. And you can't send a remittance slip with an online payment. So vendors can easily credit your account incorrectly, which can lead to problems. (My power company regularly threatens to turn off the gas to my office because even though my electric and gas charges are included on the same bill, the power company doesn't like me to send one check via the QuickBooks online bill payment system. It needs two checks — one for the electric bill and one for the gas bill.)

One other problem bears mentioning. When you use online banking, you create a vastly more complex system without clear responsibilities for problem-solving and technical support. And that means that when you have problems, you often can't call someone to get help. (No kidding. Just yesterday, some poor guy e-mailed me because his online banking stuff wasn't working: Intuit blamed the bank, the bank blamed his PC hardware, the PC company blamed Intuit. . . . This guy has a problem nobody can solve or will solve.) This is important to understand, so let me briefly outline the steps that an online payment may take:

1. You enter the transaction in QuickBooks.

2. You or QuickBooks makes an Internet connection.

3. QuickBooks uses the Internet connection to send the transaction to the bank.

4. The bank typically creates a check, which it mails to the person you're paying.

5. The person you're paying gets the check, hopefully, and credits your account.

Five simple steps, right? Wrong. Any of these five steps can go wrong, and if one does, you don't actually make the payment or transfer, and you won't know why:

✔ If QuickBooks or your computer has a bug, it may say you've entered and transmitted a transaction when in fact you haven't. This has happened to me.

- ✔ If your Internet connection doesn't work or doesn't work dependably, you can't send the online transaction. I've had problems both with online banking at home over a dial-up Internet connection (bad telephone cord) and at work using a network connection and a DSL connection (either an incorrectly configured network or a bad DSL line).

- ✔ If the bank screws up printing or mailing the check, well, of course your check won't get there. (I've had this happen, too, no kidding. QuickBooks lets you enter a five-line address on a check, but the check printed by the bank or online payment service can have only four lines. So QuickBooks just removes the fifth line of the address block.)

I don't mean to rant here, but whenever any of these problems occurs, you won't actually know what's gone wrong. Only that something has gone wrong. And you'll be responsible for solving the problem — even though it may be the fault of your bank, Intuit, your Internet service provider, the telephone company, or somebody else.

Making sense of online banking

So what should you do? Let me make a suggestion: If you use a bank that provides online banking, go ahead and try the service. It isn't very expensive — probably a few dollars a month. If, later on, you decide that you don't like the service, you can always go back to banking the old-fashioned way.

Finding a bank you can trust

Say you want to use Intuit's online banking services but your bank isn't signed up. In response to this problem, many people may say, "Well, Dodo-brain, just switch banks." But not you. You know that switching banks is harder than it sounds, especially for small businesses — and often not a smart move. Many factors go into a successful small business banking relationship:

- ✔ **Convenience:** Doing your banking should be easy.

- ✔ **Trust based on a long history:** That way, you can borrow money or set up merchant credit

card accounts without using your children for collateral.

- ✔ **Good rapport with a personal banker or loan officer:** If you ever have a problem — and I hope that doesn't happen — you have someone you can talk to.

Sure, online banking is neat. Like Cadillac fins. But online banking is neither the only nor the most important feature you need to look at when you consider a bank.

If you use a bank that doesn't provide online banking services and you're really bummed out about it, you can try the online bill payment component of online banking by using Intuit's online bill payment service. Online bill payment is the part where you send instructions either to your bank (if it provides the service) or to Intuit to write and mail checks for you. You can use the online bill payment service with any account — in essence, you just give Intuit permission to automatically deduct money from your account to make payments for you.

If you use a bank that doesn't provide online banking and you couldn't care less, don't try the online banking stuff, don't read any more of this chapter, and consider taking the rest of the afternoon off.

Signing up for the service

All you need to sign up for online banking service is to choose Banking⇨Set Up Online Financial Services⇨Apply for Online Banking. QuickBooks starts an online application wizard that walks you through the steps to apply for the online banking service. Just follow the on-screen instructions and, voilà, that's it. Another benefit of being literate.

In order to actually begin transmitting online payments or making account inquiries, you need to complete the application and have that application processed. Note, too, that you can also usually complete the application by filling out paperwork from your bank and turning that in. You don't have to use the online application process.

Making an online payment

Plan to create and send online payments a good week before they're due. For the online bill payment service to process your request and then print and send a check takes time. And a check that your bank sends doesn't go through the mail any faster than a check you send yourself. So don't expect online bill payment to save you any time over sending checks you print or handwrite yourself.

After you sign up for online banking, making payments is easy. Just follow these steps:

1. **Choose Banking⇨Write Checks.**

   Or select Banking in the Navigators list and click the Checks icon. If you've written checks with QuickBooks before, you see your old familiar friend, the Write Checks window, as shown in Figure 11-1.

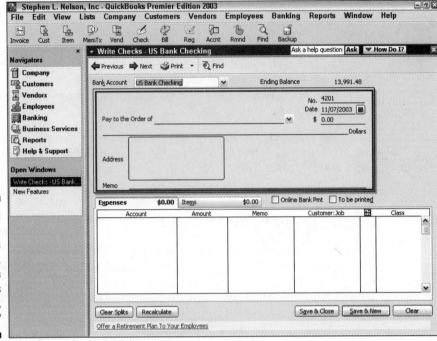

Figure 11-1:
The Write
Checks
window.
Hey, this
looks
familiar,
doesn't it?

2. **Click the Bank Account drop-down list at the top of the window and choose the account from which you want to write this check.**

   Choosing the account is a really important step. Make sure that you're accessing the right account before you write a check.

3. **Select the Online Bank Pmt check box.**

   Selecting this check box is another really important step. If you don't select this box, you're not making an online payment; you're just writing a regular check that you need to print or handwrite.

4. **Fill in the check.**

   If payee appears on one of your name lists, the AutoFill feature fills in the name of the payee in the Pay to the Order Of line after you type a few letters. For online bill payment, you must have the correct address. If the address is incomplete, QuickBooks warns you and asks you to correct it. (If you haven't entered a transaction for this person or party before or added them to a list, QuickBooks asks you to Quick Add or Set Up the payee name. Do that.

   By the way, QuickBooks makes you collect more information about anyone you're going to pay with an online payment.)

Enter the amount of the check next to the dollar sign and press Tab. QuickBooks writes out the amount for you on the Dollars line.

5. **Fill in the Expenses and Items tabs, if necessary.**

   Don't know what these tabs are? Chapter 6 explains them in minute detail. Start turning those pages.

6. **Click the Save & New or Save & Close button to finish writing the check.**

   Click Save & New to write another check or click Save & Close if you're finished writing checks for the moment. There you have it. Your check is written, entered in the Checking register, and ready to be sent so that your bank or Intuit can print and mail it.

   And you thought this stuff was going to be tough, didn't you?

People who have grown accustomed to Quicken, a cousin product of QuickBooks, may want to use the register window to make online payments. You can use the register window in QuickBooks, too, although doing so isn't quite as slick. You just enter the payment in the usual way — except that you type the word **SEND** in the Check Number text box.

Transferring money electronically

You can electronically transfer money between bank accounts, too — as long as the accounts are at the same bank. (Both accounts, of course, also need to be set for online banking.) Here's what you need to do:

1. **Choose Banking⇨Transfer Funds.**

   Or, select Banking in the Navigators list and click the Transfer Funds icon. You see the Transfer Funds Between Accounts window, as shown in Figure 11-2.

2. **In the Transfer Funds From drop-down list box, select the bank account that you're going to transfer the money from.**

   Choose the account from the drop-down list.

3. **In the Transfer Funds To drop-down list box, select the bank account to which you want to transfer the money.**

   Select the account that you want to receive the funds.

4. **Select the Online Funds Transfer check box.**

   Doing so tells QuickBooks that you want to make this transfer electronically.

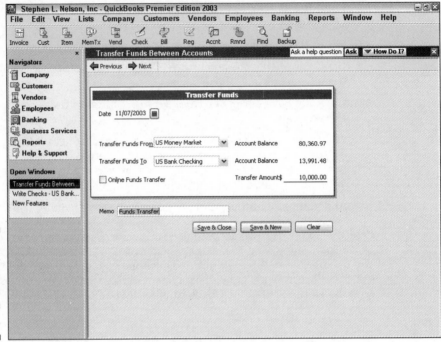

Figure 11-2:
The Transfer
Funds
Between
Accounts
window.

5. **Enter the amount that you want to transfer in the Transfer Amount field and fill in the Memo text box.**

   Someday, you may go into the register for the account you're transferring money from and wonder where you transferred this money and why. Filling in the Memo line solves this little mystery beforehand.

6. **Click the Save & Close button.**

   The transfer is recorded. After you transmit the transfer instructions (which I describe a little later in this chapter), the transfer transaction is posted to your account — maybe not immediately, but as fast as a telephone transfer or ATM machine transfer is posted.

Changing instructions

QuickBooks doesn't actually send, or transmit, your payment and transfer instructions until you tell it to. This little fact means that you can change or edit your payment instructions (what you enter with the Write Checks window) and your transfer instructions (what you enter with the Transfer Funds Between Accounts window) until you actually transmit them. You edit online payments and account transfers in the same way that you edit regular payments and account transfers. Refer to Chapter 8 if you need more information.

Transmitting instructions

After you describe the online payments and account transfers that you want QuickBooks to make, you transmit that information to the bank. To do so, follow these steps:

1. **Choose Banking⇨Online Banking Center.**

   Or, select Banking from the Navigators list and then click the Online Banking icon. You see the Online Banking Center window, as shown in Figure 11-3.

2. **In the Financial Institution list box at the top of the screen, select the bank to which you're transmitting payment and transfer instructions.**

   Choose the bank from the drop-down list.

3. **Review the payment and transfer instructions one last time.**

   Take one last peek at the Items to Send list to make sure that the payment and transfer instructions you're sending are correct. If you have questions about a particular instruction, click it and then click the Edit button. If you know that a particular payment instruction is incorrect, click it and then click the Delete button.

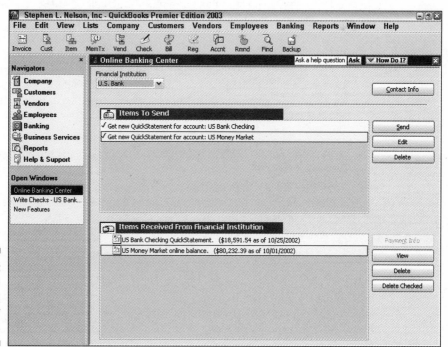

Figure 11-3:
The Online
Banking
Center
window.

4. **Click the Send button to transmit the payment and transfer instructions.**

   If you're transmitting payment and transfer instructions for the first time, QuickBooks probably prompts you to change your personal identification number, or PIN. If you've transmitted payment and transfer instructions before, QuickBooks prompts you to enter your existing PIN.

5. **Review any transactions that the bank tells you about.**

   Figure 11-3 shows two items received from the online bank — electronic statements that you can use to see cleared transactions and to reconcile your account. To view an online statement, click the statement and then click the View button.

6. **Click the Close box.**

   Hey, when you're done, you're done.

Message in a bottle

Doing all your banking electronically can be a little unsettling when you're first starting out. What if, for example, you have a question? All you do is send an e-mail message to the bank asking the people there whatever question you would normally ask in a telephone call or at the drive-through window. To do so, follow these steps:

1. **Choose Banking⇨Create Online Banking Message.**

   QuickBooks displays the Home Banking Message dialog box and fills in the bank name (as long as you use online banking services with only one bank). If you use online banking services with more than one bank, select the name of the bank to whom you want to send a message from the Message To drop-down list box.

2. **Click the Subject box and then type a brief description of your message's subject.**

   I may be telling you something you already know, but most e-mail readers simply display a list of messages that includes the sender, the message subject, and the date. Therefore, the message subject that you use is one of the first bits of message information that the bank sees.

3. **Select the online account that you're going to discuss in the message.**

4. **Click the Message box and then type your message.**

   You're on your own here.

5. **(Optional) Click the Print button to print a copy of your message.**

6. Click OK.

When you click OK, you add the message to the list of stuff that's ready to send the next time you go online with your bank. You can send the instructions immediately by following the steps in the section "Transmitting instructions," earlier in this chapter.

Using the Online Payroll Service

QuickBooks provides three payroll services: Do-It-Yourself Payroll, which is essentially the stuff I describe in Chapter 12, Premier Payroll, which is a full-blown service like the one that other outside payroll services such as ADP and PayChex provide, and QuickBooks Assisted Payroll, which is an online payroll service.

The Assisted Payroll online payroll service provides all the futures of the Do-It-Yourself Payroll plus some other features such as the filing of payroll tax returns and the payment of payroll tax deposits.

While Assisted Payroll sounds pretty good, I think it's not a good choice for most people. Unfortunately, it's too little help for about half the businesses and too much help for the other half. But let me share some comments:

- ✔ The QuickBooks online payroll service is cheaper than what you'd pay to an outside service bureau, such as QuickBooks Premier Payroll, ADP or PayChex, but you have to do more work with QuickBooks, so you're really earning your cost savings. (For what used to cost me about $1,000 a year with PayChex, I paid roughly $500 a year by using the QuickBooks Assisted Payroll service.)

- ✔ You need to watch the fees for any payroll service because they can easily nickel and dime you to death. I used to have a very small manufacturing business, for example. Usually, I was preparing fewer than six paychecks a pay period. For biweekly paychecks and all my federal and state tax returns, I paid around $1,000 to one of the large, nationally known payroll services, PayChex. When I moved to the QuickBooks service, I cut this amount in about half — which was cool. But read on . . .

- ✔ A service bureau, in my experience, provides far better service than even the Assisted Payroll Service (mostly because you deal with a real, live person you can question).

I eventually canceled the Assisted payroll service and went back to the Do-It-Yourself service (which means do all the work yourself, as described in Chapter 12, and pay Intuit about $130 a year for the tax withholding information) because of the errors the Assisted Payroll service kept making. The final straw concerning the QuickBooks Assisted Payroll service was when the Internal Revenue Service issued me a lien notice because of confusion related to the service's handling of payroll tax deposits. (A *lien notice* says that the I.R.S is about to grab money from my checking account.) For the record, the only money that I owed — roughly $1,000 in penalties — stemmed from an error that the QuickBooks Assisted Payroll service made and took weeks to clear up. Geez.

✔ The QuickBooks Do-It-Yourself and Assisted Payroll payroll services probably provide you with greater flexibility than QuickBooks Premier Payroll, PayChex or ADP, other popular payroll services. You can do payroll when you want (early, late, in the middle of the night, and so on) and easily make last minute changes to pay rates. And this is great. I admit it.

✔ If a payroll service — any payroll service — doesn't make available state payroll tax returns help for your state, use a local payroll service. The paycheck calculations and the federal payroll returns are the easy ones. The state returns are where you want the help.

✔ In spite of the new midyear conversion wizards supplied by the QuickBooks Do-It-Yourself and Assisted Payroll services, you'll probably find it easiest to convert at the start of next year (whatever year that is for you). By converting at the start of a payroll year, you can avoid recording all the year-to-date numbers for employees.

The QuickBooks.com Web site provides information about the payroll services that Intuit provides and a form you can use to request a price quote.

A Quick Review of the Other Online Opportunities

Intuit provides several other small-business-type services to QuickBooks users. For example, Intuit has also arranged for a merchant credit card service, which you can apply for online and then use online for receiving payments and even getting charge authorizations. Finally, through its Web site, Intuit also says it provides a small-business purchasing service that makes price shopping over the Internet easy, or at least easier.

If you have questions about the current state of any of these products or services, visit www.quickbooks.com and search for the name of the service.

Chapter 12

Payroll

• •

In This Chapter

▶ Creating payroll accounts

▶ Requesting an employer ID number

▶ Obtaining withholding information

▶ Computing an employee's gross wages, payroll deductions, and net wages

▶ Recording a payroll check in QuickBooks

▶ Making federal tax deposits

▶ Preparing quarterly and annual payroll tax returns

▶ Producing annual wage statements, such as W-2s

▶ Handling state payroll taxes

• •

*P*ayroll is one of the major headaches of running a small business. When I think of all the time I've wasted figuring out withholding amounts, writing checks, and trying to fill out wickedly ridiculous payroll tax returns, it just makes me want to scream. Fortunately, QuickBooks helps. And in a big way. In this chapter, I explain how.

Getting Ready to Do Payroll without QuickBooks' Help

The easiest way to do payroll, quite frankly, is to sign up with an outside service bureau, such as ADP or PayChex or QuickBooks' new Complete Payroll service. If you have an accountant, you may want to also ask him or her about other, cheaper local payroll services.

Of course, the easiest route is often the most expensive, and payroll services are no exception. In my experience, these full-meal-deal services tend to run about twice the price of the QuickBooks Assisted Payroll service after you add everything up. But all you need to do is make a phone call. (Check your telephone book for a local number or, if you're interested in the QuickBooks service, check www.quickbooks.com.) The payroll service will send someone nice out to your office. A few days later, all you'll need to do is make a phone call or send a fax when you want to pay employees.

Getting Ready to Do Payroll with QuickBooks

If you want to use either QuickBooks Do-It-Yourself Payroll or QuickBooks Assisted Payroll because you want to save money, aren't scared of a little paperwork, or maybe want the extra flexibility that comes with doing it yourself, you need to sign up for the QuickBooks Do-It-Yourself Payroll (also known as the Basic Payroll Service) or QuickBooks Assisted Payroll (previously known as Deluxe Payroll Service.)

To sign up for either service, get ready to hop on the Internet. Follow these steps:

1. **Choose the Employees⇨Set Up Payroll command.**

   Or Select Employees in the Navigators list and then click the Set Up Payroll icon.

   QuickBooks connects to the Internet and displays the first page of a multiple-page Web form that enables you to set up either the Basic Payroll Service or the Deluxe Payroll Service (see Figure 12-1).

2. **Follow the on-screen instructions.**

   I'm not going to repeat the on-screen instructions for setting up the payroll service. Providing that kind of information would be, well, extremely redundant. Just carefully follow the instructions, and you'll have no trouble.

Doing taxes the right way

You need a couple of other things if you want to do payroll the right way: an employer identification number, a state employer identification number if you withhold state income taxes, an unemployment tax identification number, and some W-4 tax forms. (If you want to do payroll the wrong way, you're reading the wrong book.)

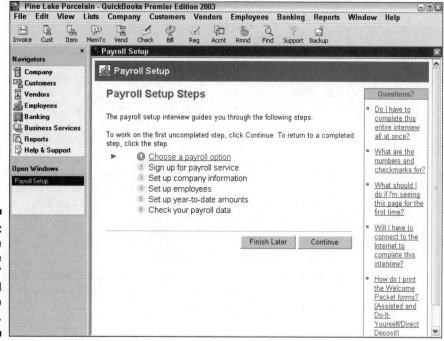

Figure 12-1:
One of the
pages of the
QuickBooks'
Payroll
Setup
wizard.

Getting an employer ID number

To get an employer ID number, you need to file an SS-4, or Request for Employer Identification Number form, with the Internal Revenue Service (IRS) so that you can get an employer identification number. You can get this form at the IRS Web site (www.irs.gov) or by calling the IRS and asking for one.

You can also apply for and receive an employer identification number over the telephone. You still need to fill out the SS-4 form, however, so that you can answer the questions that the IRS asks during the short telephone application process. (You also need to mail or fax the form to the IRS after you have your little telephone conversation.)

Having employees do their part

You also need to do something else before you can know how to handle all those taxes — you need to have each of your employees fill out a W-4 form to tell you what filing status they'll use and how many personal exemptions they'll claim. Guess where you get blank W-4s? From your friendly IRS agent or the IRS Web site (www.irs.gov).

Paying Your Employees

After you subscribe to the QuickBooks Payroll Service, set up your payroll accounts, and get an employer identification number, you're ready to pay someone. This section is going to blow your mind, especially if you've been doing payroll manually. The process makes your whole decision to use QuickBooks to do your payroll worthwhile. Here's how:

1. **Start the payroll process by choosing Employees⇨Pay Employees.**

   Or select Employees in the Navigators list and click the Pay Employees icon. The Select Employees to Pay window appears, which simply lists employees, their salaries or hourly wages, and the last payroll date. If you don't see a name that you're looking for in this list, then you never added the employee to your Employee list. If you need help adding employees to your list, read Chapter 2.

2. **Change any settings that you want to.**

   You shouldn't need to use any of the Select Employees to Pay window's boxes and buttons to change the way that QuickBooks does payroll. But you can make several changes:

   • If you're not going to print the checks — maybe you handwrite them and just use QuickBooks to keep the books — leave the To Be Printed check box selected.

   • Confirm the bank account from which the employees are paid in the Bank Account drop-down list box.

   • Typically, you want to leave the Enter Hours and Preview Check before Creating option selected, just in case. With this option selected, QuickBooks displays a summary preview for each paycheck you create. If you select the other option, Create Check Without Preview Using Hours Below and Last Quantities, QuickBooks doesn't let you check its work first — QuickBooks just creates the checks.

   • Set the Check Date and the Pay Period Ends dates appropriately.

3. **Select the employees whom you're paying and click the Create button.**

   If you're paying all the employees listed, just click the Mark All button on the right side of the Select Employees to Pay screen. If you need to mark the employees individually, just click next to each one in the left column — the column with the check mark in the heading. Then Click the Create button to have QuickBooks create "draft" versions of each of the payroll checks you need for employees. QuickBooks next displays the Preview Paycheck window if you indicated in Step 2 that you want to preview payroll checks. In essence, this window simply summarizes what you pay an employee. For example, if Joe worked 80 hours and he earns $15 an hour, the window shows you owe Joe $1,200. The window also shows the payroll tax and withholding amounts QuickBooks, ever the faithful companion, has calculated for you.

4. **Fill out the payroll information, as necessary.**

   The main thing to pay attention to in the Preview Paycheck window is the Earnings box. It shows what QuickBooks assumes you'll pay an employee. In the Earnings box, you fill in the number of hours the person worked and apply these hours to a customer or job, if necessary.

   The Preview Paycheck window also includes an Other Payroll Items input area. In the Other Payroll Items box, you enter commissions, additions (such as tips, bonuses, and expense reimbursements), deductions (such as union dues and 401(k) contributions), and company contributions (such as insurance benefits or 401(k) matching amounts). You also can change the payroll item or rate or add another payroll item, if you need to.

   Watch this. QuickBooks calculates the company and employee taxes and the amount of the net check — this information appears in the Employee Summary area of the Preview Paycheck window and the Company Summary area of the Preview Paycheck window. If some information is inaccurate, simply click the amount and change it, either by deleting it or replacing it with the correct information.

   You may also note that QuickBooks keeps totals both for the current check and for the year to date.

5. **Click the Create button to record the paycheck transaction.**

   After you check all the employees' paychecks, QuickBooks returns to the Select Employees to Pay dialog box.

6. **Print the checks.**

You can print checks from the Select Employees to Pay window by clicking the Print Paychecks button. QuickBooks prints paychecks just like it prints regular checks.

Got questions about printing checks? Take a look at Chapter 10.

Paying Payroll Liabilities

Make no mistake. Big Brother wants the money you withhold from an employee's payroll check for federal income taxes, Social Security, and Medicare. Big Brother also wants the payroll taxes you owe — the matching Social Security and Medicare taxes, federal unemployment taxes, and so on. So every so often you need to pay Big Brother the amounts you owe.

If you withhold money from employees' checks for other reasons (perhaps for health insurance or retirement savings), these amounts are payroll liabilities that need to be paid to the appropriate party.

Paying tax liabilities if you use the Deluxe Payroll Service

Fortunately, if you're using the QuickBooks Deluxe Payroll Service, your federal tax liabilities and most (perhaps all) of your state tax liabilities are paid as part of the service. In other words, Intuit withdraws money from your bank account and uses this money to pay the appropriate federal or state government agency.

Be sure to check which state payroll taxes QuickBooks calculates and will pay. In Washington state, which is where my business is located, QuickBooks won't calculate a couple of state payroll taxes, so I have to calculate these myself (on the payroll tax form) and pay them with a check.

Paying tax liabilities if you use the Basic Payroll Service

If you're using the Basic Payroll Service, you need to pay the payroll liabilities yourself. To do this, choose Employees➪Pay Payroll Liabilities, whereupon the Select Date Range for Liabilities dialog box appears. Select the appropriate date range and click OK. When you do so, QuickBooks displays the Pay Liabilities window, as shown in Figure 12-2.

All you have to do now is choose the liabilities or taxes that you want to pay by clicking in the left column and indicating the portion you want to pay of the amount due. Unless you've selected the Review Liability Check to Enter Expenses/Penalties option, QuickBooks automatically writes the check and puts it in your register. QuickBooks automatically gives the check the appropriate date and schedules it to pop up in your Reminders window at the right time.

When do you make payroll tax deposits? That's a question that frequently comes up. The general rule about United States federal tax deposits is this: If your accumulated payroll taxes are less than $500 for the quarter, you can just pay those taxes the following month with your quarterly return. This law is called the De Minimis rule. (My understanding is that the law was named after Congresswoman Dee Minimis.) If you owe $500 or more, other special rules come into play that determine whether you pay deposits monthly, semimonthly, weekly, or even immediately. The IRS tells you, by the way, how often you're supposed to make payments.

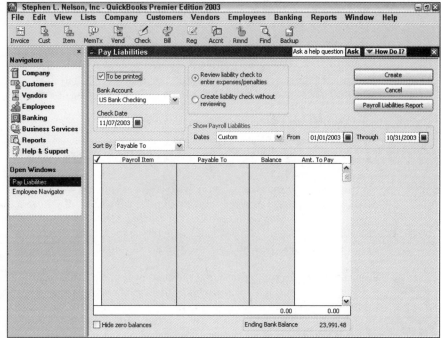

Figure 12-2:
The Pay
Liabilities
window.

If you owe a large amount of money, you're required to deposit it almost immediately. For example, if you owe $100,000 or more, you need to make the payroll tax deposit by the next banking day. Some nuances apply to these rules, so unless you don't owe very much and, therefore, can fall back on the De Minimis rule, you may want to consult a real, live tax adviser (or call the Internal Revenue Service).

The general rule when writing payroll checks is to make the last checks you write the ones that pay your federal and state tax deposits when they come due. You'll never get into late payment trouble if you follow this approach. It will also make your life a lot easier when it comes time to fill out Schedule B of Form 941, if you have to do so.

To make a payroll tax deposit, just deliver your check with a federal tax deposit coupon to a financial institution that's qualified as a depository for federal taxes or to the Federal Reserve Bank that serves your geographical area. The IRS should have already sent you a book of coupons as a result of your asking for an employer ID number. And one other thing: Make your check payable to the depository or to the Federal Reserve.

Paying Other Non-Tax Liabilities

If you're paying non-tax liabilities for things like employee health insurance or retirement savings — it doesn't matter whether you're using the Basic Payroll Service or the Deluxe Payroll Service — you also use the Pay Payroll Liabilities command (which I describe in the preceding section).

Preparing Quarterly Payroll Tax Returns

At the end of every quarter, you need to file a quarterly payroll tax return. (By quarters here, I'm referring to calendar quarters.) If you're a business owner, for example, you must file a Form 941, which is just a form that you fill out to say how much you paid in gross wages, how much you withheld in federal taxes, and how much you owe for employer payroll taxes.

If you have to fill out Schedule B of Form 941, I hope that you heeded my earlier advice and just paid the liabilities as they came due. This step makes filling out Schedule B a piece of cake: The date your liability check was due is the same as the date you wrote and deposited the check. You can use QuickBooks to create a list of all the dates on which you wrote liabilities checks in the quarter by finding just one liabilities check in your register and then clicking the QuickReport button. Then set the date for the correct quarter. QuickBooks produces a list of your liabilities checks in the blink of an eye. If, on the other hand, you didn't always pay your liabilities as they came due, you need to open your Payroll Liabilities account and scroll through the whole quarter to find the day your balance went over $500.

If you have household employees, such as a nanny, you must file a Form 942. Again, Form 942 is just a form you fill out to say how much you paid in gross wages, withheld in federal taxes, and owe in payroll taxes.

You'll find that QuickBooks makes filling out these forms darn simple.

Using the QuickBooks Assisted Payroll Service

If you're using the QuickBooks Assisted Payroll Service, the service fills out and sends the payroll tax forms for you.

Using the QuickBooks Do-It-Yourself Payroll Service

If you're using the Do-It-Yourself Payroll Service, you need to fill out and send the payroll tax forms, but don't worry — QuickBooks prepares the 941 for you. If you need to fill out the 942 or a state payroll tax form, QuickBooks can also be of great help. All you really need to know for these other forms is what the gross wages totals are.

To get the gross wages totals and the balances in each of the payroll tax liability accounts at the end of the quarter, print the payroll summary report. Choose Reports⇨Employees & Payroll⇨Payroll Summary. QuickBooks displays the Payroll Summary report. Specify the range of dates as the quarter for which you're preparing a quarterly report. Scroll across to the Total column, which shows the gross wages upon which your employer payroll taxes are calculated.

The withholding account amounts are the amounts you've recorded to date for the employee's federal income taxes withheld and the employee's Social Security and Medicare taxes, so you need to double these figures to get the actual Social Security and Medicare taxes owed. Choose Reports⇨Employees & Payroll⇨Payroll Liabilities. QuickBooks creates a report that tallies these amounts.

QuickBooks will create and print out a copy of Form 941 for you, so you don't have to get out your calculator or mess around with lining up the red form in your typewriter. Just choose Employees⇨Process Payroll Forms and then click the button for the appropriate form. QuickBooks runs you through a wizard that asks you for your state and the number of employees you had over the quarter. QuickBooks then summarizes each line of the form. When QuickBooks is all done, all you have to do is print out the form, and you're done.

By the way, if your accountant fills out the 941 or 942 form for you, you don't even need to read this stuff. Your accountant won't have any problem completing the quarterly payroll tax return by using the QuickBooks Payroll report, and in fact — I kid you not — your accountant will probably even enjoy doing it.

Filing Annual Returns and Wage Statements

At the end of the year, you need to file some annual returns — such as the 940 federal unemployment tax return — and the W-2 and W-3 wages statements.

Note that you need to prepare any state unemployment annual summary before you prepare the 940 because the 940 requires information from the state returns.

Using the QuickBooks Assisted Payroll Service

If you're using the Assisted Payroll Service, the service automatically fills out and sends these forms for you.

Using the QuickBooks Do-It-Yourself Payroll Service

If you're using the Do-It-Yourself Payroll Service, you need to fill out and send these forms in-house, but you get lots of help from QuickBooks. QuickBooks creates and prints the 940 for you. All you have to do is choose Employees⇔ Process Payroll Forms and click the button for the appropriate form. QuickBooks asks you for a little information, and then it does the calculating for you. Just check the QuickBooks records against your own, and if everything matches, print that puppy out. To look over the QuickBooks data included in the form and verify its integrity, it helps to print an Employee Earnings Summary report.

For the W-2 statements and the summary W-3 (which summarizes your W-2s), you just choose Employees⇔Process W-2s. Select the employees from the list and print away.

If you have a little trouble, call the IRS. If you have a great deal of trouble, splurge and have someone else fill out the forms for you. Filling out these forms doesn't take a rocket scientist, by the way. Any experienced bookkeeper can do it for you.

Please don't construe my "rocket scientist" comment as personal criticism if this payroll taxes business seems terribly complicated. My experience is that some people — and you may very well be one of them — just don't have an interest in things such as payroll accounting. If, on the other hand, you're a "numbers are my friend" kind of person, you'll have no trouble at all after you learn the ropes.

The State Wants Some Money, Too

Yeah. I haven't talked about state payroll taxes — at least not in any great detail. I wish that I could provide this sort of detailed, state-specific help to you. Unfortunately, doing so would make this chapter about 150 pages long. It would also cause me to go stark raving mad.

My sanity and laziness aside, however, you still need to deal with state payroll taxes. Let me say, however, that you apply to state payroll taxes the same basic mechanics that you apply to federal payroll taxes. For example, a state income tax works the same way as the federal income tax; employer-paid state unemployment taxes work like the employer-paid federal taxes; and employee-paid state taxes work like the employee-paid Social Security and Medicare taxes.

If you've tuned in to how federal payroll taxes work in QuickBooks, you really shouldn't have a problem with the state payroll taxes — at least, not in terms of mechanics. Note, however, that QuickBooks can print only federal forms, not state forms, so you'll need to fill in those yourself.

The one thing you need to figure out is what your state wants. To do that, you need to get the state's payroll tax reporting instructions. You may need to call the state. Or with a little luck, you may find online instructions at your state's Web site. If your state's Web site isn't much help, you can probably look up the state tax people's telephone in your local phone book.

Chapter 13

The Balancing Act

1 want to start this chapter with an important point: Balancing a bank account in QuickBooks is easy and quick.

I'm not just trying to get you pumped up about an otherwise painfully boring topic. I don't think that balancing a bank account is any more exciting than you do.

My point is simply this: Because bank account balancing can be tedious and boring, use QuickBooks to speed up the drudgery.

Balancing a Non-Online Bank Account

As I said, balancing a bank account is remarkably easy in QuickBooks. In fact, I'll go so far as to say that if you have any problems, they stem from . . . well, sloppy record keeping that preceded your use of QuickBooks.

Enough of this blather; I'll get started by describing how you reconcile a non-online account. By this awkward label, "non-online bank account," I just mean a bank account that isn't an account set up for online banking. I describe the steps for balancing online accounts in the section "Balancing an Online Bank Account" later in this chapter.

Giving QuickBooks information from the bank statement

As you probably know, in a *reconciliation*, you compare your records of a bank account with the bank's records of the same account. You should be able to explain any difference between the two accounts — usually by pointing to checks that you've written but that haven't cleared. (Sometimes deposits fall into the same category; you've recorded a deposit and mailed it, but the bank hasn't yet credited your account.)

The first step, then, is to supply QuickBooks with the bank's account information. You get this information from your monthly statement. Supply QuickBooks with the figures it needs, as follows:

1. **Tell QuickBooks you want to reconcile an account.**

   You can do this by choosing the Banking⇨Reconcile command or by selecting Banking from the Navigators list and clicking the Reconcile icon. QuickBooks displays the Begin Reconciliation dialog box, as shown in Figure 13-1.

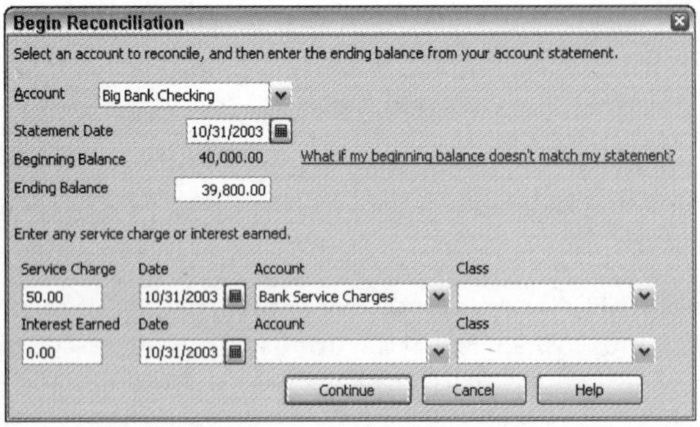

Figure 13-1:
The Begin Reconcilia-tion dialog box.

2. **Tell QuickBooks which account you want to reconcile.**

   Verify that the bank account shown in the Account list box is correct. If it isn't — and it might not be if you have several bank accounts — open the Account list box and select the correct account.

3. **Enter the bank statement date into the Statement Date box.**

   Remember that you can adjust a date one day at a time by using the plus (+) and minus (–) keys. You can also click the Calendar button on the right side of the text box to select a date from the calendar. See the Cheat Sheet at the front of this book for a list of other secret date-editing tricks.

4. **Verify the bank statement opening balance.**

   QuickBooks displays an amount in the Beginning Balance text box. (Refer to Figure 13-1.)

If the opening balance isn't correct, see the sidebar "Why isn't my opening balance the same as the one in QuickBooks?" elsewhere in this chapter.

5. **Enter the ending balance.**

   What is the ending, or closing, balance on your bank statement? Whatever it is, move the cursor to the Ending Balance text box and enter the ending balance.

6. **Enter the bank's service charge.**

   If the bank statement shows a service charge and you haven't already entered it, move the cursor to the Service Charge text box and type the amount.

7. **Enter a transaction date for the service charge transaction.**

   QuickBooks adds one month to the service charge date from the last time you reconciled. If this date isn't correct, type the correct one.

8. **Assign the bank's service charge to an account.**

   Enter the expense account to which you assign bank service charges in the first Account text box — the one beside the Date text box. Activate the drop-down list by clicking the down arrow, highlight the category by using the arrow keys, and press Enter. I bet anything that you record these charges in the Bank Service Charges account that QuickBooks sets up by default.

   If you told QuickBooks that you also want to track income and expense amounts using classes, QuickBooks adds Class boxes to the Begin Reconciliation dialog box so that you can collect this information. Figure 13-1 shows these boxes, for example.

9. **Enter the account's interest income.**

   If the account earned interest for the month and you haven't already entered this figure, type an amount in the Interest Earned text box (for example, type **9.17** for $9.17).

10. **Enter a transaction date for the interest income transaction.**

    You already know how to enter dates. I won't bore you by explaining it again (but see Step 3 if you're having trouble).

11. **Assign the interest to an account.**

    Enter the account to which this account's interest should be assigned in the second Account text box. I bet that you record this one under the Interest Income account, which is near the bottom of the Account drop-down list. To select a category from the Account list, activate the drop-down list by clicking the down arrow, highlight the category, and press Enter.

12. **Click Continue.**

After you supply the information that the Begin Reconciliation dialog box asks for, click the Continue button. QuickBooks displays the Reconcile window, as shown in Figure 13-2.

Marking cleared checks and deposits

Using the Reconcile window shown in Figure 13-2, you tell QuickBooks which deposits and checks have cleared at the bank. (Refer to the bank statement for this information.)

1. **Identify the first deposit that has cleared.**

You know how to do so, I'm sure. Just leaf through the bank statement and find the first deposit listed.

2. **Mark the first cleared deposit as cleared.**

Scroll through the transactions listed in the Deposits and Other Credits section of the Reconcile window, find the deposit, and then click it. You also can highlight the deposit by using the Tab and arrow keys and then pressing the space bar. QuickBooks places a check mark in front of the deposit to mark it as cleared and updates the cleared statement balance.

If you have a large number of deposits to make and you can identify them quickly, click the Mark All button and then simply unmark the transactions that aren't on the bank statement. To unmark a transaction, click it. The check mark disappears.

3. **Record any cleared, but missing, deposits.**

If you can't find a deposit, you haven't entered it into the Checking register yet. I can only guess why you haven't entered it. Maybe you just forgot. Close or deactivate the Reconcile window. Now open the Checking register and enter the deposit in the register in the usual way. To return to the Reconcile window, either re-open it or re-activate it.

4. **Repeat Steps 1, 2, and 3 for all deposits listed on the bank statement.**

Make sure that the dates match and that the amounts of the deposits are also correct. If they're not, go back to the transaction and correct them. To get to the transaction, click the Go To button. You see the Write Checks or Make Deposits window where the transaction was originally recorded. Make the corrections there and click Save & Close.

5. **Identify the first check that has cleared.**

No sweat, right? Just find the first check or withdrawal listed on the bank statement.

6. **Mark the first cleared check as cleared.**

Scroll through the transactions listed in the Checks and Payments section of the Reconcile window, find the first check, and then click it. You also can highlight it by pressing Tab and an arrow key. Then press the space bar. QuickBooks inserts a check mark to label this transaction as cleared and updates the cleared statement balance.

7. **Record any missing, but cleared, checks.**

If you can't find a check or withdrawal — guess what? — you haven't entered it in the register yet. Close or deactivate the Reconcile window by clicking its Close button or activating another window. Then display the Checking register and enter the check or withdrawal. To return to the Reconcile window, re-open or re-activate it.

8. **Repeat Steps 5, 6, and 7 for all withdrawals listed on the bank statement.**

By the way, these steps don't take very long. Reconciling my account each month takes me about two minutes. And I'm not joking or exaggerating. By two minutes, I really mean two minutes.

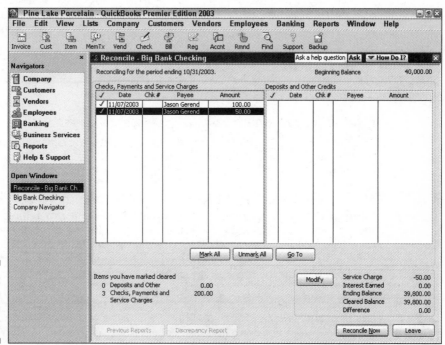

Figure 13-2:
The
Reconcile
window.

Why isn't my opening balance the same as the one in QuickBooks?

An opening balance that isn't the same as the one shown in the Opening Balance text box can mean a couple of things.

First, you may have mistakenly cleared a transaction the last time you reconciled. If you cleared a transaction last month that didn't go through until this month, your opening balance is wrong. Go back to the Checking register and start examining transactions. Each one that's cleared has a check mark next to it in the narrow column between the Payment and Deposit columns. If one of the checks that appears on this month's statement has a check mark, you made a boo-boo last month. From the Checking register, click the check mark to remove it. You're asked to confirm your actions. The check now appears in the Reconcile window.

The other reason why the opening balance is different can be that a transaction that you cleared in the past got changed. If you deleted a transaction that occurred before this reconciliation period, for example, it threw your balance off. Why? Because the transaction that you deleted helped balance your account the last time around, but now that transaction is gone.

Whatever happens, don't fret. If worse comes to worst and you can't track down the faulty transaction, you can just have QuickBooks adjust the balance for you, which I explain elsewhere in this chapter. If you frequently find that your accounts don't balance, you might want to consider using the QuickBooks Audit Trail feature to track the changes you make to transactions, and then create an Audit Trail report when it comes time to reconcile your accounts. To turn on the Audit Trail feature, choose Edit⇨ Preferences, click the Accounting icon, and select the Use Audit Trail check box on the Company Preferences tab.

If the difference equals zero

After you mark all the cleared checks and deposits, the difference between the Cleared Balance for the account and the bank statement's Ending Balance should equal zero. Notice that I said "should," not "will."

If the difference does equal zero, you're finished. Just click the Reconcile Now button. QuickBooks displays a congratulatory message box telling you that the reconciliation is complete. As a reward for being such a good boy or girl, the message box asks you whether you want to print a free, all-expenses-paid Summary or Full reconciliation report. Click Summary or Full and click OK if you want to print the report. Otherwise, just click OK.

Can't decide whether to print the reconciliation report? Unless you're a business bookkeeper or an accountant who is reconciling a bank account for someone else — your employer or a client, for example — you don't need to print the reconciliation report. All printing does is prove that you reconciled the account. (Basically, this proof is the reason why you should print the report if you're a bookkeeper or an accountant. The person for whom you're reconciling the account will know that you did your job and has a piece of paper to come back to later with any questions.)

Now each deposit, withdrawal, and check that you just cleared is marked with a check mark in your register. If you don't believe me, open the register and find out.

If the difference doesn't equal zero

If the difference doesn't equal zero, you have a problem. If you click Reconcile Now, QuickBooks shows you the Reconcile Adjustment dialog box, as shown in Figure 13-3. This dialog box tells you how unbalanced your account is and asks whether you want to adjust your maladjusted account.

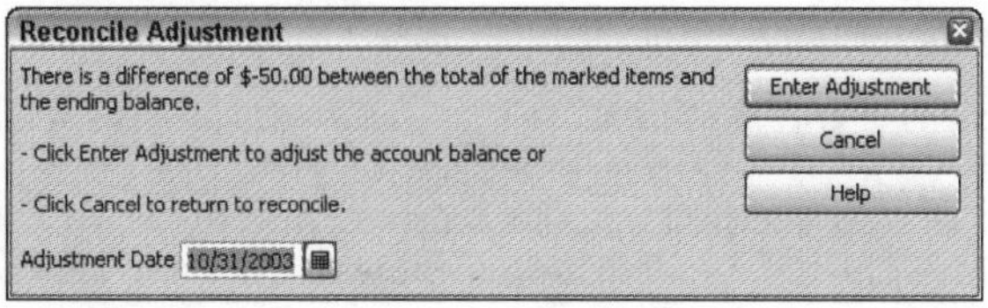

Figure 13-3:
The
Reconcile
Adjustment
dialog box.

> **Reconcile Adjustment**
>
> There is a difference of $-50.00 between the total of the marked items and the ending balance.
>
> - Click Enter Adjustment to adjust the account balance or
>
> - Click Cancel to return to reconcile.
>
> Adjustment Date 10/31/2003
>
> Enter Adjustment
> Cancel
> Help

Click Cancel if you want to go back to the Reconcile window and start the search for the missing or incorrectly entered transaction.

If you want to force the two amounts to agree, click OK. Forcing the two amounts to agree isn't a very good idea. To do so, QuickBooks adds a cleared transaction equal to the difference. (I talk about this transaction a little later in the chapter.)

Postponing a reconciliation (by clicking Cancel) and not choosing to adjust the bank account balance is usually the best approach because then you can locate and correct problems. (The next section contains some ideas that can help you determine what the problem is.) Then you can restart the reconciliation and finish your work. (You restart a reconciliation the same way that you originate one.)

Ten Things to Do If Your Non-Online Account Doesn't Balance

I want to give you some suggestions for reconciling an account when you're having problems. If you're sitting in front of your computer wringing your hands, try the tips in this section:

✔ **Make sure that you're working with the right account:** Sounds dumb, doesn't it? If you have several different bank accounts, however, ending up in the wrong account is darn easy. So go ahead and confirm, for example, that you're trying to reconcile your checking account at Mammoth International Bank by using the Mammoth International Bank checking account statement.

✔ **Look for transactions that the bank has recorded but you haven't:** Go through the bank statement and make sure that you've recorded every transaction that your bank has recorded. You can easily overlook cash machine withdrawals, special fees, or service charges (such as charges for checks or your safe-deposit box), automatic withdrawals, direct deposits, and so on.

If the difference is positive — that is, the bank thinks that you have less money than you think that you should have — you may be missing a withdrawal transaction. If the difference is negative, you may be missing a deposit transaction.

✔ **Look for reversed transactions.** Here's a tricky one: If you accidentally enter a transaction backward — a deposit as a withdrawal or a withdrawal as a deposit — your account doesn't balance. And the error can be difficult to find. The Reconcile window shows all the correct transactions, but a transaction amount appears in the wrong list. (The amount appears in the Deposits and Other Credits list if it belongs in the Checks and Payments list or vice versa.) The check that you wrote to Acme Housewreckers for the demolition of your carport appears in the Deposits and Other Credits list, for example.

✔ **Look for a transaction that's equal to half the difference:** One handy way to find the transaction that you entered backward — if you have only one — is to look for a transaction that's equal to half the irreconcilable difference. If the difference is $200, for example, you may have entered a $100 deposit as a withdrawal or a $100 withdrawal as a deposit.

✔ **Look for a transaction that's equal to the difference:** While I'm on the subject of explaining the difference by looking at individual transactions, I'll make an obvious point: If the difference between the bank's records and yours equals one of the transactions listed in your register, you may have incorrectly marked the transaction as cleared or incorrectly left the transaction unmarked (shown as uncleared). I don't know. Maybe that was too obvious. Naaaah.

✔ **Check for transposed numbers:** Transposed numbers occur when you flip-flop two digits in a number. For example, you enter $45.89 as $48.59. These turkeys always cause headaches for accountants and bookkeepers. If you look at the numbers, detecting an error is often difficult because the digits are the same. For example, when you compare a check amount of $45.89 in your register with a check for $48.59 shown on your bank statement, both check amounts show the same digits: 4, 5, 8, and 9. They just show them in different orders.

Transposed numbers are tough to find, but here's a trick that you can try. Divide the difference shown in the Reconcile window by 9. If the result is an even number of dollars or cents, chances are good that you have a transposed number somewhere.

✔ **Have someone else look over your work:** This idea may seem pretty obvious, but I'm amazed at how often a second pair of eyes can find something that I've been overlooking. Ask one of your coworkers or employees (preferably that one person who always seems to have way too much free time) to look over everything for you.

✔ **Be on the lookout for multiple errors:** If you find an error by using this laundry list and you still have a difference, start checking at the top of the list again. You may, for example, discover after you find a transposed number that you entered another transaction backward or incorrectly cleared or uncleared a transaction.

✔ **Try again next month (and maybe the month after that):** If the difference isn't huge in relation to the size of your bank account, you may want to wait until next month and attempt to reconcile your account again.

Before my carefree attitude puts you in a panic, consider the following example: In January, you reconcile your account, and the difference is $24.02. Then you reconcile the account in February, and the difference is $24.02. You reconcile the account in March and, surprise, surprise, the difference is still $24.02. What's going on here? Well, your starting account balance was probably off by $24.02. (The more months you try to reconcile your account and find that you're always mysteriously $24.02 off, the more likely that this type of error is to blame.) After the second or third month, I think that having QuickBooks enter an adjusting transaction of $24.02 is pretty reasonable so that your account balances. (In my opinion, this circumstance is the only one that merits your adjusting an account to match the bank's figure.)

If you've successfully reconciled your account with QuickBooks before, your work may not be at fault. The mistake may be (drumroll, please) the bank's! And in this case, you should do something else. . . .

✔ **Get in your car, drive to the bank, and beg for help:** As an alternative to the preceding idea — which supposes that the bank's statement is correct and that your records are incorrect — I propose this idea: Ask the bank to help you reconcile the account. Hint that you think the mistake is probably the bank's, but in a very nice, cordial way. Smile a lot. And one other thing — be sure to ask about whatever product the bank is currently advertising in the lobby (which encourages the staff to think that you're interested in that 180-month certificate of deposit, causing them to be extra nice to you).

In general, the bank's record keeping is usually pretty darn good. I've never had a problem either with my business or personal accounts. (I've also been lucky enough to deal with big, well-run banks.) Nevertheless, your bank quite possibly has made a mistake, so ask for help. Be sure to ask for an explanation of any transactions that you discover only by seeing them on your bank statement. By the way, you'll probably pay for this help.

Balancing an Online Bank Account

In a nutshell, you don't actually reconcile the bank when you balance a bank account that you've set up for online banking. Every time you send online payments or transfers to the bank, QuickBooks retrieves a list of recent bank account transactions — essentially an online bank statement. You can and should compare these statements to your own records.

To make this comparison, take the following steps:

1. **Send your online banking transactions in the usual way.**

   I won't repeat the discussion that I provide in Chapter 11; heck, you know how to turn a few pages. But all you do is choose the Banking➪ Online Banking Center command, click the Send button, and provide your PIN when prompted.

2. **Display the online statement.**

   After you exchange information with the bank, double-click the bank statement item in the Items Received From Financial Institution list. This list appears at the very bottom of the Online Banking Center window, so even though I'm not providing a figure, you'll have no trouble locating the darn thing. After you do double-click the statement, QuickBooks displays the Match Transactions window. The Match Transactions window, which isn't shown here, is just a special version of the Register window. The top half of the window, in fact, shows the bank account using the traditional Register window format. The bottom half of the window provides a list of downloaded transactions that you "match" to transactions already recorded in your register.

3. **Add missing transactions.**

   To add transactions that your bank shows (such as banking service fees or interest income) but are missing in your register, click the transaction in the online transactions list and then click the Add to Register button. QuickBooks partially records the transaction into the register. You need to complete the recording — such as by adding the account and by clicking Record.

4. **Match transactions.**

   QuickBooks attempts to match transactions in the online statement (shown in the bottom half of the Match Transactions window) with those you recorded for the bank account (shown in the top half of the Match Transactions window). If QuickBooks matches a transaction, it marks the online transaction as "match." You can manually match a transaction, however, by clicking the transaction in both the online transactions list and the bank register and then clicking the Match button. (To unmatch a transaction, duh, you click the Unmatch button.)

5. **Click Done.**

   At the point that you've added any missing transactions and matched all the transactions, you're done. You've essentially reconciled the account. Click the Done button. QuickBooks returns you to the Online Banking Center window.

Chapter 14

Reporting On the State of Affairs

. . . .

In This Chapter

▶ Printing QuickBooks reports

▶ Using the Reports menu commands

▶ QuickZooming report totals

▶ Sharing information with a spreadsheet

▶ Editing and rearranging report information

▶ Processing Multiple Reports

▶ Using QuickReports

. . . .

*O*ne of the fastest ways to find out whether your business is thriving or diving is to use the QuickBooks Reports feature. The different kinds of reports in QuickBooks cover everything from invoices to missing checks, not to mention QuickReports. QuickReports are summary reports that you can get from the information on forms, account registers, or lists by merely clicking the mouse.

In this chapter, I tell you how to prepare reports, how to print them, and how to customize reports for your special needs.

What Kinds of Reports Are There, Anyway?

If you run a small business, you don't need all the reports that QuickBooks offers, but many of these reports are extremely useful. Reports can show you how healthy or unhealthy your business is, where your profits are, and where you're wasting time and squandering resources.

To make sense of what may otherwise become mass confusion, QuickBooks organizes all its reports in categories. You can see what all the categories are by pulling down the Reports menu. The names of the reports read a bit like public television documentary names, don't they? "Tonight, Joob Taylor explores the mazelike federal budget in Budget Reports." You select a report category to see a list of actual report names.

In Table 14-1, I describe reports by category, along with a short description of the major reports in each category. To get a thorough description of a particular report, go to the Help feature. To find out what a standard profit and loss report does, for example, choose Help➪Help Index. Type **profit** in the text box and then double-click the profit and loss reports entry. The screen displays a list of topics relating to profit and loss reports. To read the details about a topic, double-click that topic in the list.

Table 14-1	QuickBooks Report Categories
Report Category	*Description*
Company & Financial	These reports give you a bird's-eye view of your company's health and cash flow. They give you a snapshot of your assets, liabilities, and equity, showing income, expenses, and net profit or loss over time.
Customers & Receivables	These accounts receivable reports are great for finding out where you stand in regard to your customer invoices. You can list unpaid invoices and group them in various ways, including by customer, job, and aging status.
Sales	These reports show what you've sold and who your customers are. You can see your sales by item, by customer, or by sales representative.
Jobs & Time	These reports let you see job and item profitability, compare job estimates versus actual costs, and view time recorded on jobs and activities.
Vendors & Payables	These accounts payable reports tell you everything you need to know about your unpaid bills. You can list bills in a variety of ways, including by vendor and by aging status. This category also includes a report for determining sales tax liability.

Report Category	Description
Purchases	These reports show from whom you bought, what you bought, and how much you paid. You can list purchases by item or by vendor. One handy report shows any outstanding purchase orders.
Inventory	These reports help answer the ever-important question, "What items do I have in stock?" You can get an enormous amount of detail from these reports. For example, you can find out how many of an item you have on hand and how many you have on order. You can group inventory by vendor or by item. If you need price lists, you can print them by using a special report from your QuickBooks file.
Employees & Payroll	These reports offer ways to track payroll or check your payroll liability accounts. Believe me, these reports come in handy.
Banking	These reports list checks and deposits.
Accountant & Taxes	These reports include income tax reports, journal and general ledger reports, and a trial balance.
Budget	These reports show you once and for all whether your budgeting skills are realistic. You can view budgets by job, by month, or by balance sheet account. Then you can compare the budgets to actual income and expense totals. (You need to have a budget already set up to use this report — something I discuss in Chapter 15.)
List	These reports let you see your lists in detail. For example, you can see the contacts, phone numbers, and addresses on your Customer, Vendor, or Other Names lists. You also can create a detailed report of your inventory.

If you're not sure which report you need to create, you can use the Report Finder. Just choose Reports⇨Report Finder, select a report type from the drop-down list box at the top of the Report Finder window (see Figure 14-1), and then select a report from the list to preview that report. You can specify the date range you want to include in the report by using the other boxes in the Report Finder window. Then click Display to display the report.

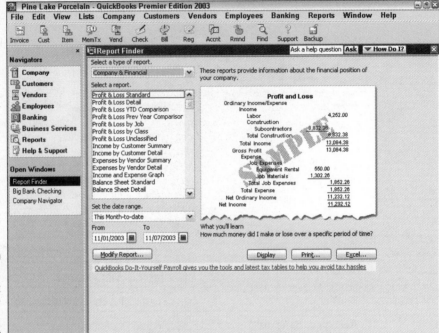

Figure 14-1:
The Report
Finder
window.

Creating and Printing a Report

After you decide what report you need, all you have to do is select it from the
appropriate menu. To create a standard profit and loss report, for example,
choose Reports⇨Company & Financial⇨Profit & Loss Standard.

Depending on how much data QuickBooks has to process, you may see a
Building Report box before the report appears on-screen in all its glory.
Figure 14-2 shows a standard profit and loss report, also called an *income
statement*. (If you see a Customize Report dialog box instead of a report,
you can tell QuickBooks to change this option. To do so, choose Edit⇨
Preferences. Then click the Reports & Graphs icon from the list on the left.
And click the My Preferences tab if you have one and it isn't already selected.
Then remove the check in the Display Customize Report Window
Automatically box.)

You can't see the entire on-screen version of a report unless your report is
very small (or your screen is monstrously large). Use the Page Up and Page
Down keys on your keyboard to scroll up and down, and use the Tab and
Shift+Tab keys to move left and right. Or, if you're a mouse lover, you can use
the scroll bar.

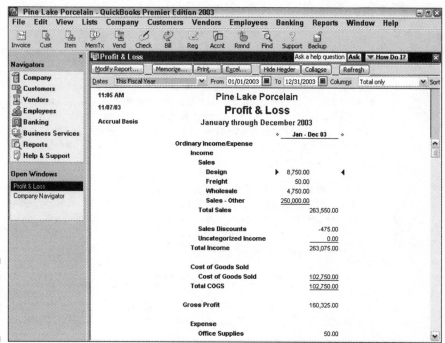

Figure 14-2:
A standard profit and loss report.

To print a report, click the Print button at the top of the report. QuickBooks displays the Print Reports dialog box, as shown in Figure 14-3. To accept the given specifications, which are almost always fine, just click the Print button. You'll never guess what happens next: QuickBooks prints the report!

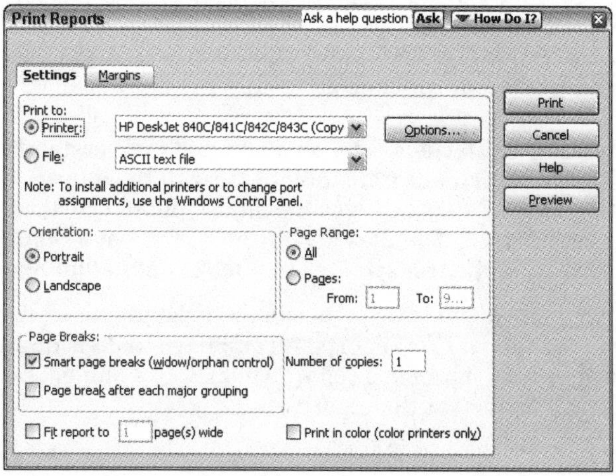

Figure 14-3:
The Print Reports dialog box.

The first time you print a report, QuickBooks displays a Printing Features dialog box that explains a few things about the mechanics of choosing and printing reports.

Before I forget, I want to tell you that you can click the File option button in the Print To panel to tell QuickBooks to save the report as a file instead of printing it. You can then choose the file format: ASCII, Comma Delimited File, and Tab Delimited File. You can use either delimited file format if you want to later open the file with a spreadsheet program such as Microsoft Excel. After you click Print, use the Create Disk File dialog box to specify the filename and storage location.

The Orientation setting tells QuickBooks how the report is supposed to appear on the paper. The Page Range settings specify the pages you want to print. The Fit Report to Page(s) Wide check box enables you to shrink the report so that it fits on the number of pages you specify. And the purpose of the Print in Color check box is probably pretty self-evident.

QuickBooks includes two page break options for creating easier-to-read reports:

✔ Click the first check box to keep items that belong in the same group on the same page.

✔ Click the second check box to give each major group its own page.

You also can preview the report by clicking the Preview button. In the next section, I describe how some of the options for the preview work.

Visiting the report dog-and-pony show

You can do some neat things with the reports you create. Here's a quick run-down of some of the most valuable tricks:

✔ **QuickZooming mysterious figures:** If you don't understand where a number in a report comes from, point to it with the mouse. As you point to numbers, QuickBooks changes the mouse pointer to a magnifying glass marked with a Z. Double-click the mouse to have QuickBooks display a list of all the transactions that make up that number.

This feature, called QuickZoom, is extremely handy for understanding the figures that appear on reports. All you have to do is double-click any mysterious-looking figure in a report. QuickBooks immediately tells you exactly how it arrived at that figure.

✔ **Sharing report data with Microsoft Excel:** If you're using QuickBooks Pro, you can export report data to a Microsoft Excel spreadsheet by clicking the Excel button in the report window. QuickBooks displays the Export Report to Excel dialog box. You can use this dialog box to specify whether you want to create a new spreadsheet for the report data or whether you want to add the report data to an existing spreadsheet.

Editing and rearranging reports

You may have noticed that when QuickBooks displays the report document window, it also displays a row of buttons: Modify Report, Print, Memorize, Excel, Refresh, and so on (as you can see in Figure 14-2 if you look carefully). Below this toolbar are some drop-down list boxes that have to do with dates and a drop-down list called Columns. (Not all these list boxes are available in every report document window. I don't know why, really. Maybe just to keep you guessing.)

You don't need to worry about these buttons. Read through the discussion that follows only if you're feeling comfortable, relaxed, and truly mellow, okay?

Modifying

When you click the Modify Report Button, QuickBooks displays the Modify Report dialog box, as shown in Figure 14-4. From this dialog box, you change the information displayed on a report and the way that information is arranged (using the Display tab), the data used to generate the report (using the Filters tab), the header and footer information (using, predictably, the Header/Footer tab), and the typeface and size of print used for a report (using the Fonts & Numbers tab).

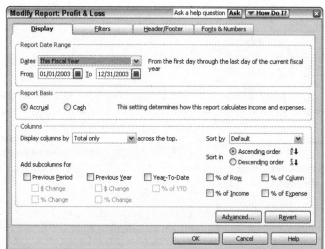

Figure 14-4: The Modify Report dialog box.

Memorizing

If you do play around with the remaining buttons, you can save any custom report specifications that you create. Just click the Memorize button. QuickBooks displays a dialog box that asks you to supply a name for the customized report and assign the memorized report to a report group. (See Figure 14-5.) After you name and assign the customized report, QuickBooks lists it whenever you choose Reports➪Memorized Reports and then the report group. Whenever you want to use your special report, all you need to do is select it from the list and click the Report button.

QuickBooks memorizes the print orientation with the report, so if the print orientation isn't the way you want it for the report, you should first change it by choosing File➪Printer Setup. Select the orientation you want to memorize, click OK, and then memorize the report.

The other buttons and boxes

If you want to see how the Hide Header, Collapse, and Dates stuff works, just noodle around. You can't hurt anything.

If you change the report dates, click the Refresh button to update the report. (To set refresh options for reports, choose Edit➪Preferences. Then click the Reports & Graphs icon from the list on the left and click the My Preferences tab if necessary. Click one of the Reports and Graphs options and click OK.)

Figure 14-5:
The Memorize Report dialog box.

Reports Made to Order

If you intend to print a large number of reports and, more importantly, if you intend to print a large number of reports and show them to customers, investors, and other significant people, you want your reports to look good and be easy to understand. I believe that beauty is in the eye of the beholder, so I'm not going to get into the aesthetics of report layouts. What I am going to do is explain how you can make QuickBooks reports look exactly the way you want them to look.

Choose Edit➪Preferences. Then click the Reports & Graphs icon from the list on the left and the Company Preferences tab to see the Preferences dialog box, shown in Figure 14-6, for reports and graphs.

You need to be logged in single-user mode as the administrator to change company preferences.

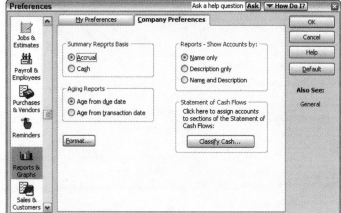

Figure 14-6:
The
Preferences
dialog box
for reports
and graphs.

Here are your options:

- ✔ **Accrual:** *Accrual* is one of those cruel accounting terms that's hard to understand at first. If you choose Accrual in the Summary Reports Basis panel, you tell QuickBooks to date all your transactions, purchases, expenses, and so on, from the moment they're recorded, not from the time you receive or pay cash for them.

   Accountants follow the accrual method because it gives a more accurate picture of profits.

- ✔ **Cash:** If you choose Cash, all the financial transactions in your reports are dated from the time payments are made.

- ✔ **Age from Due Date:** If you click Age from Due Date in the Aging Reports panel, QuickBooks counts your expenses and invoices from the day that they fall due. Otherwise, QuickBooks counts them from the day they're recorded.

- ✔ **Format:** Click the Format button if you want to improve the look of your reports. In the Report Format Preferences dialog box, shown in Figure 14-7, you can use the Header/Footer tab to choose preferences for displaying the company name, the report title, the subtitle, and so on.

    You can use the Fonts & Numbers tab to choose preferences for displaying numbers, decimal fractions, and negative numbers. You also can fool around with different fonts and point sizes for labels, column headings, titles, and other things in your reports.

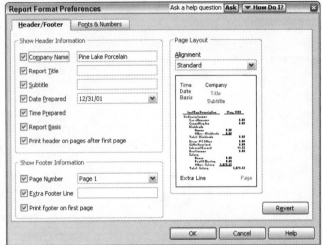

Figure 14-7:
The Report
Format
Preferences
dialog box.

Click the Revert button in the Report Format Preferences dialog box to undo your customization changes.

Processing Multiple Reports

Want to print several reports at once? No problem. Choose Reports⇨Process Multiple Reports. When QuickBooks displays the Process Multiple Reports dialog box, shown in Figure 14-8, select the reports that you want to print.

My technical editor, Mike, wants me to mention that the reports all appear in windows on-screen when you do this. He's concerned, probably rightly so, that some QuickBooks users may be confused by all the open windows. I think that if you remember you can use the Window menu to move from one window to the next, things should work out okay for you.

Figure 14-8:
The Process
Multiple
Reports
dialog box.

Last but Not Least: The QuickReport

The last kind of report is the QuickReport, which is one of the best kinds of reports, so I saved it for last. You can generate a QuickReport from a list, from invoices and bills with names of people or items on them, and from account registers. QuickReports are especially useful when you're studying a list and you see something that momentarily baffles you. Simply make sure that the item you're curious about is highlighted, click the Reports button, and choose the QuickReports command for the item from the drop-down menu.

You can also right-click an item and choose the shortcut menu's QuickReport option to create a QuickReport of the item.

Figure 14-9 shows a QuickReport produced from a Checking register. I clicked the QuickReport button to display this Register QuickReport window with the transaction information for a vendor, one Jason Gerend.

The QuickReport option is also on the Reports menu. You can display a QuickReport from a form — even though no QuickReport button appears — by choosing the menu option. For example, if you're writing a check to some vendor, you can enter the company name on the check and choose Reports⇨ QuickReport to see a report of transactions involving the Company.

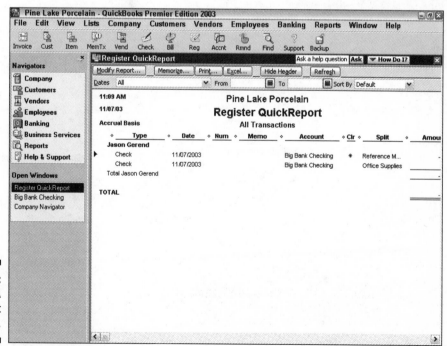

Figure 14-9:
A QuickReport report.

Chapter 15

QuickBooks Dirty Work

*O*kay, you don't need to worry about chasing dust bunnies in QuickBooks, but you do have little housekeeping tasks to take care of. In this chapter, I describe these chores and how to do them correctly with minimal hassle.

Backing Up Is (Not That) Hard to Do

Sure, I can give you some tricky, technical examples of fancy back-up strategies, but they have no point here. You want to know the basics, right?

The guiding rule is that you back up anytime you work on something that you wouldn't want to redo. Some people think that a week's worth of work is negligible, and others think that a month's worth of work is negligible.

So here's what I do to back up my files. I back up every month after I reconcile my accounts at work. Then I stick the floppy disk (you may use any removable disk, such as a Zip disk or writable CD) in my briefcase so that if something terrible happens (like a tornado hits my office building), I don't lose both my computer and the back-up disk with the data. (I carry my briefcase around with me — a sort of middle-age security blanket — so that it won't get destroyed in some after-hours disaster.) I also keep all the paperwork in a file folder through the month and do all the reconciling at one time.

Sounds like a pretty good system, huh? Actually, I admit that my strategy has its problems:

✔ Because I'm backing up monthly, I may have to re-enter as much as a month's worth of data if the computer crashes toward the end of the month. In my case, I wouldn't lose all that much work. However, if you're someone with heavy transaction volumes — if you prepare hundreds of invoices or write hundreds of checks each month, for example — you probably want to back up more frequently, perhaps once a week.

✔ A second problem with my strategy is only remotely possible but still worth mentioning: If something bad does happen to the QuickBooks files stored on my computer's hard disk and the files stored on the back-up floppy disk, CD-R, CD-RW, or Zip disk, I'll be up the proverbial creek without a paddle. (I should also note that a removable disk, especially a floppy, is far more likely to fail than a hard drive.) If this worst-case scenario actually occurs, I'll need to start over from scratch from the beginning of the year.

To prevent this scenario from happening, some people who are religiously careful circulate three sets of back-up disks to reduce the chance of this mishap. They also regularly move one copy off-site, such as to a safe-deposit box. In this scenario, whenever you back up your data, you use the oldest set of back-up disks.

Say you back up your data every week, and your hard disk not only crashes but also bursts into a ball of flames rising high into the night. To restore your files, you use the most recent set of backups — one week old, max. If something is wrong with those, you use the next recent set — two weeks old. If something is wrong with those, you use the last set — three weeks old. This way, you have three chances to get a set that works — a nice bit of security for the cost of a few extra floppy disks. I should also add that, generally, one company account's back-up file doesn't take more than one floppy disk.

You know what else? All back-up files are condensed to save disk space. If you're so inclined (I'm not), open Windows Explorer or My Computer and look in the `Program Files\Intuit\QuickBooks` folder for your company's file. (The backup file is, of course, on the disk you specify in the back-up procedure, which I describe in the following section.) If you want to set Windows Explorer to show file size — click the Views button and choose Details from the drop-down menu to do so — you'll notice that your back-up file (the one with the .QBB extension displayed, if you don't have your file extensions hidden) is a fraction of the size of its regular company file counterpart (the one with the .QBW extension). QuickBooks shrinks the back-up file in order to keep the disk from getting too crowded.

If you can't fit your back-up QuickBooks file on a single floppy, you can back up across multiple floppies or you can invest in a larger removable disk drive such as a Zip drive, CD-R, or CD-RW. Zip drives, for example, can store up to 100MB of stuff — plenty for QuickBooks backups and most other backups you'll want to make.

Backing up the quick-and-dirty way

You're busy. You don't have time to fool around. You just want to do a passable job of backing up, and you've decided how often you plan to do it. Sound like your situation? Then follow these steps:

1. **Insert a blank disk in your drive.**

   You can back up to any removable disk, including floppy disks, Zip disks, and writable CDs.

   Heck, I should admit that you can back up to any fixed disk, such as your hard disk or a network disk too, but the advantage of a removable disk is that you can store it in some other location. As a compromise, you can also use a network disk. You typically don't want to use your hard disk (although this is better than nothing) because one of the disasters that may befall your QuickBooks data is a hard disk failure.

2. **If you store data for more than one company, make sure that the company whose data you want to back up is the active company.**

   Yes, I know that all your companies are active — I'm hoping they're not dead in the water. My point is that you want to back up the right company. To find out whether the right company is active, just look at the QuickBooks application window's title bar, which names the active company. (If you don't remember setting up multiple files, don't worry. You probably have only one file — the usual case.)

3. **Choose File⇨Back Up to begin the backup operation.**

   QuickBooks displays the Back Up Company File dialog box, as shown in Figure 15-1.

   If you use QuickBooks in multiple user mode, you need to switch to single user mode before you back up your file. For more information on how to make this switch, see Chapter 3.

4. **Identify the back-up drive.**

   Click the Disk button and then the Browse button. QuickBooks displays the Back Up Company To dialog box (see Figure 15-2). Click the Save In drop-down list and select the letter of the drive that you stuffed the disk into.

   QuickBooks 2003 includes new backup options, Verify Data Integrity and Format Each Floppy During Backup, which appear as check boxes on the Back Up Company File dialog box (see Figure 15-1). You can check these boxes to have QuickBooks double-check the data it copies to the backup disk and, if necessary, to have QuickBooks first format the backup floppy disk. As the Back Up Company To dialog box indicates, however, these options do slow down the backup process.

5. **Click Save.**

   QuickBooks returns to the Back Up Company File dialog box shown in Figure 15-1.

6. **Click Back Up.**

   QuickBooks backs up your company file. When it finishes, it displays a
   message telling you that the backup worked.

Figure 15-1:
The Back Up
Company
File dialog
box.

Figure 15-2:
The Back Up
Company To
dialog box.

Backing up files online

You can quickly and easily back up your data online. By doing so, you no longer need to remember to make backups and take them off-site. To learn more about online backup, click the Tell Me More button on the Back Up Company File dialog box. (Refer to Figure 15-1.) To back up online, click the Online button shown in Figure 15-1 and then click Backup.

The Online Backup service, by the way, is a pretty good idea if you've got a fast Internet connection, but the service isn't cheap. You pay

at least $80 a year and as much as $240 a year depending on the level of service. But you can actually set up the service so that QuickBooks is automatically backing up your data on a regular basis.

Just for the record, I don't think you need to worry about the security. You can read more about the security measures at the QuickBooks Web site, but your data is as secure online as it is in your office.

Getting back the QuickBooks data you've backed up

What happens if you lose all your QuickBooks data? First of all, I encourage you to feel smug. Get a cup of coffee. Lean back in your chair. Gloat for a couple of minutes. You, my friend, have no problem. You have followed instructions.

Okay, you may have one or two problems, but you probably can blame PC gremlins for those. If the disaster that caused you to lose your data also trashed other parts of your computer, you may need to reinstall QuickBooks. You also may need to reinstall all your other software.

After you've gloated sufficiently (and pieced your computer back together again if it was the cause of the disaster), carefully do the following to reinstate your QuickBooks data:

1. **Get your back-up disk.**

   Find the back-up disk you created and carefully insert it into one of the disk drives.

2. **Start QuickBooks and choose File⇨Restore.**

   QuickBooks closes whatever company file you have open. QuickBooks displays the Restore Company Backup dialog box.

3. **Use the Filename and Location boxes in the Get Company Backup From area to identify the backup file you want to use.**

   If you know the company filename and location, you can enter this information into the boxes provided. If you don't know this information, click the Change button. QuickBooks displays the Restore From dialog box. Use the Look In box to identify the drive that contains the file you want to back up. Then select the file you want to restore and click Open.

4. **Use the Filename and Location boxes in the Restore Company Backup To area to identify the file you want to replace.**

   If you know the company filename and location, you can enter this information in the boxes provided. If you don't know this information, click the Change button. QuickBooks displays the Restore To dialog box. Use the Save In drop-down list box to make sure that you place the restored file in the correct folder on the correct drive.

5. **Click the Restore button.**

   If the file you're trying to restore already exists, you see a message box telling you so. Either click Yes to overwrite or replace the file with the one stored on the floppy disk, or click No to keep the original copy.

QuickBooks may ask you for your password to verify that you have administrative permission to restore the file. Then, if everything goes okay, you see a message box that says so. Breathe a deep sigh of relief and give thanks.

Oops. I almost forgot:

✔ When you restore a file, you replace the current version of the file with the back-up version stored on the floppy disk. Don't restore a file for fun. Restore a file only if the current version is trashed and you want to start over by using the version stored on the back-up disk.

✔ You need to re-enter everything you entered since you made the back-up copy. I know. You're bummed out. Hopefully, it hasn't been all that long since you backed up.

Accountant's Review

Hey. While I'm on the subject of the housecleaning stuff you can do with your QuickBooks files, let me mention the Accountant's Review feature.

Accountant's Review allows your accountant to make adjustments in a special copy of your QuickBooks data file while you continue to enter your daily transactions in the master file. When your accountant returns the updated file, you can then merge the changes back into the master file.

To use Accountant's Review, choose File⇨Accountant's Review⇨Create Accountant's Copy. Select a location for the accountant's copy and click Save. To import the accountant's changes, choose File⇨Accountant's Review⇨ Import Accountant's Changes. If you need help with this feature, you should talk to your accountant.

Shrinking Files That Are Too Big for Their Own Good

You can enter a large number of transactions in a QuickBooks company file. Even so, you may want to shrink or condense the .QBW or working set of your data file. Working with files of a manageable size means that QuickBooks runs faster because your computer has more memory and disk space available.

QuickBooks files can become dangerously large, just for the record. The QuickBooks support Web site warns that QuickBooks files shouldn't be larger than 40MB in size, for example. But, you know what? I've noticed strange, inexplicable problems with files that get larger than 20MB in size — like you have trouble condensing and archiving the files — and I suspect the real explanation is that the files are just getting too large to be easily handled.

Condensing defined

If your company file has become too big for its own good, you can knock it down to size by condensing it. As part of condensing the file, QuickBooks lets you decide which parts should be condensed and which parts should be readily accessible. You make this decision based on a cutoff date of your choice. In other words, if you have two or three years' worth of data records and the stuff from three years ago doesn't pertain to you for the most part, you can condense it. You also can delete unused accounts, information on inactive customers and vendors, old invoices, and Audit Trail information.

Condensing means that you get to work with a smaller file. And that, in turn, means QuickBooks runs faster. (The memory thing comes into play again.) And a smaller file should make backing up easier because you can probably keep your file small enough to fit on a single floppy disk.

Condensed information isn't lost — it's merely summarized. QuickBooks retains numeric totals and dates of the transactions but deletes other details, such as the names. In other words, if you wrote a check to Tuggey's Hardware on July 31, 1997, QuickBooks retains the amount of the check and the date it was written but loses the name of the hardware store.

Don't despair, however, about losing crucial data. In all its wisdom, QuickBooks can tell if a data item that you want to condense still bears on transactions that you enter in the future, and QuickBooks won't condense these transactions. If you choose to condense all information from before January 1, 1999, and you just so happen to have skipped a monthly rent payment in December 1998, for example, QuickBooks still retains all accounts payable information pertaining to your missed payment. And quit trying to pull a fast one, you rascal.

Here's some other stuff QuickBooks won't condense, even if you ask it to nicely:

✔ Unpaid invoices, bills, and credit memos; undeposited customer payments that have been applied to invoices; unreconciled transactions in credit card and checking accounts; and anything whatsoever that has been checked To Be Printed are not condensed.

✔ For the purposes of tax liability, QuickBooks doesn't condense any of your tax data. QuickBooks retains all information about taxable items and tax vendors. If you are audited, you won't be able to point to your computer and say, "There you are. Just uncondense that, Mr. Taxman." (Technically, what QuickBooks actually does is create general ledger journal entries that summarize each month's activity, so you can still create financial statements and explain tax return data.)

Condensing made simple

To condense a QuickBooks file, follow these steps:

1. **Start from a blank QuickBooks screen.**

   Close registers, reports, or anything else on-screen.

   If you use QuickBooks in multiple user mode, you need to switch to single user mode before you back up your file. For more information on making this switch, see Chapter 3.

2. **Choose File➪Utilities➪Archive & Condense Data.**

   QuickBooks displays a portrait of Barry Nelson, the first actor to portray James Bond. No, not really — I just wanted to see whether you were awake. Actually, QuickBooks displays the first dialog box of the Archive and Condense wizard, as shown in Figure 15-3.

3. **Specify a cutoff date.**

   In the Remove Closed Transactions On or Before line, enter a cutoff date. QuickBooks keeps all transactions with dates that fall after this cutoff date. But all transactions with dates that fall on or before this cutoff date are condensed (with the exceptions I note earlier in this chapter). Figure 15-4 shows you how the first of these babies looks.

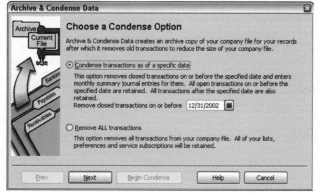

Figure 15-3:
The first
Archive &
Condense
Data dialog
box.

Figure 15-4:
The second
Archive &
Condense
dialog box.

4. **(Optional) Select other items in the Select Unused Items to Remove list.**

   Click Next to move to the next dialog boxes of the Archive and Condense
   wizard. These subsequent dialog boxes enable you to tell QuickBooks
   which items to remove or summarize.

5. **Click Next a few times.**

   Because QuickBooks is an exceptionally courteous program, it may
   display a few messages to make sure it's doing what you want it to.

6. **Click Begin Condense, finally, to begin scrunching the file.**

   By the way, before condensing the data file, QuickBooks asks you to
   make a back up file.

   Condensing your file may take a while, depending on how large it is.
   So expect a little whirring and humming from the computer. After
   QuickBooks condenses the file, you see a message box confirming the
   process.

How condensing is summarized on registers

QuickBooks summarizes data on registers into the generic GENJRNL entry. So if you condense all data from 2000, your Accounts Payable register for May 2000 shows a GENJRNL entry totaling all accounts payable transactions from that month. You don't see the individual transactions that have been condensed.

Condensed data affects some reports. Summary reports about your total equity aren't affected, but any report concerning details — classes, items, and so on — isn't as complete.

Chapter 16

Building the Perfect Budget

In This Chapter

▶ Powerful tips for business budgets

▶ Setting up a budget

▶ Reviewing QuickBooks' new Planning & Budgeting tools

1 don't think that a budget amounts to financial handcuffs, and neither should you. A budget is just a plan that outlines the way you plan to generate sales, the way you should spend your money, and your ideas about how you can best organize your firm's financial affairs.

Is This a Game You Want to Play?

If you've created a good, workable chart of accounts, you're halfway to a good, solid budget. (In fact, for 99 out of 100 businesses, the only step left is to specify how much you earn in each income account and how much you spend in each expense account.)

Does every business need a budget? No, of course not. Maybe you've got a simple financial plan that you can monitor some other way. Maybe in your business, you make money so effortlessly that you don't need to plan your income and outgo. Maybe Elvis Presley really is still alive and living somewhere in the Midwest.

For everyone else, though, a budget improves your chances of getting your business wherever you want it to go financially. It gives you a way to "plan your work and work your plan." In fact, I'll stop calling it a budget. The word has such negative connotations. I know — I'll call it The Secret Plan.

All Joking Aside: Some Basic Budgeting Tips

Before I walk you through the mechanics of outlining your Secret Plan, I want to give you a few tips. After that, I want to tell you a secret. A very special secret.

Following are five ways to increase the chances that your Secret Plan works:

- ✔ **Plan your income and expenses as a team, if that's possible.** For this sort of planning, two heads are invariably better than one. What's more, although I don't really want to get into marriage counseling or partnership counseling here, a business's budget — oops, I mean Secret Plan — needs to reflect the priorities and feelings of everyone who has to live within the plan: partners, partners' spouses, key employees, and so on. So don't use a Secret Plan as a way to minimize what your partner spends on marketing or on long-distance telephone charges talking to pseudocustomers and relatives in the old country. You need to resolve such issues before you finalize your Secret Plan.

- ✔ **Include some cushion in your plan.** In other words, don't budget to spend every last dollar. If you plan from the start to spend every dollar you make, you'll undoubtedly have to fight the mother of all financial battles: paying for unexpected expenses when you don't have any money. (You know the sort of things I mean: the repair bill when the delivery truck breaks down, a new piece of essential equipment, or that cocktail dress or tuxedo you absolutely must have for a special party.)

- ✔ **Regularly compare your actual income and outgo to your planned income and outgo.** This comparison is probably the most important part of budgeting, and it's what QuickBooks can help you with the most. As long as you use QuickBooks to record what you receive and spend and to describe your budget, you can print reports that show what you planned and what actually occurred.

  If you find that you've budgeted $1,000 a month for shipping costs but you discover that you consistently spend twice that amount, you may need to shift some money from your monthly cocktail dress and tuxedo allowance. Unless you like coming in over budget on shipping charges.

- ✔ **Make adjustments as necessary.** When you encounter problems with your Secret Plan — and you will — you'll know that part of your plan isn't working. You can then make adjustments (by spending a little less on calling the old country, for example).

- ✔ **A Word to the Wise:** One final suggestion related to budgeting and cost management: Don't gear up your business overhead or your personal living and lifestyle when you have a great year (or even a few great years) in the business. When you have a good year or even a few good years, keep your overhead and expenses modest. Stash the extra cash. If you can, build up some financial wealth that's independent and apart from your business assets. (One great way to do this, for example, is by contributing to an IRA or by setting up a SIMPLE-IRA or a SEP/IRA for you and any other employees.)

A Budgeting Secret You Won't Learn in College

I also have a secret tip for you. (I'm going to write very quietly now so that no one else hears. . . .)

Here's the secret tip: Go to the library, ask for the *Robert Morris & Associates Survey,* the *Risk Management Association, or RMA, Reference,* the *Dun & Bradstreet Annual Financial Statement Survey,* and any similar references of business financial statistics. Once you get these books, find a nice quiet corner of the library and look up the ways that other businesses like yours (that is, businesses that are the same size, sell the same stuff or services, and have the same gross and net profits) spend money.

These references are really cool. For example, Robert Morris & Associates surveys bank lending officers, creating a summary of the information that these bankers receive from their customers, and publishes the results. You can look up what percentage of sales the average tavern spends on beer and peanuts.

Plan to spend an hour or so at the library. Getting used to the way that the Robert Morris & Associates, for example, displays information takes a while. The taverns page doesn't actually have a line for beer and peanuts, for example. Instead, you see some vague accounting term, like "cost of goods sold."

Make a few notes so that you can use the information you glean to better plan your own business financial affairs. If you spend about the same amount on beer and peanuts every year as the average tavern, you're in good shape — well, unless you own a shoe store.

The point is that you can and should use this information to get a better handle on what businesses like yours earn and spend.

Setting Up a Secret Plan

Okay, enough background stuff. The time has come to set up your budget — er, your Secret Plan in QuickBooks. Follow these steps:

1. **Choose Company⇨Budget & Planning⇨Set Up Forecast.**

   If you haven't yet set up a budget, QuickBooks displays the New Budget window, as shown in Figure 16-1. If you have already set up a budget, another window appears and you need to click the Create New Budget button to get to the New Budget window.

2. **Select the year that you want to budget.**

   Use the Year and Type boxes to specify the fiscal year. You use the arrows at the end of the box to adjust the year number incrementally.

3. **Choose the type of budget you want to create.**

   See those two option buttons on the New Budget window? They let you tell QuickBooks whether you want to create a budget of income and expense amounts (done with a pro forma profit & loss statement) or a budget of year-end asset, liability and owners equity account balances (done with a pro forma balance sheet). Typically, I'll just say here, you want to budget income and expense amounts. After you indicate for what year you want to budget and whether you want to budget income statement amounts or balance sheet amounts, click Next.

4. **Provide any additional budgeting criteria and instructions.**

   QuickBooks next asks if you want to budget using additional criteria, such as customer:job information or class information. You answer this question by marking the option button that corresponds to budgeting criteria you want and click Next. (If you're just starting out, don't worry about specifying additional criteria. Keep things simple to start.)

5. **Indicate whether you want to start from scratch.**

   QuickBooks next asks whether you want it to create a first-cut at your budget using last year's numbers or whether you just want to start from scratch. To answer this question, you just mark the option button that corresponds to your choice. For example, to budget from scratch, mark the Create Budget from Scratch button.

6. **Do your budget.**

   After you answer the question discussed in Step 5, click Finish. QuickBooks displays the Set Up Budgets window (see Figure 16-2). You use this window to identify the budgeted amounts you plan for each account. If you said you want to budget by scratch, by the way, QuickBooks shows a window with a bunch of empty columns. If you said that you want to base the coming year's budget on last year's real numbers, you'll see numbers in the columns.

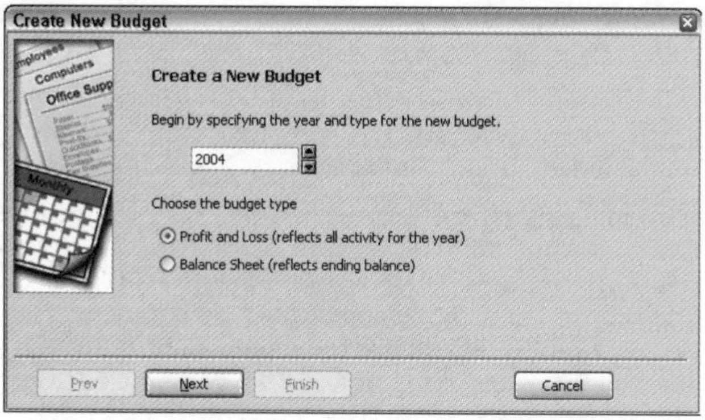

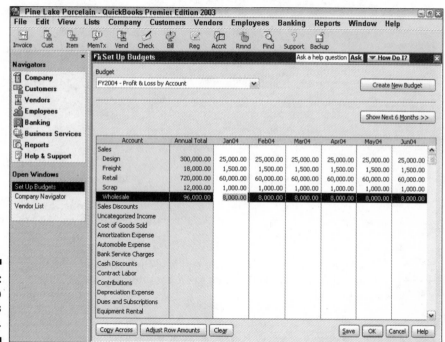

Figure 16-1:
The New
Budget
window.

Figure 16-2:
The Set Up
Budgets
window.

QuickBooks only shows a few months of budgeted data at a time. Click the Show Next 6 Months button to move to the next part of the budget year. To move back to the first part of the year, click the Show Prev 6 Months button. (Only one of these "Show" buttons appears at a time.)

The Budget box, at the top of the Set Up Budgets window, lets you name the budget you're creating. Why? You can work with several different versions of your budget. To create a new budget, click the Create New Budget button that then steps you through the six-step process described here.

Note: QuickBooks essentially uses the terms budget and forecast as synonyms.

To copy the amount shown in the selected box across the row, click the Copy Across button. (This lets you copy, for example, some amount you've budgeted for January into February, March, April, May, and so on.)

If you want to be a little fancier, you can also select some budgeted amount and click the Adjust Row Amounts button. QuickBooks displays the Adjust Row Amounts dialog box (see Figure 16-3), which lets you adjust the selected amount by some specified percentage increase or decrease. For example, if you want to increase the budgeted amount by, say, .25% a month, you use the Adjust Row Amounts button.

Figure 16-3:
The Adjust
Row
Amounts
dialog box.

7. Save your budgeting work.

After you enter your secret plan, click Save to save your work and leave the Set Up Budgets window open. Or click OK to save your work but close the Set Up Budgets window.

I should mention, too, that you can just click Cancel if you don't want to save your work (in case you've just been noodling around).

Adjusting a Secret Plan

To later make additional changes to a budget, choose the Company⇨ Planning & Budgets⇨Set Up Budget command. QuickBooks displays the Set Up Budgets window. Choose the budget you want to work with from the Budget drop-down list box, and then make your changes. All of the same tools that you have for initially setting up your forecast (described in the preceding section) are available for editing your budget.

Using the Formal Business Planner Tool

The Planning & Budgets submenu provides a command you can use to start the QuickBooks Business Planner, a wizard-like thing that walks you through the steps to writing a business plan. The planner isn't a bad tool. In fact, it's pretty powerful. I will say that you need to be pretty darn proficient in accounting and finance to get through it. I can't, for example, in a few paragraphs supply the information you need. Heck, I can only suggest you take the core requirements in an undergraduate business major. You'd need about that much information to do the plan and understand the results. Sorry.

Using the Expert Analysis Tool

The Expert Analysis Tool, also available from the Planning & Budgets submenu, lets you assess your firm's financial condition and performance against those of similar businesses. The Expert Analysis Tool, just so you know, steps you through a wizard that asks you about your business, grabs information from the QuickBooks data file, and then does some simple analysis.

I'd suggest that you experiment with this tool after you've used QuickBooks for a year or two. It may provide you with some interesting insights into your business. Nothing ground-shaking, mind you. But it's worth the ten minutes or so the wizard takes. (I will say that you'll find it far more valuable to make the field trip to the library that I suggested earlier in the chapter.)

Using the Decision Tools

One final command available on the Planning & Budgets submenu deserves mention: Decision Tools. The Decision Tools command displays a sub-submenu of commands you can use to learn more about accounting and finance and how to apply accounting and financial concepts to your business. For example, the Decision Tools sub-submenu includes a command that steps you through a wizard that explains what depreciation is and how you calculate depreciation.

If you're a regular Joe or Jane trying to be smart about managing your financial affairs, the Decision Tools sub-submenu offers some real nuggets of gold. I recommend it.

Part IV
The Part of Tens

The 5th Wave · By Rich Tennant

"For 30 years I've put a hat and coat on to make sales calls and I'm not changing now just because I'm doing it on the Web from my living room."

In this part . . .

As a writing tool, laundry lists aren't something high school English teachers encourage. But you know what? The old laundry list format is pretty handy for certain types of information.

With this in mind (and, of course, with deepest apologies to my high school English teacher, Mrs. O'Rourke), this part simply provides you with ten-item (or almost ten-item) lists of information about QuickBooks.

Chapter 17

(Almost) Ten Knowledge Nuggets about Web-ifying Your Business

I'm not sure where to start this. Most of the time when a software company like Intuit (or any other big developer) adds some new whistles or bells to a program, I'm not all that excited. Most of the gizmos and gadgets that get added to mature products like QuickBooks aren't — in my opinion — really worth all that much. Sorry, but that's just the way it is.

That said, I have to emphasize that this Web publishing stuff is different. Way different. It's more than just a whistle or bell. It's a very powerful new capability. The weird part is that, while the technology and mechanics are deceptively simple (as you find out in a few paragraphs), the strategy is a tough nut to crack. Maybe you should do this. Maybe you shouldn't. You have got to think carefully.

So this not-so-simple capability puts me in a difficult place with regard to the Web Site Builder that's part of QuickBooks 2003. I want to talk about both things a bit — both mechanics and strategy — but I need to emphasize the strategy stuff. After much hand-wringing, I'm going to treat this subject by providing you with the best knowledge nuggets I can about how to use the Web in your business. Along the way, I'll first briefly go over the new Web Site Builder tool.

My discussion of that simple wizard will be pretty fast-paced because that's not the main thing you need to know about. Quite frankly, you need to think about and understand a bunch of big, important, strategic decisions before you take the 20 or so minutes required to run the Web Site Builder Wizard.

The Mechanics Are Simple

Here's the first thing I want to tell you. In terms of mechanics, Web publishing is very simple. All you're really doing when you publish Web pages is creating HTML documents that combine text and pictures and then storing them on a central Web server. All of the tricky stuff, I should point out, gets taken care of by the Web server and the poor souls who have to maintain that sucker.

By the way, you probably know that HTML stands for HyperText Markup Language; you don't really need to know how HTML works — just that it's a special programming language that enables Web browsers to view Web pages.

After your HTML documents are stored on the Web server, people with Web browsers and Internet connections can easily view them at any time of the day or night. That's it. Really.

If you want a good solid introduction to building your own site, check out *Creating Web Pages For Dummies,* 6th Edition, by Bud Smith and Arthur Bebak. This comprehensive guide is published by the good people at Wiley Publishing, Inc.

Creating your new site

You can use a variety of Web publishing and Web editing programs to create these HTML documents, or Web pages. Web browsers, such as Internet Explorer and Netscape Navigator, provide simple Web editing capabilities. More powerful Web publishing programs, such as FrontPage and Dreamweaver, enable you to create and administer very sophisticated collections of HTML documents, including Web documents that are interactive. (By interactive, I just mean that you can collect information from the Web site visitor by using a form and that you can also dynamically change the information shown on the Web page.)

But if you have QuickBooks 2003 — and of course you do because that's why you're reading this book — you can easily create a Web site in just a few minutes by choosing Company⇨Company Web Site. When you choose this command, QuickBooks 2003, through its Web Site Builder feature, starts a wizard that guides you through the steps to building a Web site.

To use the wizard, you answer simple questions about your business, such as what its name is and about what information you want to appear on your Web site. To provide this information, you either type the information into text boxes, or you copy the information from another program.

This is maybe obvious, but I recommend that you type your information into a word processor document, spell-check and grammar-check the text, and then copy and paste the information from the document into the appropriate text boxes. In this way, you're liable to reduce any textual errors. Especially the embarrassing ones, like (oops!) misspelling your company's name.

To move text between a word processor and the Web Site Builder wizard, select the text in the word processor, choose the Edit⇨Copy command, switch to the Web Site Builder, click the text box where you want the selected text to appear, and then choose the Edit⇨Paste command.

Previewing your new site

After you finish stepping through the wizard, the Web Site Builder constructs the Web site. Presto. You can preview it from inside the Web Site Builder window. And a few days after you finish it, you and anyone else in the world will be able to view the Web site over the Internet. Yes, that's right. As part of your running the Web Site Building wizard, QuickBooks 2003 sets up an Internet domain for your Web site and publishes your pages.

You can view your Web site at any time from within QuickBooks by choosing the Company⇨Company Web Site command.

And that, my friend, is really it. I know you're going to find it hard to believe that setting up your Web site can be so simple. But, aside from the work of figuring out what you're going to say (which I talk about later in this chapter), using the Web Site Builder is laughably easy.

Changing your new site

The QuickBooks 2002 Web publishing capabilities fall somewhere between the simple Web editing capabilities of a browser and the sophisticated Web publishing capabilities of a full-blown Web authoring program, such as FrontPage. That's good, and that's bad. The good part is that the Web Site Builder in QuickBooks 2003 is very easy to use, as noted. The bad part — maybe the bad part — is that you can't build a really sophisticated Web site with QuickBooks 2003. In essence, what you do with the Web Site Builder is create an online catalog or brochure.

Oh, wait. One other thing. If you want to change something on one of your Web pages, you use the Web Site Builder, too. Choose the Company⇨ My Company Web Site⇨Edit Web Site command. Doing this lets you rerun the wizard so that you can modify your Web site.

Web Publishing Is Relatively Cheap

Let me say something else here at the very beginning: Web publishing doesn't have to be very expensive. In fact, you can keep your Web publishing expenses very low. If you have QuickBooks 2003, for example, you don't need to purchase any special software to do Web publishing. And the cost to actually operate a Web site is affordable and worthwhile for many small businesses — about $20 a month at the time I'm writing this if you use the Web Site Builder that comes with QuickBooks 2003. (Check with Intuit at www.intuit.com for up-to-date pricing information.)

Not surprisingly, if you're unconcerned about costs or if you have a big budget, you can spend a lot of money on your Web publishing. And, predictably, if you spend a lot of money, you can create a fantastic Web site.

By the way, if you want to create a fantastically sophisticated Web site and have the financial resources to do so — understand that you may be spending thousands of dollars — what you need to do is locate a good *Web designer*. This is a person who understands not only the aesthetic issues of designing Web pages but also the technical issues. Your best bet may be to look at the Web sites designed for other local businesses and see who has put together a really good site. (Usually, Web designers identify themselves someplace on the sites they create for people, so maybe you can track down a good designer this way.) Another idea: Ask your accountant or attorney for a recommendation. You may think it's odd that accountants would know more than you do about Web design. Think about it, though. Accountants have got other business clients besides you. And hopefully, they should know somebody or somebody who knows somebody.

Why the Web Is Better Than Paper

In the rush to get online, some people kinda forget what it is about Web publishing that's better than paper publishing. You maybe already know this stuff, but humor me by letting me recount that Web publishing provides three advantages as compared with traditional paper publishing:

- ✔ Lower publishing costs
- ✔ Faster publishing schedules
- ✔ Easier editing

You know what else? There's another subtle benefit. Be careful, though, because this one has been overemphasized by the recent herd of dot-com entrepreneurs: Customers can access your business 24/7. All day, all night.

Of course, they have to know that your site exists in order to access it, but that's another issue altogether — one that I address later in this chapter.

If you're seriously interested in taking your business online, read the rest of this chapter. If you're still interested, check out *E-Commerce For Dummies* by Don Jones, Mark D. Scott, Richard Villars, and John Gantz, published by Wiley Publishing, Inc.

Big benefit number one

The first advantage, and maybe the biggest, is that you don't have printing or mailing costs when you publish on the Web. This cost saving sounds small and almost insignificant, I guess, but it's really extremely useful.

Consider, for example, an expensive color brochure that you supply to your customers. You pay a pretty penny — perhaps several dollars a copy — to print in low volumes of a few hundred or a thousand copies. And while printing at larger volumes, say 5,000 to 20,000 copies, drives down your per-unit cost, those sorts of print volumes can easily push your total cost to tens of thousands of dollars.

Web publishing works very differently. After you finish creating your HTML documents, you don't really have any additional costs. Oh sure, you pay something to store Web pages on a Web server someplace, and that adds up to a few dollars a month. But you won't have any printing costs or mailing costs. In essence, the cost to print, mail, and view your information is borne by the people who are browsing your Web site. Their computers, Internet connections, and printers do the work of retrieving and then displaying or printing your Web pages.

Big benefit number two

Okay. Let me talk for a minute about the second big advantage of Web publishing. After you finish with your HTML documents, or Web pages, you can publish them. That's it. You don't take time to ship stuff to a printer. You don't take time to wait for your printer to complete your job. You don't take time to have your printer return the job to you.

This is all obvious, right? Printing takes time — at least a few days and, in some cases, several weeks. In comparison, with Web publishing, it takes a few seconds or maybe a few minutes to move your HTML documents, or Web pages, to the Web server.

After you move your Web documents to the server, you're done. So (and this is a pretty cool thing) Web publishing allows you to distribute your publications instantaneously. Great, unless you're in the printing business!

Big benefit number three

Let me quickly mention the third big benefit of Web publishing: Making changes is simple.

This makes sense, right? To correct some typographical error on a Web page, you simply edit the HTML document — you've stored a copy on your computer, of course — and then you move this correct copy to the Web server, thereby replacing the old erroneous copy.

The ease of fixing small mistakes this way (or adding to your catalog a new item that you just got in) is actually pretty cool if you think about the embarrassment of simple typos. And it maybe becomes lifesaving if you think about the really serious ramifications of bad telephone numbers or addresses, prices, or part numbers. Clearly, one of the Web's big benefits is that you get to make corrections immediately.

Mom, Don't Read This

I feel a little nervous about broaching this next subject. But because I'm talking about something very serious here — how you can use the Web as a business tool — I want to talk with you a bit about the only type of Web publisher that, to date, has really made serious money from the Web: the adult entertainment sites.

Hear me out, please. This topic is very relevant to small businesses. Note that many large businesses — including companies like Microsoft — have not, to date, found a way to make money on the Internet from Web publishing (except, of course, by selling hardware and software to people who want to use the Internet).

In comparison, the adult entertainment sites (the porn sites) reportedly have made lots of money. And while I'm not suggesting that you or I get into the adult entertainment industry, I do think that we can learn to think more intelligently and creatively about our own Web publishing efforts. We can look at the adult entertainment sites and, in particular, at why they've been successful. So here I go. (We're both adults, right? We can do this.) I won't get embarrassed, if you won't.

Lessons from those "other" Web sites

Here are the lessons to be learned from the success of the adult entertainment Web publishers:

✔ **You need to heavily promote and actively advertise your Web site:** You need to do this in order to build traffic, and you need to maintain traffic by providing reasons for people to revisit.

The first thing to note about the adult Web sites is this: Typically, they heavily promote and advertise their product — usually photographs and videos — by posting product samples in, er, appropriate newsgroups and on free Web sites. These adult Web site operators also typically create lots and lots of new content so that their customers and prospective customers have a reason to continually revisit the Web sites.

This free content, active promotion, and fresh content results in heavy Web site traffic — the first lesson those of us outside of the adult entertainment industry should learn from the porn site operators.

If your Web site is to have a big impact on your business, you need to build and maintain heavy traffic. There's nothing magical about being on the Web. People won't visit your Web site unless they have a reason, such as free content. And they won't revisit your Web site unless you continually add fresh content.

✔ **You may want to consider making money through incremental sales:** $3 to subscribe, $12 for a special book, $25 for a video, and so forth.

The second thing I want to note about these, er, Web publishers is that, according to articles in business publications, such as *The Wall Street Journal,* the adult entertainment Web sites typically rely on incremental sales. (Mom? If you're reading this, please note that I'm basing my information not on personal experience but rather on written reports in the press.)

Here's how this incremental sales stuff works. If you visit one of these Web sites, you may be asked or may be required to prove your age by allowing the site to charge your credit card for some nominal amount like $3. And then you'll get an offer to buy a CD of pictures for $12 so you don't have to spend time downloading. And then you'll get the chance to buy a special video for $25.

You see the pattern: $3 here, $12 there, $25 over there. With perhaps tens of thousands of Web site visitors, if even a handful of these visitors spends a few dollars, the Web site makes money. By some reports — and these numbers are a bit out of date at this point — some of the adult sites produce $4,000 to $6,000 a day from small incremental sales.

✔ **You may need to use your Web site to reengineer some part of your business:** For example, you may be able to save your customers money, time, or hassle.

Okay, the third and final thing I want to note about the adult entertainment Web sites is this: In essence, the adult entertainment Web publishers have reengineered the process by which people acquire so-called adult entertainment and adult products. Rather than expecting a customer to stand in line at a local convenience store or visit some garish retail outlet on the other side of the railroad tracks, someone can anonymously visit a Web site and place an order. This reengineering presumably gives the Web-based providers of adult entertainment a big competitive advantage over their non-Web-based competitors.

Applying the lessons to your business

The three points in the previous section seem pretty abstract, I guess. So let me give you some concrete examples about how the points might be applied in a specific small business situation. Suppose that you own and operate a small accounting or bookkeeping firm. Nothing fancy. Just a meat-and-potatoes business. You might think that the whole Internet thing is just another fad that you can ignore.

But you know what? I think that you could try to use the Web to reengineer your service. Call me crazy, but what if you attempted to copy the tactics employed by the successful adult entertainment Web publishers?

For example, maybe you can build and maintain heavy traffic by maintaining a Web page that collects news links to business or financial stories of interest to your clients or that posts the best prices available on frequently used business products. Or given the way that tax reporting requirements work, maybe you could include a weekly to-do list that reminds people when they need to make tax deposits and file payroll returns.

Maybe you could also easily and economically generate fresh, good content by letting people write in and ask questions that you then answer online. In other words, you could create a FAQ (Frequently Asked Questions) area that enables clients and potential clients ask things like: "What do I need to do to start a business in our town?" "What are my chances of getting audited?" or "Does the new tax law provide any small business tax breaks?" You're probably answering these questions anyway, right? Why not type up the questions and answers and post them to your Web site.

Finally, maybe you could get incremental sales by selling business forms or specialty, hard-to-get business how-to books. Or maybe you could include a local business profile of one of your customers each week. Doing that doesn't directly produce sales . . . but it builds goodwill and loyalty. (What business owners wouldn't like to see an article on the Web about their business and what it sells?)

To sum things up — and, of course, I don't know enough about your business to appear very smart here — maybe you could use the Web to essentially reengineer some part of the small accounting or bookkeeping firm business. And you could do so in a way that the large financial services companies neither can do nor will do. And maybe you'd charge for this service, thereby boosting profits. Or maybe you'll use this service to boost sales, thereby boosting profits. And maybe, just maybe, you would do both.

The Web's Information-sharing Risk

Let me make a quick point here. Despite all the advantages of Web-based publishing, despite the fact you may be able to use the Web or the Internet to reengineer your business in some powerful way, the Web presents a noteworthy risk: Whatever you put on the Web is available immediately to everybody, including your competitors. This means that you don't really have any secrets (or at least you don't have them for long). Lower prices (or higher prices), new services, new ways of doing business, fresh new content — all these began to get old and stale and outdated very quickly with the Internet. And, I would say, the better and bigger your good idea, the more quickly it loses its value.

The Web Site Builder Wizard that comes with QuickBooks Pro alludes to this, by the way. The wizard warns you more than once that you need to be careful about what you publish on the Web. I want to echo that warning here.

About Those Content Costs, Dude

Earlier, in my discussion about using the Web Site Builder, I noted that the actual mechanical process of creating Web pages takes only a few minutes. That's true. But one of the things a lot of people miss is that creating good, rich, interesting Web page content is very time-consuming. Good content, my friend, costs money and time.

The hard part of becoming a Web publisher isn't running the Web Site Builder Wizard. That's easy. The hard part is coming up with a bunch of content to stick on your Web site. Think for a moment about how you felt in high school when Mrs. Magilabush asked for that six-page term paper. Ha. That was nothing. A few hundred words of text. A Web site requires, probably, some multiple of that . . . and a bunch of art as well.

One related point bears mentioning again here, too: In the previous paragraphs, I discussed my notion that one of the secrets to making your Web site successful is continually refreshing its content. If you think about that a bit, you quickly realize that a Web site becomes an ongoing responsibility. If you're going to do anything striking, you effectively become like a newsletter or magazine publisher who, each week or month, is trying to publish a batch of new, interesting, and fresh content.

Most of us realize that undertaking such a venture would require more time than we have available and would perhaps not deliver the benefits needed to make it worthwhile.

A Scary Thought I Shouldn't Share

Here's a scary thought: Maybe Web publishing — especially the simple Web publishing that you do with something like QuickBooks 2003 — doesn't really make sense for your small business.

Think about it. If you don't have time to produce good content, if you're busy running your business, a Web site may turn out to be more work than it's worth — especially in the case where you have a targeted market.

Maybe, just maybe, if you do anything, you should treat your Web site as just a big "yellow pages" ad. If you're thinking this way, take a look at my Web site at www.stephenlnelson.com. What I've done is really simple. Some may even say crude. But it's easy to update, cheap to maintain, and (when needed) gives me a convenient way to make digital information available to my clients.

By the way, the information at my Web site took me just a few hours to collect and polish. Your own efforts shouldn't take much more time than that if you go with the "quick-and-dirty" approach. I should also mention that I used Microsoft FrontPage rather than QuickBooks to create my little Web site. I wanted to use one of FrontPage's Web design themes because I liked them better than QuickBooks' design themes.

Remember that the Web is a mass-market medium that lets you reach millions of users around the world. In some businesses, that breadth and reach is really cool. In targeted, niche-based businesses, promoting your business on the Web may not make sense.

A scary prediction I shouldn't share

A few years ago, I was at a Web publishing and electronic commerce seminar. A big, unnamed software company headquartered in Redmond, Washington, sponsored the event. I won't name names. But pretty much what every speaker kept saying was "Well, girls and boys, the Web is really going to change things. With half of your customers on the Internet, people want to shop this way. . . ."

People in the audience were nodding their heads, glad to be included in this thought-provoking seminar. Everybody was pumped up. And it seemed as if all the people in the audience had decided that this Web-based business stuff was the cat's meow.

So at one particular high point in the day's festivities, this one guy stands up — okay it was me — and says, "Don't people worry that this will erode prices?"

I got the "Hey dude, what do you mean?" stare, so I explained myself: If you can easily compare prices on the Web simply by clicking a couple hyperlinks, price shopping becomes incredibly easy and incredibly exact. It's way easier and way more precise than telephone shopping, for example. I went on to say that because the Web is free, even if you provide wonderful additional content on your Web site to really build traffic, the Web's anonymous nature doesn't help build customer loyalty. That is, people can happily visit your site, grab your content for free, and then go buy the item they need from somebody selling the item for less money.

In the end, I wondered aloud whether the Web would simply create new, priced-based, virtual retail businesses like Costco or Wal-Mart. Sure. You could, of course, provide free advice and wonderful content to get people to visit your site, but a Web site visitor is always only a click away from some discounter's Web site.

After I finished my little speech, one of the principal sponsors of the conference stood up, beat around the bush for a bit, and then admitted that price erosion is a risk. He also noted that he wondered whether it was something businesses could work around, such as by not providing prices over the Net.

I didn't want to say anymore or try to rebut his position. I was a guest, after all. But inside I was thinking, "You know, this Web stuff really isn't a good idea for everyone. It's a special tool for special situations."

Chapter 18

(Almost) Ten Tips for Business Owners

*I*f you run a business and you use QuickBooks, you need to know the information in this chapter. You can get this information by sitting down with your certified public accountant over a cup of coffee at $100 an hour. Or you can read this chapter.

Sign All Your Own Checks

I have nothing against your bookkeeper. In a small business, however, people — especially full-charge bookkeepers — can bamboozle you too darn easily. By signing all the checks yourself, you keep your fingers on the pulse of your cash outflow.

Yeah, I know this practice can be a hassle. I know that you can't easily spend three months in Hawaii. I know that you have to wade through paperwork every time you sign a stack of checks.

By the way, if you're in a partnership, I think that you should have at least a couple of the partners cosign checks.

Don't Sign a Check the Wrong Way

If you sign many checks, you may be tempted to use a John Hancock–like signature. Although scrawling your name illegibly makes great sense when you're autographing baseballs, don't do it when you're signing checks. A clear signature, especially one with a sense of personal style, is distinctive. A wavy line with a cross and a couple of dots is really easy to forge.

Which leads me to my next tip. . . .

Review Canceled Checks Before Your Bookkeeper Does

Be sure that you review your canceled checks before anybody else sees the monthly bank statement.

This chapter isn't about browbeating bookkeepers. But a business owner can determine whether someone is forging signatures on checks only by being the first to open the bank statement and by reviewing each of the canceled check signatures.

If you don't examine the checks, unscrupulous employees — especially bookkeepers who can update the bank account records — can forge your signature with impunity. And they won't get caught if they never overdraw the account.

I won't continue this rant, but let me mention just one last thing: Every time I teach CPAs about how to better help their clients with QuickBooks, I hear again and again about business owners who haven't been careful about keeping an eye on the bookkeeper — and have suffered from embezzlement and forgery as a result.

If you don't follow these procedures, you will probably eat the losses, not the bank.

Choose a Bookkeeper Who Is Familiar with Computers and Knows How to Do Payroll

Don't worry. You don't need to request an FBI background check.

In fact, if you use QuickBooks, you don't need to hire people who are familiar with small-business accounting systems. Just find people who know how to keep a checkbook and work with a computer. They shouldn't have a problem understanding QuickBooks.

Of course, you don't want someone who just fell off the turnip truck. But even if you do hire someone who rode into town on one, you're not going to have much trouble getting that person up to speed with QuickBooks.

A bookkeeper who knows double-entry bookkeeping is super-helpful. But, to be fair, such knowledge probably isn't essential. I will say this, however: When you're hiring, find someone who knows how to do payroll — not just the federal payroll tax stuff (see Chapter 12) but also the state payroll tax monkey business.

Choose an Appropriate Accounting System

When you use QuickBooks, you use either cash-basis accounting or accrual-basis accounting. (I describe the difference between these two methods in Appendix B.)

Cash-basis accounting is fine when a business's cash inflow mirrors its sales and its cash outflow mirrors its expenses. This situation isn't the case, however, in many businesses. A contractor of single-family homes, for example, may have cash coming in (by borrowing from banks) but may not make any money. A pawnshop owner who loans money at 22 percent may make scads of money, even if cash pours out of the business daily.

As a general rule, when you're buying and selling inventory, accrual-basis accounting works better than cash-basis accounting.

This news may not be earthshaking, but making the switch is something that you should think about doing. Note that you can easily switch to accrual-basis accounting simply by telling QuickBooks that you want reports prepared on an accrual basis and by promptly recording customer invoices and vendor bills.

If QuickBooks Doesn't Work for Your Business

QuickBooks is a great small-business accounting program. In fact, I'd even go as far as saying that QuickBooks is probably the best small-business accounting program available.

However, if QuickBooks doesn't seem to fit your needs — if, for example, you need a program that works better for a manufacturer or that includes some special industry-specific feature — you may want one of the more complicated (but also more powerful) small-business accounting packages.

One possibility is another popular (and more powerful) full-featured Windows accounting program: Peachtree Accounting for Windows from Peachtree. If that program doesn't work, you may want to talk to your accountant about industry-specific packages. (For example, if you're a commercial printer, some vendor may have developed a special accounting package just for commercial printers.)

I'm amazed that PC accounting software remains so affordable. You can buy a great accounting package — one that you can use to manage a $5 million or a $25 million business — for a few hundred bucks. Accounting software is truly one of the great bargains in life.

Keep Things Simple

Let me share one last comment about managing small-business financial affairs: Keep things as simple as possible. In fact, keep your business affairs simple enough that you can easily tell whether you're making money and whether the business is healthy.

This advice may sound strange, but as a CPA, I've worked for some very bright people who have built monstrously complex financial structures for their businesses, including complicated leasing arrangements, labyrinthine partnership and corporate structures, and sophisticated profit-sharing and cost-sharing arrangements with other businesses.

I can only offer anecdotal evidence, of course, but I strongly believe that these super-sophisticated financial arrangements don't produce a profit when you consider all the costs. What's more, these super-sophisticated arrangements almost always turn into management and record-keeping headaches.

Chapter 19

Tips for Handling (Almost) Ten Tricky Situations

In This Chapter

▶ Selling an asset

▶ Tracking owner's equity

▶ Doing multiple-state accounting

▶ Obtaining and repaying loans

As your business grows and becomes more complex, your accounting does, too. I can't describe and discuss all the complexities you'll encounter, but I can give you some tips on handling (just about) ten tricky situations.

In QuickBooks, you make journal entries by using the General Journal Entry window, which you get to by choosing Company➪Make Journal Entry. If you don't understand double-entry bookkeeping but you'd like to, take a gander at Appendix B.

To track the depreciation of an asset that you've already purchased (and added to the chart of accounts), you need two new accounts: an asset account called something like Accumulated Depreciation and an expense account called something like Depreciation Expense.

By the way, if you have a large number of assets, keeping track of the accumulated depreciation associated with specific assets is a good idea. You can do this either outside of QuickBooks (like in an Excel spreadsheet or with your tax return) or inside QuickBooks (by using individual accounts for each asset's original cost and accumulated depreciation).

After you set up these two accounts, you can record the asset depreciation with a journal entry such as the following one that records $500 of depreciation expense:

	Debit	Credit
Depreciation expense	$500	
Accumulated depreciation		$500

The federal tax laws provide a special form of depreciation called Section 179 depreciation. Section 179 depreciation enables you to depreciate the entire cost of some assets, which is a big break for small businesses. You can't, however, use more than a certain amount of Section 179 depreciation in a year: $24,000 in 2002, for example, and $25,000 thereafter. You also need to know about some other nitty-gritty details, so confer with your tax adviser if you have questions.

Selling an Asset

When you sell an asset, you need to back out (get rid of) the asset's account balance, record the payment of the cash (or whatever) that somebody pays you for the asset, and record any difference between what you sell the asset for and its value as a gain or loss.

If you purchase a piece of land for $5,000 but later resell it for $4,000, for example, you use the following journal entry to record the sale of this asset:

Debit	Credit	
Cash	$4,000	
Loss	$1,000	
Asset	$5,000	

You may need to set up another income account for the gain or another expense account for the loss. Refer to Chapter 1 for information on setting up new accounts.

Selling a Depreciable Asset

Selling a depreciable asset works almost identically to selling an asset that you haven't been depreciating. When you sell the asset, you need to back out (or get rid of) the asset's account balance. You also need to back out the asset's accumulated depreciation (which is the only thing that's different from selling an asset that you haven't been depreciating). You need to record the payment of the cash (or whatever) that somebody pays you for the asset. Finally, you count as a gain or a loss any difference between what you sell the asset for and what its net-of-accumulated-depreciation value is.

This process sounds terribly complicated, but an example will help. Suppose that you purchased a $5,000 piece of machinery and have accumulated $500 of depreciation thus far. Consequently, the asset account shows a $5,000 debit balance, and the asset's accumulated depreciation account shows a $500 credit balance. Suppose also that you sell the machinery for $4,750 in cash.

To record the sale of this depreciable asset, you would use the following journal entry:

	Debit	*Credit*
Cash	$4,750	
Accumulated depreciation	$500	
Asset		$5,000
Gain		$250

As noted earlier in the chapter, if you have a bunch of assets, you probably want to set up individual accounts for each asset's original cost and its accumulated depreciation. The individual accounts make it much, much easier to make the journal entry shown in the preceding table.

Owner's Equity in a Sole Proprietorship

Actually, tracking owner's equity in a sole proprietorship is easy. You can use the single account that QuickBooks sets up for you, called Opening Bal Equity, to track what you've invested in the business. (You may want to rename this account something like Contributed Capital.)

To track the money you withdraw from the business, you can set up and use a new owner's equity account called something like Owner's Draws. Table 19-1 gives an example of owner's equity accounts in a sole proprietorship.

Table 19-1	An Example of Owner's Equity Accounts in a Sole Proprietorship
Account	**Amount**
Contributed capital	$5,000
Retained earnings	$8,000
Owner's draws	($2,000)
Owner's equity (total)	$11,000

Owner's Equity in a Partnership

To track the equity for each partner in a partnership, you need to create three accounts for each partner: one for the partner's contributed capital, one for the partner's draws, and one for the partner's share of the distributed income.

Amounts that a partner withdraws, of course, get tracked with the partner's draws account.

The partner's share of the partnership's profits gets allocated to the partner's profit share account. (Your partnership agreement, by the way, should say how the partnership income is distributed among the partners.) Table 19-2 gives an example of owner's equity accounts in a partnership.

Table 19-2	An Example of Owner's Equity Accounts in a Partnership	
Account	**Partner A's Amount**	**Partner B's Amount**
Contributed capital	$5,000	$7,000
Profit share	$6,000	$6,000
Draws	($3,000)	($4,000)
Equity (total)	$8,000	$9,000

Owner's Equity in a Corporation

Yikes! Accounting for the owner's equity in a corporation can get mighty tricky mighty fast. In fact, I don't mind telling you that college accounting textbooks often use several chapters to describe all the ins and outs of corporation owner's equity accounting.

As long as you keep things simple, however, you can probably use three or four accounts for your owner's equity:

- ✔ **A par value account** for which you get the par value amount by multiplying the par value per share by the number of shares issued.

- ✔ **A paid-in capital in excess of par value account** for the amount investors paid for shares of stock in excess of par value. You get this amount by multiplying the price paid per share less the par value per share by the number of shares issued.

- ✔ **A retained earnings account** to track the business profits left invested in the business.

- ✔ **A dividends paid account** to track the amounts distributed to shareholders.

Table 19-3 shows an example of owner's equity accounts in a corporation.

Table 19-3	An Example of Owner's Equity in a Corporation
Account	*Amount*
Par value	$500
Paid-in capital in excess of par value	$4,500
Retained earnings	$8,000
Dividends paid	($3,000)
Shareholder's equity	$10,000

Multiple-State Accounting

For multiple-state accounting, you can either use classes to track sales in each state or set up a chart of accounts that includes a complete set of income and expense accounts (and, if necessary, a complete set of asset and liability accounts) for each state. After you set up this chart of accounts, all you have to do is use the correct state's income and expense accounts to record transactions.

If you do business in both Washington and Oregon, for example, you would record sales in Oregon as Oregon sales and sales in Washington as Washington sales. You would treat other income accounts and all your expense accounts in the same way. If you use class tracking for sales in different states, you wouldn't have duplicate accounts for each state.

Getting a Loan

Getting a loan is the hard part. After you get the money, recording it in QuickBooks is easy. All you do is record a journal entry that increases cash and that recognizes the new loan liability. For example, if you get a $5,000 loan, you record the following journal entry:

Debit	Credit
Cash	$5,000
Loan payable	$5,000

You'll already have a cash account set up, but you may need to set up a new liability account to track the loan.

Repaying a Loan

To record loan payments, you need to split each payment between two accounts: the interest expense account and the loan payable account.

For example, suppose that you're making $75-a-month payments on a $5,000 loan. Also, suppose that the lender charges 1 percent interest each month. The following journal entry records the first month's loan payment:

Debit	Credit	Explanation
Interest expense	$50	Calculated as 1 percent of $5,000
Loan payable	$25	The amount left over and applied to principal
Cash	$75	The total payment amount

The next month, of course, the loan balance is slightly less (because you made a $25 dent in the loan principal, as shown in the preceding loan payment journal entry). The following journal entry records the second month's loan payment:

Debit	Credit	Explanation
Interest expense	$49.75	Calculated as 1 percent of $4,975, the new loan balance
Loan payable	$25.25	The amount left over and applied to principal
Cash	$75.00	The total payment amount

Get the lender to provide you with an amortization schedule that shows the breakdown of each payment into interest expense and loan principal reduction.

You can record loan payments by using either the Write Checks window or the Enter Bills window. Just use the Expenses tab to specify the interest expense account and the loan liability account.

Chapter 20

(Almost) Ten Little Ideas for Saving Big on Business Taxes

. . . .

In This Chapter

▶ Use pension plan devices

▶ Stop taking personal vacations

▶ Choose to expense, not depreciate

▶ Incorporate your business

▶ Think about using the Sub S election

▶ Opt for the best of both worlds

▶ Put your kids to work

▶ Move your business

. . . .

*O*kay. I'm a little nervous about this. In fact, I had this crazy idea that maybe I should somehow camouflage this chapter. Perhaps name it something like "Don't Read This" or "Really Boring Stuff You Probably Don't Want to Know Anyway." My nervousness, I should point out, doesn't stem from the material. I daresay that what you can find here in this little chapter may provide you more value than almost anything else in this book. And because this chapter talks about how you can probably save at least hundreds — and very probably thousands — of dollars on taxes, well, by definition, the material is interesting.

No, here's the problem: What I talk about here is easily misunderstood. And if you misunderstand something I say here and then get just slightly mixed up in the way that you implement some strategy or follow some snidbit of advice, well, all bets are off. I can pretty well guarantee you a real mess.

So here's what I need you to do if you really want to save money on taxes:

1. Read through the tax-saving ideas that I present in this chapter.

Make sure that you understand (as best you can) the gist of each gambit.

2. **Sit down with your tax adviser and ask for help implementing the two or three ideas that make the most sense in your situation.**

By following these two steps, two other important things happen. One, you do the background research (just by reading this chapter) into which tax-saving tricks work in your situation. And, two, you get the expert advice typically necessary to make sure that you don't mess up and, thereby, find yourself in a heap of trouble.

And now let the tips begin.

Trick 1: Benefit from the Appropriate Pension Device

Let me start with the biggie. Pension plans. Here's the deal. If you're self-employed, you can set up a pension fund that pretty much lets you stash as much money as you want into things like Individual Retirement Accounts, SEP/IRAs, Simple-IRAs, 401(k)s, and some of their more exotic brothers and sisters — plans that go by the names of Paired Plan Keoghs and Defined Benefit Plans.

Although this angle doesn't sound very exciting, if your business is profitable, these plans give you a way to put money into tax-deductible, tax-deferred investment choices. In doing so, not only do you build wealth outside of your business — which is important for reducing risk — but you also save a heap of taxes.

I should clarify the risk-reduction angle here. In most states, money that you store in pension plans is not available to creditors. This protection means that if you go bankrupt, you may be able to save the money in your pension. And if someone sues you, again, you may be able to save the money in your pension. If you have questions about this possibility, ask your attorney.

The tax savings is easy to underestimate, so let me explain how this works. Say you have $10,000 of profit and are considering saving this money. Further, suppose that your marginal income tax rate — the top combined state and federal rate you pay on your last income — is 33 percent. In this case, if you save the $10,000 into a pension plan, you'll actually get a $3,300 tax savings, which is pretty impressive. With this method, much of the money you save actually comes from the tax savings.

You can calculate how big a tax savings you'll enjoy by multiplying your pension plan contribution by the marginal income tax rate. Remember, though, that you can further boost your tax savings and your pension plan contributions by saving your tax savings. In other words, you can also use the initial tax savings — $3,300 in this example — to augment the amount of the pension contribution. By saving your savings, you generate further savings.

Okay, all this business about pension fund contributions probably doesn't sound all that exciting. But before you say to yourself, "Man, this guy is boring," let me tell you two things you may not know.

- ✔ **The first thing you should know:** My guess is that your marginal tax rate is higher than you think. If you have a successful business in a state with income tax, you may easily be paying a 33-percent tax rate on your last dollars of income. And if you have a really successful business, you may be paying close to 50 percent. People often miss this fact — and get confused because average tax rates are lower. But we live in a country with very progressive tax rates. And small businesses often get hit harder by this progressivity than they realize. But anyway, that's the first thing you need to take away from this discussion of pension plan angles.

- ✔ **The second thing you should know:** You can probably save way more money in pension plan accounts than you realize. What you're probably thinking is, "Oh, yeah, I know you put a couple of grand into an IRA and a bit more into a 401(k)." But you don't realize that other, almost-secret pension plans, are available. And some of these other, almost-secret pension plans let you stash away oodles and oodles of money. For example, something called a paired plan lets you save up to $40,000 a year. With the help of a pension consultant, you can even set up pension plans that let you save $50,000 or $100,000 a year by using something called a Defined Benefit Plan.

I'm not going to spend any more time on this pension plan stuff. I have other tax tips to talk about. But do recognize that if you want to build wealth outside of your business, you can do so by using pension plan devices that provide you with just scads of tax savings.

While the tax breaks associated with pension fund options like those described in the preceding paragraphs seem like no-brainers, don't go to the work of setting up a pension plan for yourself or for employees if you can save just as much through traditional IRA accounts. For example, an individual can save up to $3,000 of earned income, and a married couple can save up to $6,000 of earned income in an IRA if the taxpayer or taxpayers aren't covered by some other qualified pension plan. If these IRA contribution limits are all you want to save, therefore, you don't need a formal pension plan. And you're only wasting your money by paying some plan administrator $2,000 or $3,000 a year to maintain such a plan.

Trick 2: Don't Take Any More Personal Vacations

Okay, I really, really want you to talk to your tax adviser about this gambit. In fact, I'm not going to tell you about this trick unless you promise me that you'll consult a tax adviser first. Okay?

Okay, that caveat given, let me point out something that a tax adviser told me a while back. He said to me, "Steve, you're basically an idiot to be taking personal vacations."

Now this guy wasn't telling me I should stop taking my family to Hawaii. He knows firsthand how gloomy and gray Seattle looks in February. His point, really, was that I could probably get many of the same benefits from business travel.

Rather than Hawaii, for example, he suggested a really good conference in sunny Phoenix. In this way, my plane ticket, the car rental, and the hotel all become business travel deductions. Of course, I can't write off my family's airplane tickets. But, in truth, many of the family's typical travel expenses — the hotel and car rental, to name just two — do become deductible by my following his suggestion.

The only real trick to this gambit is that the travel needs to be real business travel. You can't simply call a family vacation a business trip. You need to be doing real business.

By the way, I haven't actually taken this "don't take any family vacations" advice. I have a little problem unwinding on vacation anyway. And trying to take a working vacation just doesn't work for someone with my particular set of personality disorders. But you may be different. If what you really want from a vacation is some sun (or snow), a change of scenery, and a chance to see another part of the country or world, well, you may be able to get all these things on a tax-deductible business trip.

You promised me earlier that you would check with a tax adviser before attempting this gambit on your own. You need to meet very specific criteria in order to deduct travel expenses as business expenditures.

Trick 3: Don't Depreciate — Expense

I mention the Section 179 election in a handful of places elsewhere in this book. But because this is a powerful tax-saving gambit, let me again say that, in general, you can immediately expense up to the first $24,000 of depreciable stuff you buy in a year. (Usually, you have to depreciate depreciable stuff, thereby spreading out the deduction over the estimated economic life of the thing you bought.) In this way, you boost your deductions without actually having to suffer a cash outflow. Note that if you buy more than $200,000 of stuff in a year, the election amount gets phased out.

If you ask your tax adviser about how the Section 179 election works, ask him or her, too, about a *small tools policy.* This policy means that for some inexpensive items, you don't depreciate them — you just write them off.

For example, even though a $5 pen will last for perhaps three years, you don't actually have to depreciate the pen. You can instead write it off immediately. You can obviously apply the same rule to a $25 lamp — and maybe a $100 chair. And, well, here I better stop. Ask your tax adviser for more information.

Trick 4: Incorporate

In some circumstances, you can incorporate a business and save substantial income taxes. This step is tricky, though, because when you incorporate, the new corporation typically becomes a new taxpayer, which means that it's also subject to income taxes (except in the special case where you make the Sub S election, which I talk about in the very next trick).

The neat thing about corporations — at least for shareholder employees — is that they let you provide lots of tax-free fringe benefits to all your employees, including you.

But let me explain exactly how the corporation thing works. First, say you have a sole proprietorship that makes $100,000 a year. In this situation, you can't provide any tax-deductible fringe benefits to yourself, and you must pay taxes on the entire $100,000 of income. (By the way, a partnership can't for the most part provide tax-deductible fringe benefits to partners either.)

Okay. Now say you incorporate the exact same business, pay yourself a salary of $60,000, and provide a generous fringe benefits package worth around $20,000. In this case, the money you spend on the fringe benefits isn't taxable. And you can provide an incredibly rich fringe benefits package, including complete health insurance and even a generous medical expenses reimbursement plan. The medical expenses reimbursement plan, by the way, may include money for things like kids' orthodontia, new air conditioning that your allergist recommends for your house, and the backyard swimming pool your physician prescribes for your arthritis.

Now before you run off to your attorney's office and incorporate, let me share with you the two complicating factors in this "incorporate and provide yourself with massive fringe benefits" trick:

✔ **You must provide the same set of fringe benefits to all your employees.** Obviously that's not a big deal if the only employees are you and your spouse or maybe you and the other shareholder. But what if your kids work for the business, too? Or maybe you employ a bunch of other people? Do they all deserve, for example, a physician-prescribed backyard swimming pool? You see the problem.

✔ **You also face what people usually call the double-taxation problem.** Here's how this works. You can only pay yourself a fair salary. So, in the case where your business makes $100,000 and, out of this amount, you pay $60,000 in salary and another $20,000 in fringe benefits, you have another $20,000 in leftover profits. These profits — these corporate profits — are taxed at the corporate tax rates. Corporate tax rates run 15 percent on the first $50,000 of income and then rather quickly rise to rates that roughly run 35 percent to 40 percent. Now that doesn't sound so bad, I guess, but any money the corporation distributes to shareholders is taxed again as a dividend. So here's what happens to that last $20,000 of profit you can't pay out as a salary and can't pay out in fringe benefits.

- First, it's subjected to a 15-percent corporate tax, which reduces the $20,000 to $17,000 because the corporate tax amounts to $3,000.

- Then, when you pay out the remaining $17,000 as a dividend, you are subjected to another income tax — this time, the individual income tax, which will probably run roughly another 30 percent, or $5,100.

So you are taxed twice on the same money. And as a result, your $20,000 rather quickly dwindles to around $12,000 because of the roughly $3,000 corporate income tax and the roughly $5,000 personal income tax. Bummer.

Now before you shake your head, let me share a little secret. And this is another thing you need to discuss with your tax adviser. The double-taxation thing maybe isn't as bad as it seems if you're saving a good deal of money on the fringe benefits thing. For example, returning again to the case in which you're thinking about incorporating a business that makes $100,000 a year, the $20,000 of deductible fringe benefits may save you around $6,000 in taxes. The double-taxation penalty may cost you an extra $3,000 in corporate income taxes. So in that case, you're still $3,000 ahead.

I want to say one other thing about the double-taxation thing. Although the IRS looks very closely at the salaries that corporations pay to shareholder employees, I think that, in practice, you have a bit of wiggle room. Check with your tax adviser; but maybe in good years, you can pay yourself a $10,000 bonus, which adds to your salary and reduces your taxable corporate profits. Or maybe in good years, you invest extra money in the business. Perhaps the good years, for example, are when you buy the new equipment you regularly need. These sorts of tricks may further reduce the damage done by double taxation.

One other way to avoid the double-taxation problem is to elect Sub S status. If you do so, however, you don't get to deduct fringe benefits for shareholder employees.

Trick 5: Consider the Sub S Election

Okay, here's another tricky technique. And again, this is not something that you want to do without the help of a tax adviser! Those two warnings in place, let me say that you can sometimes save quite a bit of money by incorporating a business and then electing S corporation status. A corporation that elects S status doesn't get taxed at the corporate level on its profits. The profits just get allocated to the shareholders, and they then pay the personal income taxes on the corporate profits. What you save by using this option isn't income taxes but something that's often equally annoying: self-employment taxes.

Self-employment taxes are what self-employed persons pay in lieu of Social Security and Medicare taxes. In effect, they are equivalent to Social Security and Medicare taxes.

To explain how this election works, I need to set up an example. Say that you run a sole proprietorship and that you make $60,000 a year in profits. In this case, you must pay self-employment taxes (equivalent to Social Security and Medicare taxes) of 15.3 percent, or roughly $9,000. That's a bummer, right?

Well, if you incorporate and then tell the IRS that you want to be treated as a special type of corporation called an S corporation, you can split your $60,000 into two categories: wages and dividends. The weird part is that only your wages are subject to the self-employment taxes. You see where I'm going, right? Say, for example, that you're now incorporated, and that you take $30,000 of your $60,000 of profit and treat that money as wages. And then you take the other $30,000 of profit and treat that money as dividends. In this case, you pay self-employment taxes of around $4,500. Why? Because the 15.3-percent self-employment taxes you pay are only levied on the wages you make — not on the dividends.

The only trick in this deal is that you have to pay yourself a reasonable salary. If you're a plumber and plumbers make $50,000 a year where you live, for example, you can't pay yourself $30,000.

Trick 6: Enjoy the Best of Both Worlds

If you read Trick 4, you know that regular corporations, called C corporations, provide a neat tax-saving opportunity in the form of deductible fringe benefits. And that's pretty sweet. But if you read Trick 5, you know that Sub S corporations provide a different tax-savings opportunity — the self-employment taxes gambit (plus they let you avoid the double-taxation trap).

If you have to choose between one classification and the other, you need to sit down and work out the numbers, of course. But consider that this may not be an "either-or" option. Maybe you really have two businesses. In this case, you may want to treat the smaller business as a C corporation and the larger, more-profitable business as an S corporation. In this way, you may actually get to enjoy the best of both worlds.

Just so you don't waste any time on this, you can't be artificial in creating the second business. The I.R.S. has the ability to come in, look at the reality of your situation, and recategorize whatever you've done so it matches reality. For example, I have a CPA practice. But I can't decide to put individual tax returns and planning into a C corporation and then business tax returns and planning into an S corporation. That's clearly me being bogus. But if I also had, say, a travel agency, I could set up separate corporations for the travel agency business and for the public accounting practice. And one could be an S corporation, and one could be a C corporation.

Trick 7: Create Some Legitimate Job for Your Kids

Here's a clever trick I saw the partners of a CPA firm recently do. They put together a brochure that described all the services their firm offers to individuals. The brochure, of course, included pictures of the sorts of families they serve. And the models in the pictures were the partners' kids, who were, of course, fairly paid.

The neat thing about this trick is that the first bit of money a kid earns isn't taxable because of the standard deduction. So the partners effectively turned several thousand dollars of taxable "partner" income into nontaxable "partners' kids" income.

A side note: My understanding, by the way, is that the partners took the money that each kid was paid and stashed it away into that kid's college savings fund.

Trick 8: Relocate Your Business

Different states and cities have different income tax rates, so you want to be careful about where you locate your business. Now clearly, you don't want to pick a location purely for tax reasons. That truly would be a case of letting the tail wag the dog. But you ought to look at the tax burden of each of the locales from which you can operate your business. I save about $4,000 a year, for example, by operating my business from the suburbs rather than from downtown Seattle.

If you do consider the tax consequences of relocating your business, be sure to consider not just income taxes but also other taxes, such as payroll taxes like unemployment and workmen's compensation and even indirect taxes, such as minimum wage requirements. Recently, I was happy (Not!) to see that Washington state, where I live, forces employers to pay the nation's highest hourly minimum wage and the nation's second highest unemployment tax rate.

Chapter 21

(Almost) Ten Secret Business Formulas

. . . .

In This Chapter

▶ The first "most expensive money you can borrow" formula

▶ The second "most expensive money you can borrow" formula

▶ The "How do I break even?" formula

▶ The "You can grow too fast" formula

▶ The first "What happens if . . ." formula

▶ The second "What happens if . . ." formula

▶ The economic order quantity formula

▶ The Rule of 72

. . . .

1 have some good news and some bad news for you. The good news is that you can use some powerful formulas to better your chances of business success and increase your profits. No, I'm not joking. These formulas do exist. You can and should use them. And in the pages that follow, I explain the formulas and how to use them.

Now for the bad news: To use these formulas, you need to feel comfortable with a bit of arithmetic. You don't need to be a serious mathematician or anything. But you do need to feel comfortable with percentages and calculators. By the way, you can use the standard Windows Calculator accessory, available from within QuickBooks, to calculate any of the secret formulas.

Even if you're not particularly fond of (or all that good at) math, I want to encourage you to skim through this chapter. You can pick up some weird insights into the world of finance.

The First "Most Expensive Money You Can Borrow" Formula

Here's something you may not know: The most expensive money that you can borrow is from vendors who offer cash or early payment discounts that you don't take. For example, perhaps your friendly office supply store offers a 2 percent discount if you pay cash at the time of purchase instead of paying within the usual 30 days. You don't pay cash, so you pay the full amount (which is 2 percent more than the cash amount) 30 days later. In effect, you pay a 2-percent monthly interest charge. A 2-percent monthly interest charge works out to a 24-percent annual interest charge. And that's a great deal of money.

Here's another example that is only slightly more complicated. Many, many vendors offer a 2-percent discount if you pay within the first 10 days an invoice is due instead of 30 days later. (These payment terms are often described and printed at the bottom of the invoice as "2/10, Net 30.")

In this case, you pay 2 percent more by paying 20 days later. (The 20 days later is the difference between 10 days and 30 days.) Two percent for 20 days is roughly equivalent to 3 percent for 30 days, or a month. So, a 2-percent 20-day interest charge works out to a 36-percent annual interest charge. And now you're talking serious money.

Table 21-1 shows how some common early payment discounts (including cash discounts) translate into annual interest rates. By the way, I've been a bit more precise in my calculations for this table, so these numbers vary slightly from (and are larger than) those given in the preceding paragraph.

Table 21-1	Annual Interest Rates for Early Payment Discounts	
Early Payment Discount	*For Paying 20 Days Early*	*For Paying 30 Days Early*
1%	18.43%	12.29%
2%	37.24%	24.83%
3%	56.44%	37.63%
4%	76.04%	50.69%
5%	96.05%	64.04%

Is it just me, or do those numbers blow you away? The 2 percent for 20 days early payment discount that you often see works out (if you do the math precisely) to more than 37-percent annual interest. Man, that hurts. And if you don't take a 5 percent for 20 days early payment discount when it's offered, you're effectively borrowing money at an annual rate of 96 percent. You didn't read that last number wrong. Yes, a 5 percent for 20 days early payment discount works out to an annual interest rate of almost 100 percent.

I want to make a couple more observations, too. Turning down a 1-percent discount for paying 30 days early isn't actually a bad deal in many cases. Look at Table 21-1. It shows that the 1-percent discount for paying 30 days early is 12.29 percent. Sure, that rate is pretty high. But that interest rate is less than for many credit cards. And it's less than for many small-business credit lines. So if you would have to borrow money in some other way in order to pay 30 days early, making an early payment may not be cost-effective.

The bottom line on all this ranting is that early payment discounts, if not taken, represent one of the truly expensive ways to borrow money. I'm not saying that you won't need to borrow money this way at times. I can guess that your cash flow gets pretty tight sometimes (a circumstance that is true in most businesses, as you probably know). I am saying that you should never skip taking an early payment discount unless borrowing money at outrageous interest rates makes sense.

Oh, yes. The secret formula. To figure out the effective annual interest rate that you pay by not taking an early payment discount, use this formula:

Discount % / (1 – Discount %) × (365 / Number of Days of Early Payment)

So, to calculate the effective annual interest rate that you pay by not taking a 2-percent discount for paying 20 days early, calculate this formula:

.02 / (1 – .02) × (365 / 20)

Work out the mathematics, and you get .3724, which is the same thing as a 37.24-percent interest rate. (Note that the discount percents are entered as their equivalent decimal values.)

The Scientific view of the Windows Calculator includes parentheses keys that you can use to calculate this formula and the others I give in the chapter. Choose View➪Scientific to switch to the Scientific view of the calculator.

The Second "Most Expensive Money You Can Borrow" Formula

You know that "most expensive money you can borrow" stuff that I talk about in the preceding section? The very tragic flip side to that story occurs when you offer your customers an early payment discount and they take the discount. In effect, you borrow money from your customers at the same outrageous interest rates. For example, if customer Joe Schmoe gets a 2-percent early payment discount for paying 20 days early, you, in effect, pay ol' Joe roughly 2-percent interest for a 20-day loan. Using the same formula I give for the first "most expensive money you can borrow" formula, the rate works out to 37.24 percent.

In some industries, customers expect early payment discounts. You may have to offer them, but you should never offer them willingly. You should never offer them just for fun. Borrowing money this way is just too expensive. A rate of 37.24 percent? Yikes!

Let me also offer a rather dour observation. In my experience, anytime someone offers big early payment discounts — I've seen them as big as 5 percent — they're either stupid or desperate, and probably both.

The "How Do I Break Even?" Formula

I know that you're not interested in just breaking even. I know that you want to make money in your business. But knowing what quantities you need to sell just to cover your expenses is often super-helpful. If you're a one-person accounting firm (or some other service business), for example, how many hours do you need to work to pay your expenses and perhaps pay yourself a small salary? Or, if you're a retailer of, say, toys, how many toys do you need to sell to pay your overhead, the rent, and sales clerks?

You see my point, right? Knowing how much revenue you need to generate just to stay in the game is essential. Knowing your break-even point enables you to establish a benchmark for your performance. (Anytime you don't break even, you know that you have a serious problem that you need to resolve quickly to stay in business.) And considering break-even points is invaluable when you think about new businesses or new ventures.

As you ponder any new opportunity and its potential income and expenses, you need to know how much income you need to generate just to pay those expenses.

To calculate a break-even point, you need to know just three pieces of information: your *fixed costs* (the expenses you have to pay regardless of the business's revenue, or income), the revenue you generate for each sale, and the variable costs that you incur in each sale. (These variable costs, which also are called *direct expenses,* in case you care, aren't the same thing as the fixed costs.)

- ✔ Whatever you sell — be it thingamajigs, corporate jets, or hours of consulting services — has a price. That price is your revenue per item input.

- ✔ Most of the time, what you sell has a cost, too. If you buy and resell thingamajigs, those thingamajigs cost you some amount of money. The total of your thingamajigs' costs varies depending on how many thingamajigs you buy and sell, which is why these costs are referred to as *variable costs*. A couple of examples of variable costs include hourly (or contract) labor and shipping. Sometimes, the variable cost per item is zero, however. (If you're a consultant, for example, you sell hours of your time. But you may not pay an hourly cost just because you consult for an hour.)

- ✔ Your fixed costs are all those costs that you pay regardless of whether you sell your product or service. For example, if you have to pay an employee a salary regardless of whether you sell anything, that salary is a fixed cost. Your rent is probably a fixed cost. Things like insurance and legal and accounting expenses are probably also fixed costs because they don't vary with fluctuations in your revenue.

Fixed costs may change a bit from year to year or may bounce around a bit during a year. So maybe *fixed* isn't a very good adjective. People use the term *fixed costs,* however, to differentiate these costs from *variable costs,* which are those costs that do vary with the number of goods you sell.

Take the book-writing business as an example. Suppose that as you read this book, you think, "Man, that guy is having too much fun. Writing about accounting programs . . . working day in and day out with buggy beta software . . . yeah, that would be the life."

Further suppose that for every book you write, you think that you can make $5,000, but that you'll probably end up paying about $1,000 per book for such things as long-distance telephone charges, overnight courier charges, and extra hardware and software. And suppose that you need to pay yourself a salary of $20,000 a year. (In this scenario, your salary is your only fixed cost because you plan to write at home at a small desk in your bedroom.) Table 21-2 shows how the situation breaks down.

Table 21-2	**Costs and Revenue**	
Variable	*Amount*	*Explanation*
Revenue	$5,000	What you can squeeze out of the publisher
Variable costs	$1,000	All the little things that add up
Fixed costs	$20,000	You need someplace to live and food to eat

With these three bits of data, you can easily calculate how many books you need to write to break even. Here's the formula:

Fixed Costs / (Revenue – Variable Costs)

If you plug in the writing business example data, the formula looks like this:

$20,000 / ($5,000 – $1,000)

Work through the math, and you get five. So you need to write (and get paid for) five books a year to pay the $1,000 per book variable costs and your $20,000 salary. Just to prove that I didn't make up this formula and that it really works, Table 21-3 shows how things look if you write five books.

Table 21-3	**The Break-Even Point**	
Description	*Amount*	*Explanation*
Revenue	$25,000	Five books at $5,000 each
Variable costs	($5,000)	Five books at $1,000 each
Fixed costs	($20,000)	A little food money, a little rent money, a little beer money
Profits	$0	Subtract the costs from the revenue, and nothing is left

Accountants, by the way, use parentheses to show negative numbers. That's why the $5,000 and the $20,000 in Table 21-3 are in parentheses.

But back to the game. To break even in a book-writing business like the one that I describe here, you need to sell and write five books a year. If you don't think that you can write and sell five books in a year, getting into the book-writing business makes no sense.

Your business is probably more complicated than book writing, but the same formula and logic for calculating your break-even point apply. You need just three pieces of information: the revenue you receive from the sale of a single item, the variable costs of selling (and possibly making) the item, and the fixed costs that you pay just to be in business.

QuickBooks doesn't collect or present information in a way that enables you to easily pull the revenue per item and variable costs per item off some report. Nor does it provide a fixed-costs total on some report. But if you understand the logic of the preceding discussion, you can easily massage the QuickBooks data to get the information you need.

The "You Can Grow Too Fast" Formula

Here's a weird little paradox: One of the easiest ways for a small business to fail is by being too successful. I know. It sounds crazy, but it's true. In fact, I'll even go out on a limb and say that business success is by far the most common reason that I see for business failure.

"Oh, geez," you say. "This nut is talking in circles."

Let me explain. Whether you realize it, you need a certain amount of financial horsepower, or net worth, to do business. (Your *net worth* is just the difference between your assets and your liabilities.) You need to have some cash in the bank to tide you over the rough times that everybody has at least occasionally. You probably need to have some office furniture and computers so that you can take care of the business end of the business. And if you make anything at all, you need to have adequate tools and machinery. This part all makes sense, right?

How net worth relates to growth

Okay, now on to the next reality. If your business grows and continues to grow, you need to increase your financial horsepower, or net worth. A bigger business, for example, needs more cash to make it through the tough times than a smaller business does — along with more office furniture and computers and more tools and machinery. Oh sure, you may be able to have one growth spurt because you started off with more financial horsepower (more net worth) than you needed. But — and this is the key part — you can't sustain business growth without increasing your net worth. Some of you are now saying things like, "No way, man. That doesn't apply to me." I assure you, my new friend, it does.

As long as your creditors will extend you additional credit as you grow your business — and they should, as long as the business is profitable and you don't have cash-flow problems — you can grow your business as fast as you can grow your net worth. If you can grow your net worth by 5 percent a year, your business can grow at an easily sustained rate of only 5 percent a year. If you can grow your net worth by 50 percent a year, your business can grow at an easily sustained rate of only (only?) 50 percent a year.

You grow your business's net worth in only two ways:

- **By reinvesting profits in the business.**

  Note that any profits that you leave in the business instead of drawing them out — such as through dividends or draws — are reinvested.

- **By getting people to invest money in the business.**

  If you're not in a position to continually raise money from new investors — and most small businesses aren't — the only practical way to grow is by reinvesting profits in the business.

Calculating sustainable growth

You can calculate the growth rate that your business can sustain by using this formula:

Reinvested Profits / Net Worth

I should say, just for the record, that this formula is a very simple *sustainable growth* formula. But even so, it offers some amazingly interesting insights. For example, perhaps you're a commercial printer doing $500,000 in revenues a year with a business net worth of $100,000; your business earns $50,000 a year, but you leave only $10,000 a year in the business. In other words, your reinvested profits are $10,000. In this case, your sustainable growth is calculated as follows:

$10,000 / $100,000

Work out the numbers and you get .1, or 10 percent. In other words, you can grow your business by 10 percent a year (as long as you grow the net worth by 10 percent a year by reinvesting profits). For example, you can easily go from $500,000 to $550,000 to $605,000 and continue growing annually at this 10 percent rate. But your business can't grow any faster than 10 percent a year. That is, you'll get into serious trouble if you try to go from $500,000 to $600,000 to $720,000 and continue growing at 20 percent a year.

CASE STUDY

How growth kills businesses

I don't want to beat this sustainable growth thing to death, but let me close with a true and mercifully short story.

I just saw another entrepreneur fail because he was successful. At first, he ignored the symptoms of fast growth. He needed another computer, so he bought it. He had to hire another person, so he just did it. Cash flow was tight and getting tighter, but he ignored the problems. After all, he was making a large number of sales, and the business was growing. Sure, things were getting awkward, but he didn't need to worry, right?

Unfortunately, because his cash flow was so tight, he paid his vendors later and later. This situation went on for a few weeks until some vendors started insisting on cash payments. One

Friday, he couldn't make his payroll. He then committed the unpardonable sin of borrowing payroll tax money — something you should never, ever do.

Finally, he had a large number of bills to pay and with no cash to pay the bills and no cash in sight. Employees quit. Vendors said, "No more." This lack of cash is what ultimately killed the business. When the telephone company cuts off your telephone service, you're in serious trouble. When your landlord locks you out of your business location, you're pretty much out of luck.

The paradox in this story is that the guy had a successful business. He just spread his financial resources too thin by growing too fast.

REMEMBER

You can convert a decimal value to a percentage by multiplying the value by 100. For example, $.1 \times 100$ equals 10, so .1 equals 10 percent. You can convert a percentage to a decimal value by dividing the value by 100. For example, 25 (as in 25 percent) divided by 100 equals .25.

TIP

By the way, the sustainable growth formula inputs are pretty easy to get after you have QuickBooks up and running. You can get the net worth figure off the balance sheet. You can calculate the reinvested profits by looking at the net income and deducting any amounts that you pulled out of the business.

REMEMBER

I'm not going to go through the mathematical proof of why this sustainable growth formula is true. My experience is that the formula makes intuitive sense to people who think about it for a few minutes. If you aren't into the intuition thing or you don't believe me, get a college finance textbook and look up its discussion of the sustainable growth formula. Or do what all the kids today are doing — search online for "sustainable growth formula."

The First "What Happens if . . ." Formula

One curiosity about small businesses is that small changes in revenue or income can have huge impacts on profits. A retailer who cruises along at $200,000 in revenue and struggles to live on $30,000 a year never realizes that boosting the sales volume by 20 percent to $250,000 may increase profits by 200 percent to $60,000.

In fact, if you take only one point away from this discussion, it should be this curious little truth: If fixed costs don't change, small changes in revenue can produce big changes in profits.

The following example shows how this point works and provides a secret formula. For starters, say that you currently generate $100,000 a year in revenue and make $20,000 a year in profits. The revenue per item sold is $100, and the variable cost per item sold is $35. (In this case, the fixed costs happen to be $45,000 a year, but that figure isn't all that important to the analysis.)

Accountants like to whip up little tables that describe these sorts of things, so Table 21-4 gives the current story on your imaginary business.

Table 21-4	Your Business Profits	
Description	*Amount*	*Explanation*
Revenue	$100,000	You sell 1,000 doohickeys at $100 a pop
Variable costs	($35,000)	You buy 1,000 doohickeys at $35 a pop
Fixed costs	($45,000)	All the little things: rent, your salary, and so on
Profits	$20,000	What's left over

Okay, Table 21-4 shows the current situation. But suppose that you want to know what will happen to your profits if revenue increases by 20 percent but your fixed costs don't change. Mere mortals, not knowing what you and I know, might assume that a 20 percent increase in revenue would produce an approximate 20 percent increase in profits. But you know that small changes in revenue can produce big changes in profits, right?

To estimate exactly how a change in revenue affects profits, use the following secret formula:

$$\text{Percentage} \times \text{Revenue} \times (1 - \text{Variable Cost per Item} / \text{Revenue per Item})$$

Using the sample data provided in Table 21-4 (I'm sorry this example is starting to resemble those story problems from eighth-grade math), you make the following calculation:

$$.20 \times \$100{,}000 \times (1 - 35 / 100)$$

Work out the numbers, and you get 13,000. What does this figure mean? It means that a 20 percent increase in revenue produces a $13,000 increase in profits. As a percentage of profits, this $13,000 increase is 65 percent ($13,000 / $20,000 = 65 percent).

Let me stop here and make a quick observation. In my experience, entrepreneurs always seem to think that they need to grow big to make big money. They concentrate on doing things that will double or triple or quadruple their sales. Their logic, though, isn't always correct. If you can grow your business without having to increase your fixed costs, small changes in revenues can produce big changes in profits.

Before I stop talking about this first "What happens if . . ." formula, I want to quickly describe where you get the inputs you need for the formula:

- ✔ The percentage change input is just a number that you pick. If you want to see what happens to your profits with a 25 percent increase in sales, for example, use .25.

- ✔ The revenue input is your total revenue. You can get it from your profit and loss statement. (In Chapter 14, I describe how you can create a profit and loss statement by using QuickBooks.)

- ✔ The revenue per item sold and variable costs per item sold figures work the same way as I describe for the break-even formula earlier in this chapter.

The Second "What Happens if . . ." Formula

Maybe I shouldn't tell you this. But people in finance, like me, usually have a prejudice against people in sales. And it's not just because people who are good at sales usually make more money than people who are good at finance. It's really not. Honest to goodness.

Here's the prejudice: People in finance think that people in sales always want to reduce prices.

People in sales see things a bit differently. They say, in effect, "Hey, you worry too much. We'll make up the difference in additional sales volume." The argument is appealing: You just undercut your competitor's prices by a healthy chunk and make less on each sale. But because you sell your stuff so cheaply, your customers will beat a path to your door.

Just for the record, I love people who are good at sales. I think that someone who is good at sales is more important than someone who is good at finance.

But, that painful admission aside, I have to tell you that I see a problem with the "Cut the prices; we'll make it up with volume" strategy. If you cut prices by a given percentage — perhaps by 10 percent — you usually need a much bigger percentage gain in revenue to break even.

The following example shows what I mean and how this strategy works. Suppose that you have a business that sells some doohickey or thingamajig. You generate $100,000 a year in revenue and make $20,000 a year in profits. Your revenue per item, or doohickey, sold is $100, and your variable cost per item, or doohickey, sold is $35. Your fixed costs happen to be $45,000 a year; but, again, the fixed costs aren't all that important to the analysis. Table 21-5 summarizes the current situation.

Table 21-5	Your Current Situation	
Description	*Amount*	*Explanation*
Revenue	$100,000	You sell 1,000 doohickeys at $100 a pop
Variable costs	($35,000)	You buy 1,000 doohickeys at $35 a pop
Fixed costs	($45,000)	All the little things: rent, your salary, and so on
Profits	$20,000	What's left over

Then business is particularly bad for one month. Joe-Bob, your sales guy, comes to you and says, "Boss, I have an idea. I think that we can cut prices by 15 percent to $85 a doohickey and get a truly massive boost in sales."

You're a good boss. You're a polite boss. Plus, you're intrigued. So you think a bit. The idea has a certain appeal. You start wondering how much of an increase in sales you need to break even on the price reduction.

You're probably not surprised to read this, but I have another secret formula that can help. You can use the following formula to calculate how many items (doohickeys, in the example) you need to sell just to break even on the new, discounted price. Here's the formula:

(Current Profits + Fixed Costs) / (Revenue per Item – Variable Cost per Item)

Using the example data provided earlier, you make the following calculation:

($20,000 + $45,000) / ($85 – $35)

Work out the numbers and you get 1,300. What does this figure mean? It means that just to break even on the $85 doohickey price — just to break even — Joe-Bob needs to sell 1,300 doohickeys. Currently, per Table 21-3, Joe-Bob sells 1,000 doohickeys a year. As a percentage, then, this jump from 1,000 doohickeys to 1,300 doohickeys is exactly a 30 percent increase. (Remember that Joe-Bob proposes a 15 percent price cut.)

Okay, I don't know Joe-Bob. He may be a great guy. He may be a wonderful salesperson. But here's my guess: Joe-Bob isn't thinking about a 30 percent increase in sales volume. (Remember, with a 15 percent price reduction, you need a 30 percent increase just to break even!) And Joe-Bob almost certainly isn't thinking about a 50 percent or 75 percent increase in sales volume — which is what you need to make money on the whole deal, as shown in Table 21-6.

Table 21-6	How Profits Look at Various Sales Levels		
Description	*1,300 Units Sold*	*1,500 Units Sold*	*1,750 Units Sold*
Revenue	$110,500	$127,500	$148,750
Variable costs	($45,500)	($52,500)	($61,250)
Fixed costs	($45,000)	($45,000)	($45,000)
Profits	$20,000	$30,000	$42,500

In summary, you can't reduce prices by, say, 15 percent and then go for some penny-ante increase. You need huge increases in the sales volume to get big increases in profits. If you look at Table 21-6, you can see that if you can increase the sales from 1,000 doohickeys to 1,750 doohickeys — a 75 percent increase — you can more than double the profits. This increase assumes that the fixed costs stay level, as the table shows.

I want to describe quickly where you get the inputs that you need for the formula:

✔ The profit figure can come right off the QuickBooks profit and loss statement.

✔ The fixed costs figure just tallies all your fixed costs. (I talk about fixed costs earlier in this chapter in "The 'How Do I Break Even?' Formula" section.)

✔ The revenue per item is just the new price that you're considering.

✔ Finally, the variable cost per item is the cost of the thing you sell. (I discuss this cost earlier in the chapter, too.)

Please don't construe the preceding discussion as proof that you should never listen to the Joe-Bobs of the world. The "cut prices to increase volume" strategy can work wonderfully well. The trick, however, is to increase the sales volume massively. Sam Walton, the late founder of Wal-Mart, used the strategy and became, at one point, the richest man in the world.

The Economic Order Quantity (a.k.a. Isaac Newton) Formula

Isaac Newton invented differential calculus, a fact that is truly amazing to me. I can't imagine how someone could just figure out calculus. I could never, in a hundred years, figure it out. But I'm getting off the track.

The neat thing about calculus — besides the fact that I'm not going to do any for you here — is that it enables you to create optimal values equations. One of the coolest such equations is called the *economic order quantity,* or *EOQ,* model. I know that this stuff all sounds terribly confusing and totally boring, but stay with me for just another paragraph. (If you're not satisfied in another paragraph or so, skip ahead to the next secret formula.)

Perhaps you buy and then resell — oh, I don't know — 2,000 cases of vintage French wine every year. The EOQ model enables you to decide whether you should order all 2,000 cases at one time, order 1 case at a time, or order some number of cases in between 1 case and 2,000 cases.

Another way to say the same thing is that the EOQ model enables you to choose the best, or optimal, reorder quantity for items that you buy and then resell.

If you're still with me at this point, I figure that you want to know how this formula works. You need to know just three pieces of data to calculate the optimal order quantity: the annual sales volume, the cost of placing an order, and the annual cost of holding one unit in inventory. You plug this information into the following formula:

$$\sqrt{(2 \times \text{Sales Volume} \times \text{Order Cost})/\text{Annual Holding Cost per Item}}$$

You buy and resell 2,000 cases a year, so that amount is the sales volume. Every time you place an order for the wine, you need to buy an $800 round-trip ticket to Paris (just to sample the inventory) and pay $200 for a couple of nights at a hotel. So your cost per order is $1,000. Finally, with insurance, interest on a bank loan, and the cost of maintaining your hermetically sealed, temperature-controlled wine cellar, the cost of storing a case of wine is about $100 a year. In this example, then, you can calculate the optimal order quantity as follows:

$$\sqrt{(2 \times 2000 \times \$1000) / \$100}$$

Work through the numbers, and you get 200. Therefore, the order quantity that minimizes the total cost of your trips to Paris and of holding your expensive wine inventory is 200 cases. You could, of course, make only one trip to Paris a year and buy 2,000 cases of wine at once, thereby saving travel money, but you would spend more money on holding your expensive wine inventory than you would save on travel costs. And, although you could reduce your wine inventory carrying costs by going to Paris every week and picking up a few cases, your travel costs would go way, way up. (Of course, you would get about a billion frequent flyer miles a year.)

You can use the Standard view of the Windows Calculator to compute economic order quantities. The trick is to click the √ (square root) key last. For example, to calculate the economic order quantity in the preceding example, you enter the following numbers and operators:

$$\sqrt{(2 \times 2000 \times 1000) / 100}$$

The Rule of 72

The Rule of 72 isn't exactly a secret formula. It's more like a general rule. Usually, people use this rule to figure out how long it will take for some investment or savings account to double in value. The Rule of 72 is a cool little trick, however, and it has several useful applications for businesspeople.

What the rule says is that if you divide the value 72 by an interest rate percentage, your result is approximately the number of years it will take to double your money. For example, if you can stick money into some investment that pays 12 percent interest, it will take roughly 6 years to double your money because 72 / 12 = 6.

The Rule of 72 isn't exact, but it's usually close enough for government work. For example, if you invest $1,000 for 6 years at 12 percent interest, what you really get after 6 years isn't $2,000 but $1,973.92.

If you're in business, you can use the Rule of 72 for a couple other forecasts, too:

- ✔ **To forecast how long it will take inflation to double the price of an item, divide 72 by the inflation rate.** For example, if you own a building with a value that you figure will at least keep up with inflation and you wonder how long the building will take to double in value if inflation runs at 4 percent, you just divide 72 by 4. The result is 18, meaning that it will take roughly 18 years for the building to double in value. Again, the Rule of 72 isn't exactly on the money, but it's dang close. A $100,000 building increases in value to $202,581.65 over 18 years if the annual inflation rate is 4 percent.

- ✔ **To forecast how long it will take to double sales volume, divide 72 by the given annual growth rate.** For example, if you can grow your business by, say, 9 percent a year, you will roughly double the size of the business in 8 years because 72 / 9 = 8. (I'm becoming kind of compulsive about this point, I know, but let me say again that the rule isn't exact, but it's very close. If a $1,000,000-a-year business grows 9 percent annually, its sales equal $1,992,562.64 after 8 years of 9 percent growth. This figure really means that the business will generate roughly $2,000,000 of sales in the ninth year.)

Part V
Appendixes

The 5th Wave — By Rich Tennant

"We can monitor our entire operation from one central location. We know what the 'Wax Lips' people are doing; we know what the 'Whoopee Cushion' people are doing; we know what the 'Fly-in-the-Ice Cube' people are doing. But we don't know what the 'Plastic Vomit' people are doing. We don't want to know what the 'Plastic Vomit' people are doing."

In this part . . .

Appendixes are like basements. Why? You use them to store stuff that you want to keep but don't know where else to put. The appendixes that follow provide instructions for installing QuickBooks, an overview of accounting, and help with project estimating, and a description of the QuickBooks Timer program.

Appendix A

How to Install QuickBooks in Ten Easy Steps

- -

*I*f you haven't already installed QuickBooks, get it over with right now:

1. **Turn on the PC.**

   Find and flip on the computer's power switch. (Depending on whether you're using Windows 95, 98, NT, Windows 2000, Windows Me, or Windows XP, your screen may look a little different than the figures here.) I'm using Windows XP Professional, by the way. Not that you care or that it matters. . . .

   If you're installing QuickBooks on a computer running Windows NT, Windows 2000, or Windows XP Professional, you need to log on as either the administrator or a user with administrator rights. With these operating systems, Windows security features require an administrator to install the QuickBooks program.

2. **Get the QuickBooks CD.**

   Rip open the QuickBooks package and get out the CD (which looks exactly like the ones that play music).

3. **Insert the CD in your CD-ROM drive.**

   If you have any amount of luck, Windows recognizes that you've inserted the QuickBooks CD and displays the dialog box shown in Figure A-1, which asks if you want to install QuickBooks. If you see this dialog box — you might have to wait a few minutes — click the Yes button and skip to Step 6.

Figure A-1:
The Do You
Want to
Install
QuickBooks
Now dialog
box.

4. **If nothing happens when you insert the QuickBooks CD, open the Control Panel window.**

   In Windows XP, click the Start button and then choose Control Panel. In most versions of Windows, including Windows 2000, you click the Start button and then choose Settings⇨Control Panel from the Start menu. Figure A-2 shows the Windows XP Control Panel window that appears.

5. **Start the Windows Install program.**

   In most versions of Windows, you can do this by double-clicking the Add or Remove Programs icon. When the dialog box in Figure A-3 appears, click Add New Programs and follow the on-screen instructions. You need to press the Enter key a couple-three times to move through some dialog boxes. Figure A-3, I should mention, is the Windows XP Add/Remove Programs tool. If you're using some other flavor of Windows, the tool looks different. But it works in roughly the same way.

6. **Tell QuickBooks how you want it to install itself.**

   The QuickBooks setup window appears. Enter the CD key code and click Next to begin the installation process. Then follow the on-screen instructions. If you have a question about an installation option, just accept the QuickBooks suggestion by pressing Enter. (The suggested, or default, installation options are fine for 999 out of 1,000 users.)

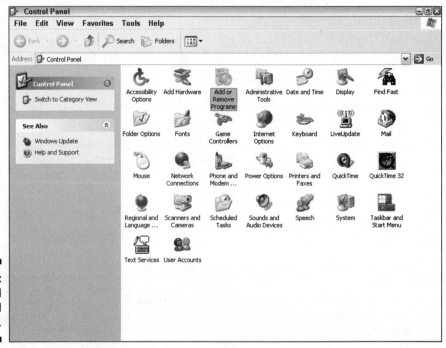

Figure A-2:
The Control Panel window.

Figure A-3:
The Add/
Remove
Programs
tool in
Windows XP
Professional.

7. **Click Next to begin copying the files.**

   QuickBooks gives you a summary of your installation choices and then tells you to click Next to begin copying the files. Do so. As the installation program runs, you should see a little bar that shows your progress.

   If you need to cancel the installation at any time, click Cancel. QuickBooks warns you that the setup is incomplete. That's okay — just start the setup from scratch next time around.

8. **Take 30 seconds or so to contemplate the meaning of life or get a drink of water.**

9. **After the Install program finishes, click Restart.**

   Congratulations. You're finished with the installation. You have a new item on the Programs menu and probably new shortcuts on your desktop.

10. **(Optional) Celebrate.**

    Stand up at your desk, click your heels together three times, and repeat the phrase, "There's no place like home, Toto; there's no place like home." And watch out for flying houses.

As soon as you're done celebrating, you may want to flip to Chapter 1 and find out how to register the program. You'll probably want to register QuickBooks before you begin using it.

If you work on a network and want to be able to share a QuickBooks file stored on one computer with other computers on the network, you need to install QuickBooks on all of the other computers that you want to use to work with the file. ***Note:*** You need a separate copy of QuickBooks — such as from the five-pack version — for each computer on which you want to install QuickBooks. And by the way, just because I've had a couple of clients ask about this in the last week: Running QuickBooks on a network with multiple QuickBooks users isn't super-tricky or terribly complicated. QuickBooks takes care of the hard stuff. If you've got more than one person using QuickBooks, you owe it to yourself (and your business) to set up a network and then purchase and install multiple copies of QuickBooks. Refer to Chapter 3 for more information.

Appendix B

If Numbers Are Your Friends

● ●

You don't need to know much about accounting or about double-entry bookkeeping to use QuickBooks, which, as you know, is most of its appeal. But if you're serious about this accounting business or serious about your business, consider finding out a bit more; setting up QuickBooks and understanding all the QuickBooks reports will be easier, and you'll be more sophisticated in your accounting, too.

Now, just because the accounting in this appendix is a little more complicated doesn't mean that you can't understand it. To make this whole discussion more concrete, I use one big example. Hope it helps you out! If nothing else, it'll inspire you to get into the rowboat rental business.

Keying In on Profit

Start with the big picture. The key purpose of an accounting system is to enable you to answer the burning question, "Am I making any money?"

Accounting is that simple. Really. At least conceptually. So, throughout the rest of this appendix, I just talk about how to calculate a business's profits in a reasonably accurate but still practical manner.

Let me introduce you to the new you

You just moved to Montana for the laid-back living and fresh air. You live in a cute log cabin on Flathead Lake. To support yourself, you plan to purchase several rowboats and rent them to visiting fly fishermen. Of course, you'll probably need to do quite a bit of fly-fishing, too. But just consider that the price you pay for being your own boss.

The first day in business

It's your first day in business. About 5 a.m., ol' Peter Gruntpaw shows up to deliver your three rowboats. He made them for you in his barn, but even so, they aren't cheap. He charges $1,500 apiece, so you write him a check for $4,500.

Peter's timing, as usual, is impeccable. About 5:15 a.m., your first customers arrive. Mr. and Mrs. Hamster (pronounced ohm-stair) are visiting from Phoenix. They want to catch the big fish. You're a bit unsure of your pricing, but you suggest $25 an hour for the boat. They agree and pay $200 in cash for eight hours.

A few minutes later, another couple arrives. The Gerbils (pronounced go-bells) are very agitated. They were supposed to meet the Hamsters and fish together, but the Hamsters are rowing farther and farther away from the dock. To speed the Gerbils' departure, you let them leave without paying. But you're not worried. As the Gerbils leave the dock, Ms. Gerbil shouts, "We'll pay you the $200 when we get back!"

Although you don't rent the third boat, you do enjoy a sleepy summer morning.

About 2 p.m., the Hamsters and Gerbils come rowing back into view. Obviously, though, a problem has occurred. You find out what it is when the first boat arrives. "Gerbil fell into the lake," laughs Mr. Hamster. "Lost his wallet, too." Everybody else seems to think that the lost wallet is funny. You secretly wonder how you're going to get paid. No wallet, no money.

You ask Mr. Gerbil if he would like to come out to the lake tomorrow to pay you. He says he'll just write you a check when he gets home to Phoenix. Reluctantly, you agree.

Look at your cash flow first

I've just described a fairly simple situation. But even so, answering the question, "Did I make any money?" isn't going to be easy. You start by looking at your cash flow: You wrote a check for $4,500, and you collected $200 in cash. Table B-1 shows your cash flow.

Table B-1	The First Day's Cash Flow	
	Cash In and Out	*Amount*
Add the cash in:	Rent money from Hamsters (pronounced ohm-stairs)	$200
	Rent money from Gerbils (pronounced go-bells)	$0
Subtract the cash out:	Money to purchase rowboats	($4,500)
Equals your cash flow:		($4,300)

To summarize, you had $200 come in but $4,500 go out. So your cash flow was –$4,300. (That's why the $4,300 is in parentheses.) From a strictly cash-flow perspective, the first day doesn't look all that good, right? But does the cash flow calculation show you whether you're making money? Can you look at it and gauge whether your little business is on the right track?

The answer to both questions is no. Your cash flow is important. You can't, for example, write a $4,500 check unless you have at least $4,500 in your checking account. But your cash flow doesn't tell you whether you're making money. In fact, you may see a couple of problems with looking just at the cash flow of the rowboat rental business.

Depreciation is an accounting gimmick

Here's the first problem: If you take good care of the rowboats, you can use them every summer for the next few years. In fact, say that the rowboat rental season, which runs from early spring to late autumn, is 150 days long and that your well-made rowboats will last 10 years.

✔ **You can probably rent the rowboats for 1,500 days.**

(150 days a year times 10 years equals 1,500 days)

✔ **Each rowboat costs $1,500.**

The depreciation expense for each rowboat is only $1 per day over 1,500 days. That's a whopping $3 for all three boats.

Do you see what I'm saying? If you have something that costs a great deal of money but lasts for a long time, spreading out the cost makes sense. This spreading out is usually called *depreciation*. The little $1 chunks that are allocated to a day are called the *depreciation expense*.

Different names, same logic

I don't see any point in hiding this nasty little accounting secret from you: Accountants call this cost-allocation process by different names, depending on what sort of cost is being spread out.

Most of the time, the cost allocation is called *depreciation.* You depreciate buildings, machinery, furniture, and many other items as well. But allocating the cost of a natural resource — such as crude oil that you pump, coal that you dig up, or minerals that you extract — is called *depletion.* And allocating the cost of things that aren't tangible — copyrights and patents, for example — is *amortization.*

Accountants use the terms *cost* and *expense* to mean distinctly different things. A cost is the price you pay for something. If you pay Peter Gruntpaw $1,500 for a rowboat, the rowboat's cost is $1,500. An expense, on the other hand, is what you use in a profit calculation. The little $1 chunks of the rowboat's $1,500 cost (that are allocated to individual days) are expenses.

If this depreciation stuff seems wacky, remember that what you're really trying to do is figure out whether you made any money your first day of business. And all I'm really saying is that you shouldn't include the whole cost of the rowboats as an expense in the first day's profit calculation. Some of the cost should be included as an expense in calculating the profit in future days. That's fair, right?

Accrual-basis accounting is cool

You don't want to forget about the $200 that the Gerbils owe you either. Although Mr. Gerbil (remember that the name's pronounced go-bell) may not send you the check for several days, or even for several weeks, he will pay you. You've earned the money.

The principles of accounting say that you should include sales in your profit calculations when you earn the money and not when you actually collect it. The logic behind this "include sales when they're earned" rule is that it produces a better estimate of the business you're doing.

Say that the day after the Gerbils and Hamsters rent the rowboats, you have no customers, but Mr. Gerbil comes out and pays you $200. If you use the "include sales when they're earned" rule — or what's called *accrual-basis accounting* — your daily sales look like this:

	Day 1	Day 2
Sales	$400	$0

If you instead use what's called *cash-basis accounting* (in which you count sales when you collect the cash), your daily sales look like this:

	Day 1	Day 2
Sales	$200	$200

The traditional accrual-based accounting method shows that you have a good day when you rent two boats and a terrible day when you don't rent any boats. In comparison, when you use cash-basis accounting your sales record looks as if you rented a boat each day, even though you didn't. Now you know why accrual-basis accounting is a better way to measure profit.

Accrual-basis accounting also works for expenses. You should count an expense when you make it, not when you pay it. For example, you call the local radio station and ask the people there to announce your new boat rental business a couple of times for a fee of $25. Although you don't have to pay the radio station the day you make the arrangements for your announcement, you should still count the $25 as an expense for that day.

Now you know how to measure profits

With what you now know, you're ready to measure the first day's profits. Table B-2 is a profit and loss statement for your first day in business.

Table B-2	A Profit and Loss Statement for the First Day	
Description	**Amount**	**Explanation**
Sales	$400	Rental money from the Hamsters and Gerbils
Expenses		
Depreciation	$3	3 rowboats × $1/day depreciation
Advertising	$25	Radio advertising
Total expenses	$28	Depreciation expense plus the advertising
Profit	$372	Sales minus the total expenses

Although the first day's cash flow was terrible, your little business is quite profitable. In fact, if you really do make about $370 a day, you'll recoup your entire $4,500 investment in less than three weeks. That's pretty darn good.

Some financial brain food

Now that you know how to measure profits, I can fill you in on some important conceptual stuff.

✔ **You measure profits for a specific period of time.**

In the rowboat business example, you measured the profits for a day. Some people actually do measure profits (or they try to measure profits) on a daily basis. But most times, people use bigger chunks of time. Monthly chunks of time are common, for example. And so are three-month chunks of time. Everybody measures profits annually — if only because the government makes you do so for income tax accounting.

✔ **When people start talking about how often and for what chunks of time profits are measured, they use a couple of terms.**

The year you calculate profits for is called the *fiscal year*. The smaller chunks of time for which you measure profits over the year are called *accounting periods* or *interim accounting periods*.

You don't need to memorize the two new terms. But now that you've read them, you'll probably remember them.

✔ **The length of your accounting periods involves an awkward trade-off.**

Daily profit and loss calculations show you how well you did at the end of every day, but you have to collect the data and do the work every day. And preparing a profit and loss statement is a great deal of work.

I made the example purposefully easy by including only a few transactions, but in real life, you have many more transactions to worry about and fiddle with.

✔ **If you use a quarterly interim accounting period, you don't have to collect the raw data and do the arithmetic very often, but you know how you're doing only every once in a while.**

In my mind, checking your profits only four times a year isn't enough. A lot can happen in three months.

In the Old Days, Things Were Different

If you're new to the arithmetic and logic of profit calculation — which is mostly what modern accounting is all about — you won't be surprised to hear that not all that long ago, most people couldn't and didn't do much profit calculating.

What they did instead was monitor a business's financial condition. They used — well, actually, they still use — a *balance sheet* to monitor the financial condition. A balance sheet just lists a business's assets and its liabilities at a particular point in time.

Say that at the start of your first day in the rowboat rental business — before you pay Peter Gruntpaw — you have $5,000 in your checking account. To make the situation interesting, $4,000 of this money is a loan from your mother-in-law, and $1,000 is cash that you've invested in your business.

Here's a key to help you understand the balance sheets and cash flow in this section:

- A business's *assets* consist of the things the business owns.

- *Liabilities* consist of the amounts the business owes.

- *Equity* is the difference between the business's assets and its liabilities. Interestingly, equity also shows the money the owners or shareholders or partners have left in the business.

- If you correctly calculate each of the numbers that go on the balance sheet, the total assets value always equals the total liabilities and total owner's equity value.

A balance sheet lists asset, liability, and owner's equity balances on a specific date. It gives you a financial snapshot at a point in time. Usually, you prepare a balance sheet whenever you prepare a profit and loss statement. The balance sheet shows account balances for the last day of the fiscal year and interim accounting period.

Your balance sheet at the beginning of the day looks like the one in Table B-3.

Table B-3	The Balance Sheet at the Beginning of the Day	
Description	*Amount*	*Explanation*
Assets	$5,000	The checking account balance
Total assets	$5,000	Your only asset is cash, so it's your total, too

Table B-3 *(continued)*

Liabilities and owner's equity	$4,000	The loan from your mother-in-law
Total liabilities and owner's equity	$4,000 $1,000	Your only liability is that crazy loan The $1,000 you put in
Total liabilities and owner's equity	$5,000	The total liabilities plus the owner's equity

If you construct a balance sheet at the end of the first day, the financial picture is only slightly more complicated. Some of these explanations are too complicated to give in a sentence, so the paragraphs that follow describe how I got each number.

Even if you don't pay all that much attention, I recommend that you quickly read through the explanations. Mostly, I want you to understand that if you try to monitor a business's financial condition by using a balance sheet, as I've done here, the picture gets messy. Later in this appendix, I talk about how QuickBooks makes all this stuff easier.

Table B-4 shows the balance sheet at the end of the first day.

Table B-4	The Balance Sheet at the End of the Day
Description	*Amount*
Assets	
Cash	$700
Receivable	$200
Rowboats	$4,497
Total assets	**$5,397**
Liabilities and owner's equity	
Payable	$25
Loan payable	$4,000
Total liabilities	**$4,025**
Owner's equity	$1,000
Retained earnings	$372
Total liabilities and owner's equity	**$5,397**

Cash, the first line item shown in Table B-4, is the most complicated line item to prove. If you were really in the rowboat rental business, of course, you could just look at your checkbook. But if you were writing an appendix about being in the rowboat rental business — as I am — you'd need to be able to calculate the cash balance. Table B-5 shows the calculation of the cash balance for your rowboat rental business.

Table B-5		The First Day's Cash Flow	
Description	*Payment*	*Deposit*	*Balance*
Initial investment		$1,000	$1,000
Loan from mother-in-law		$4,000	$5,000
Rowboat purchase	$4,500		$500
Cash from Hamsters		$200	$700

The $200 receivable, the second line item shown in Table B-4, is just the money the Gerbils owe you.

The third line shown in Table B-4, the Rowboats balance sheet value, is $4,497. This is weird, I'll grant you. But here's how you figure it: You take the original cost of the asset and deduct all the depreciation expense that you've charged to date. The original cost of the three rowboats was $4,500. You've charged only $3 of depreciation for the first day, so the balance sheet value, or net book value, is $4,497.

The only liabilities are the $25 you owe the radio station for those new business announcements (shown on the seventh line in Table B-4) and that $4,000 you borrowed from your mother-in-law (shown on the eighth line in Table B-4). I won't even ask why you opened that can of worms.

Finally, the owner's equity section of the balance sheet shows the $1,000 you originally contributed (see line 10 in Table B-4) and also the $372 of money you earned (see line 11 in Table B-4).

It's not a coincidence that the total assets value equals the total liabilities and total owner's equity value. If you correctly calculate each of the numbers that go on the balance sheet, the two totals are always equal.

A balance sheet lists asset, liability, and owner's equity balances as of a specific date. It gives you a financial snapshot at a point in time. Usually, you prepare a balance sheet whenever you prepare a profit and loss statement. The balance sheet shows account balances for the last day of the fiscal year and interim accounting period. (I think that it's kind of neat that after only a few pages of this appendix you're reading and understanding such terms as *fiscal year* and *interim accounting period*.)

What Does an Italian Monk Have to Do with Anything?

So far, I've provided narrative descriptions of all the financial events that affect the balance sheet and the income statement. I described how you started the business with $5,000 of cash (a $4,000 loan from your mother-in-law and $1,000 of cash that you yourself invested). At an even earlier point in this appendix, I noted how you rented a boat to the Hamsters for $200, and they paid you in cash.

Although the narrative descriptions of financial events — such as starting the business or renting to the Hamsters — make for just-bearable reading, they are unwieldy for accountants to use in practice. Partly, this awkwardness is because accountants are usually (or maybe always?) terrible writers. But an even bigger problem is that using the lots-and-lots-of-words approach makes describing all the little bits and pieces of information that you need difficult and downright tedious.

Fortunately, about 500 years ago, an Italian monk named Lucia Pacioli thought the same thing. No, I'm not making this up. What Pacioli really said was, "Hey, guys. Hello? Is anybody in there? You have to get more efficient in the way that you describe your financial transactions. You have to create a financial shorthand system that works when you have a large number of transactions to record."

Pacioli then proceeded to describe a financial shorthand system that made it easy to collect all the little bits and pieces of information needed to prepare income statements and balance sheets. The shorthand system he described? *Double-entry bookkeeping.*

This system enabled people to name the income statement or balance sheet line items or accounts that are affected and then give the dollar amount of the effect. The profit and loss statement and the balance sheet line items are called *accounts*. You need to remember this term.

Just for your information, a list of profit and loss statement and balance sheet line items is called a *chart of accounts*. You may already know this term from using QuickBooks.

Pacioli also did one wacky thing. He used a couple of new terms — *debit* and *credit* — to describe the increases and decreases in accounts.

✔ Increases in asset accounts and in expense accounts are debits. Decreases in liability, owner's equity, and income accounts are also debits.

✔ Decreases in asset and expense accounts are credits. Increases in liability, owner's equity, and income accounts are also credits.

Keeping these terms straight is a bit confusing, so refer to Table B-6 for help.

I'm sorry to have to tell you this, but if you want to use double-entry bookkeeping, you need to memorize the information in Table B-6. If it's any consolation, this information is the only chunk of data in the entire book that I ask you to memorize. Or, failing that, mark this page with a dog-ear so that you can flip here quickly, or just refer to the Cheat Sheet.

Table B-6	The Only Stuff in This Book That I Ask You to Memorize	
Account Type	*Debits*	*Credits*
Assets	Increase asset accounts	Decrease asset accounts
Liabilities	Decrease liability accounts	Increase liability accounts
Owner's equity	Decrease owner's equity accounts	Increase owner's equity accounts
Income	Decrease income accounts	Increase income accounts
Expenses	Increase expense accounts	Decrease expense accounts

And now for the blow-by-blow

The best way to help you understand this double-entry bookkeeping stuff is to show you how to use it to record all the financial events that I've discussed thus far in this appendix. Start with the money that you've invested in the business and the money that you foolishly borrowed from your mother-in-law. You invested $1,000 in cash, and you borrowed $4,000 in cash. Here are the double-entry bookkeeping transactions — called *journal entries*, in case you care — that describe these financial events.

Journal entry 1: To record your $1,000 investment

	Debit	Credit
Cash	$1,000	
Owner's equity		$1,000

Journal entry 2: To record the $4,000 loan from your mother-in-law

	Debit	Credit
Cash	$4,000	
Loan payable to mother-in-law		$4,000

If you add up all the debits and credits in a journal entry, you get something called a *trial balance*. A trial balance isn't all that special, but you use it to prepare profit and loss statements and balance sheets easily. If you add up the debits and credits shown in journal entries 1 and 2, you get the trial balance shown in Table B-7.

Table B-7	Your First Trial Balance	
	Debit	Credit
Cash	$5,000	
Loan payable to mother-in-law		$4,000
Owner's equity		$1,000

This trial balance provides the raw data needed to construct the rowboat business balance sheet at the start of the first day. If you don't believe me, take a peek at Table B-3. Oh sure, the information shown in Table B-7 isn't as polished. Table B-7 doesn't provide labels, for example, that tell you that cash is an asset. And Table B-7 doesn't provide subtotals showing the total assets (equal to $5,000) and the total liabilities and owner's equity (also equal to $5,000). But it does provide the raw data.

Take a look at the journal entries you would make to record the rest of the first day's financial events:

Journal entry 3: To record the purchase of the three $1,500 rowboats

	Debit	Credit
Rowboats	$4,500	
Cash		$4,500

Journal entry 4: To record the rental to the Hamsters

	Debit	Credit
Cash	$200	
Sales		$200

Journal entry 5: To record the rental to the Gerbils

	Debit	Credit
Receivable	$200	
Sales		$200

Journal entry 6: To record the $25 radio advertisement

	Debit	Credit
Advertising expense	$25	
Payable		$25

Journal entry 7: To record the $3 of rowboat depreciation

	Debit	Credit
Depreciation expense	$3	
Accumulated depreciation		$3

To build a trial balance for the end of the first day, you add all the first day journal entries to the trial balance shown in Table B-7. The result is the trial balance shown in Table B-8.

Table B-8	The Trial Balance at the End of the First Day	
	Debit	*Credit*
Balance sheet accounts		
Cash	$700	
Receivable	$200	
Rowboats — cost	$4,500	
Accumulated depreciation		$3
Payable		$25
Loan payable		$4,000
Owner's equity		$1,000
Profit and Loss Statement accounts		
Sales		$400
Depreciation expense	$3	
Advertising expense	$25	

The trial balance shown in Table B-8 provides the raw data used to prepare the balance sheet and profit and loss statement for the first day.

If you look at the accounts labeled "Balance sheet accounts" in Table B-8 and compare these to the balance sheet shown in Table B-4, you see that this trial balance provides all the raw numbers needed for the balance sheet. The only numbers in Table B-4 that aren't directly from Table B-8 are the subtotals you get by adding up other numbers.

If you look at the accounts labeled as "Profit & Loss Statement accounts" in Table B-8 and compare them to the profit and loss statement shown in Table B-2, you see that this trial balance also provides all the raw numbers needed for the profit and loss statement. Again, the only numbers in Table B-2 that aren't directly from Table B-8 are the subtotals you get by adding up other numbers.

Blow-by-blow, part II

If you understand what I've discussed so far, you grasp how accounting and double-entry bookkeeping work. I want to show you about a half dozen more example transactions, however, to plug a few minor holes in your knowledge.

When you collect money you've previously billed, you record the transaction by debiting cash and crediting receivables (or accounts receivable). In the rowboat business, you make this basic entry when Mr. Gerbil later pays you the $200 he owes you for the first day's rental.

Journal entry 8: To record a payment by a customer

	Debit	Credit
Cash	$200	
Receivable		$200

Don't record a sale when you collect the cash. The sale has already been recorded in Journal entry 5. When you pay the radio station for the advertising, you record the transaction by debiting accounts payable and crediting cash.

Journal entry 9: To record your payment of $25 to the radio station

	Debit	Credit
Payable	$25	
Cash		$25

The one other thing I want to cover — ever so briefly — is *inventory accounting*. Accounting for items you buy and resell or the items you make and resell is a bit trickier. And I don't have room to go into a great deal of detail.

When you buy items to resell, you debit an asset account, often named Inventory. If you purchase 300 of the $10 thingamajigs you hope to resell for $25 each, you record the following journal entry:

Journal entry 10: To record the cash purchase of thingamajigs

	Debit	Credit
Inventory	$3,000	
Cash		$3,000

When you sell a thingamajig, you need to do two tasks: record the sale and record the cost of the sale. If you need to record the sale of 100 thingamajigs for $25 each, for example, you record the following journal entry:

Journal entry 11: To record the sale of 100 thingamajigs for $25 apiece

	Debit	Credit
Receivable	$2,500	
Sales		$2,500

You also need to record the cost of the thingamajigs that you've sold as an expense and record the reduction in the value of your thingamajig inventory. That means that if you reduce your inventory count from 300 items to 200 items, you need to adjust your inventory's dollar value. You record the following journal entry:

Journal entry 12: To record the cost of the 100 thingamajigs sold

	Debit	Credit
Cost of goods sold	$1,000	
Inventory		$1,000

The cost of goods sold account, by the way, is just another expense. It appears on your profit and loss statement.

How does QuickBooks help?

If you (or someone else) keep the books for your business manually, you actually have to make these journal entries. But if you use QuickBooks to keep the books, all this debiting and crediting business usually goes on behind the scenes. When you invoice a customer, QuickBooks debits accounts receivable and credits sales. When you write a check to pay some bill, QuickBooks debits the expense (or the accounts payable account) and credits cash.

In the few cases in which a financial transaction isn't recorded automatically when you fill in some on-screen form, you need to use the General Journal Entry window. To display the General Journal Entry window, choose Company⇨Make Journal Entry. You use the General Journal Entry window to create journal entries.

QuickBooks automatically builds a trial balance, using journal entries it constructs automatically and any journal entries that you enter by using the General Journal Entry window. If you want to see the trial balance, just choose Reports⇨Accountant & Taxes⇨Trial Balance. QuickBooks prepares balance sheets, profit and loss statements, and several other reports as well, using the trial balance.

Two Dark Shadows in the World of Accounting

The real purpose of accounting systems, such as QuickBooks, is simple: Accounting systems are supposed to make succeeding in your business easier for you. You may think, therefore, that the world of accounting is a friendly place. Unfortunately, this scenario isn't quite true. I'm sorry to report that two dark shadows hang over the world of accounting: *financial accounting standards* and *income tax laws*.

The first dark shadow

"Financial accounting standards," you say. "What the heck are those?"

Here's the quick-and-dirty explanation: *Financial accounting standards* are accounting rules created by certified public accountants. These rules are supposed to make reading financial statements and understanding what's going on easier for people. (I happen to believe that just the opposite is true, in case you're interested.) But because of what financial accounting standards purport to do, some people — such as bank loan officers — want to see profit and loss statements and balance sheets that follow the rules. The exact catchphrase is one that you might have heard before: "Prepared in accordance with generally accepted accounting principles."

Unfortunately, the rules are very complicated. The rules are inconsistently interpreted. And actually applying the rules would soon run most small businesses into the ground. (And as you were running your business into the ground — you'll be happy to know — your certified public accountant would make a great deal of money helping you figure out what you were supposed to be doing.) So what should you do about this first dark shadow?

Glad you asked:

- ✔ **Well, first of all, know that it exists.** Know that people like your banker honestly think that you should follow a super-complicated set of accounting rules.

- ✔ **Also, don't get sucked into the financial accounting standards tar pit.** Tell people — your banker included — that you do your accounting in the way that you think enables you to best manage your business. Tell people a small business like yours can't afford to have an in-house staff of full-time CPAs. And finally, tell people that you don't necessarily prepare your financial statements "in accordance with generally accepted accounting principles."

Do attempt to fully and fairly disclose your financial affairs to people who need to know about them. Lying to a creditor or an investor about your financial affairs or getting sneaky with one of these people is a good way to end up in jail.

The second dark shadow

And now here's the second dark shadow: income tax accounting laws. You know that Congress enacts tax legislation to raise revenue. And you know that it does so in a political environment strewn with all sorts of partisan voodoo economics and social overtones. So you won't be surprised to find out that the accounting rules that come out of the nation's capital and your state capital don't make much sense for running a business.

You need to apply the rules when you prepare your tax return, of course. But you don't have to use them the rest of the year. A far better approach is to do your accounting in a way that enables you to best run your business. That way, you don't use accounting tricks and gambits that make sense for income tax accounting but foul up your accounting system. At the end of the year, when you're preparing your tax return, have your tax preparer adjust your trial balance so that it conforms to income tax accounting laws.

The Danger of Shell Games

This appendix is longer than I initially intended. I'm sorry about that. I want to share one more thought with you, however. And I think that it's an important thought, so please stay with me just a little longer.

You could use the accounting knowledge that this appendix imparts to do the bookkeeping for a very large business. As crazy as it sounds, if you had 3,000 rowboats for rent — perhaps you have rental outlets at dozens of lakes scattered all over the Rockies — you might actually be able to keep the books for a $200,000,000-a-year business. You would have to enter many more transactions, and the numbers would all be bigger, but you wouldn't necessarily be doing anything more complicated than the transactions in this appendix.

Unfortunately, the temptation is great — especially on the part of financial advisers — to let the money stuff get more complicated as a business grows. People start talking about sophisticated leasing arrangements that make sense because of the tax laws. Some customer or vendor suggests some complicated profit-sharing or cost-reimbursement agreement. Then your attorney talks you into setting up a couple new subsidiaries for legal reasons.

All these schemes make accounting for your business terribly complicated. If you choose to ignore this complexity and go on your merry way, very soon you won't know whether you're making money. (I've seen plenty of people go this route — and it isn't pretty.) On the other hand, if you truly want to do accurate accounting in a complex environment, you need to spend a great deal of cash for really smart accountants. (This tactic, of course, supposes that you can find, hire, and afford these really smart accountants.)

If you're unsure about how to tell whether something is just too complicated, here's a general rule you can use: If you can't easily create the journal entries that quantify the financial essence of some event, you're in trouble.

So, what should you do? I suggest that you don't complicate your business's finances — not even if you think that the newfangled, tax-incentivized, sale-leaseback profit plan is a sure winner. Keep things simple, my friend. To win the game, you have to keep score.

Appendix C

Timing Yourself

· ·

*Q*uickBooks Pro and QuickBooks Premier include a handy timer feature for those of you — consultants, contractors, and other professionals — who need to keep a close eye on your billable time.

The Timer program is also available as a standalone program, just in case you find it handier to be able to track your time without pulling up QuickBooks. Or maybe you want employees to track their time with the timer, but you don't want them using the full QuickBooks program. Or maybe you have masochistic tendencies. In any case, the program's there if you want it. All you have to do is install it off the QuickBooks CD-ROM.

Timing Activities

The Timer gives you two ways to record the time you spend. You can track the time you spend as you work — actually using the Timer to track the minutes and hours you toil. And you can use the Timer, after the fact, to record a list of the ways you've spent your time. If you work in front of your computer, it makes sense to use the real-time recording approach. If you don't work in front of your computer, you have to use the record-your-time-later approach.

If you didn't tell QuickBooks that you wanted to track time as part of setting up, you need to do so before you can noodle around with the stuff I talk about here. To do this, choose the Edit➪Preferences command and click the Time Tracking icon. Then check the Yes button to answer the Do You Track Time? question.

Real-time recording of the time you're spending

To record the time you spend on a task or job or project as you work, choose Employees➪Time Tracking➪Time/Enter Single Activity. QuickBooks displays the Time/Enter Single Activity dialog box, as shown in Figure C-1.

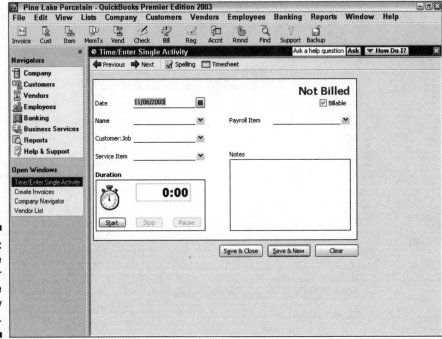

Figure C-1:
The
Time/Enter
Single
Activity
dialog box.

To describe the new activity, follow these steps:

1. **Type the date in the Date text box.**

   You can use the same date entry tricks that you use in QuickBooks. See Chapter 4 or the Cheat Sheet at the front of this book for a list of these tricks.

2. **Type your name in the Name text box.**

   You enter the name by which QuickBooks Pro knows you in the Name box. If you haven't yet been set up as an employee or vendor, QuickBooks asks whether you want to add the name to a Vendor, Employee, or other list. Indicate that you do, indicate which list, and then fill out the dialog box that QuickBooks displays. If you have questions about how to do this, refer to the chapter on payroll (Chapter 12) or the chapter on paying vendor bills (Chapter 6). (If you're entering time for someone identified as an employee, QuickBooks displays a dialog box that lets you indicate you want the time data that's collected to get transferred to the person's payroll records. You can do this — just follow the on-screen instructions.)

3. **Select the Billable check box if you're going to bill a customer for the time recorded for the activity.**

4. **If the activity is billable, enter the name of the customer or job you're billing for the activity.**

   Select a customer or a job from the Customer:Job drop-down list box.

5. **Enter a Service Item if you want to track the service in reports.**

   If you're billing a customer for the activity, you need to have a service item set up in your QuickBooks file. If you want to make the activity billable and you haven't yet set up a service item, do so right now. (I describe setting up items in Chapter 2.)

6. **If you already spent time on the activity, enter the time in the Duration box.**

   Enter the time spent on the activity. If you worked two and a half hours on the activity, enter 2.5 or 2:30. The Timer then uses this time as a starting time and adds minutes to this time whenever you choose this activity and start the Timer.

7. **If you're an employee and set up for using time data to create paychecks, select the description of the appropriate payroll item from the Payroll Item drop-down list.**

   The payroll item you choose essentially tells QuickBooks how to expense the cost of your time. Obviously, if you're not an employee, you don't enter anything here.

8. **(Optional) Enter any notes you have about the activity.**

   I don't really need to tell you what to say here. This is for your own records. You might collect information here that you'll want to know or have handy for when you prepare any invoices based on the time you're recording.

9. **Click Start to begin timing the activity and click Stop to finish.**

   You can click Stop at any time or click Save & Close, and QuickBooks automatically closes the Time/Enter Single Activity dialog box and asks whether you want to stop the timer. You can also, by the way, edit the time shown in the big box next to the stopwatch.

10. **Click Save & New or Save & Close when you're done.**

    If you click Save & New, QuickBooks then opens up a new Activity for you to fill out, which you can use by repeating Steps 1 through 10. Or, if you won't want to record the time spent on an additional activity, you can close the Time/Enter Single Activity dialog box.

You can also use the Timesheet feature in QuickBooks to record time spent on jobs. Choose Employees⇨Time Tracking⇨Time/Enter Single Activity to enter information for activities singly as you accomplish them during the day, or click the Use Weekly Timesheet icon to enter a whole week's activities at once.

After-the-fact recording of the time you spent

To record the time you spend on a task or job or project after you work on it, choose Employees⇨Time Tracking⇨Use Weekly Timesheet. QuickBooks displays the Weekly Timesheet dialog box, as shown in Figure C-2. While this looks different from the Time/Enter Single Activity dialog box shown in Figure C-1, it actually collects the same set of information — except for more than one activity. As a result, you can use it to record the time spent on several activities — not just one.

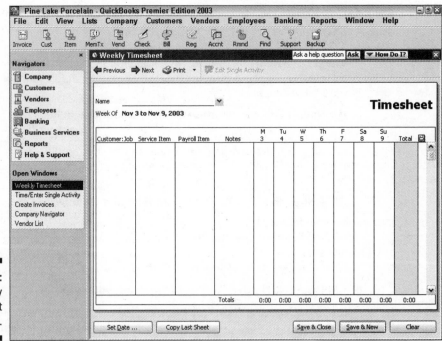

Figure C-2:
The Weekly
Timesheet
dialog box.

Index

• D •

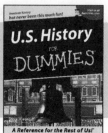

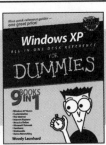

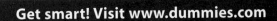

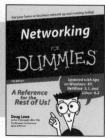